Education!
Education!
Education!

Education!
Education!
Education!

Managerial ethics and the
law of unintended consequences

Edited by Stephen Prickett and
Patricia Erskine-Hill

IMPRINT ACADEMIC
in conjunction with the
Higher Education Foundation

Published in the UK by Imprint Academic
PO Box 1, Thorverton EX5 5YX, UK

Published in the USA by Imprint Academic
Philosophy Documentation Center
PO Box 7147, Charlottesville, VA 22906-7147, USA

ISBN 0907845363

A CIP catalogue record for this book is available from the
British Library and US Library of Congress

Cover design: stevek@conceptstudio.co.uk

Contents

Acknowledgements vi

About Authors vii

Introduction 1

Part I:
The Mismanagement of Universities

Bruce Charlton, *Audit, Accountability and All That* 13

Anthony Smith, *The Laura Spence Affair*. 29

Evan Harris, *Higher Education: A Question of Access* 39

Robert Grant, *Education, Utility and the Universities* 49

Roger Scruton, *The Idea of a University* 73

Stephen Prickett, *Polyphony, the Idea of Education,
and Social Utility*. 85

Desmond Ryan, *Neo-Luddism*. 103

Part II:
Testing to Destruction: the New School Environment

Diana Mabbutt, *From Board School to Boardroom:
Changes and Consequences of Education Policy
in Primary Schools*. 139

Margaret Sutcliffe, *Bureaucracy and the Growth of Anxiety
in a Small Independent School* 149

Libby Purves, *Against the Grain*. 159

Rowan Williams, *Statements, Acts and Values:
Spiritual and Material in the School Environment* 167

Afterword

Stephen Prickett, *Managerial Ethics and the Corruption
of the Future*. 181

Acknowledgements

Our prime debt must be to members of the Higher Education Foundation who did so much to stimulate the discussions form which this book arose. In particular I would like to thank Anand Chitnis and Donald Tranter, who originally prepared work on parts of this book, and whose knowledge of the administrative side of higher education and its history have proved invaluable.

To conversations with Desmond Ryan, of the University of Edinburgh, I owe a sense of the profound historical and sociological changes implicit in recent British educational policy.

Others, including David Aers of Duke University, Frank Furedi of the University of Kent, Susan Basnett of the University of Warwick, and Richard Whitaker of the BBC's *File on Four*, as well as many colleagues at the University of Glasgow, have contributed ideas that have taken hold and maybe germinated in ways they might not recognize.

Though this book has been very much a team effort, any errors that may remain must be laid at the feet of the contributors themselves, and, above all, at those of their grateful editors.

Stephen Prickett
Duke University, 2002

Authors

Bruce Charlton is Reader in Evolutionary Psychiatry in the Department of Psychology at Newcastle University and Visiting Professor at the UEL Centre for Public Health Policy and Health Services Research. He graduated in medicine from Newcastle Medical School in 1982 and following a year as a junior psychiatrist, went into full time research as a Wellcome Fellow in Disorders of Mental Health at the MRC Neuroendocrinology Unit in Newcastle where he completed an MD thesis on the subject of hormonal and brain changes in depression. As resident don at University College Durham, he completed an English Literature MA on the Scottish author Alasdair Gray. Returning to biological research, he worked as a lecturer in Anatomy at Glasgow University (gaining a reference to his work in Gray's Anatomy), and then as a lecturer in Epidemiology and Public Health. During AD 2000 he was a Visiting Distinguished Millennial Fellow at King's College, London. Dr Charlton has published more than one hundred papers on scientific, medical, literary, philosophical and other topics; co-authored a book on medical education; contributed journalism to many magazines and newspapers; and written a BBC Radio 3 experimental drama. He serves on the editorial boards of *Medical Hypotheses*, *Journal of Evaluation in Clinical Practice*, and *Reason in Practice: the journal of philosophy of management*.

Robert Grant is Reader in English Literature at Glasgow University. In 1999 he was Visiting Research Fellow in the Social Philosophy and Policy Center, Bowling Green State University, Ohio. He has lectured widely in Britain, the USA, Eastern Europe and Japan, and has published two books. *Oakeshott* (1990) was the first single-handed study of the philosopher Michael Oakeshott's complete *oeuvre*, and *The Politics of Sex and Other Essays* (2000) is the first of a three-volume collection drawn from over one hundred previously published essays, articles, and reviews across a variety of fields. A frequent contributor to the *Times Literary Supplement*, he is also on the editorial boards of *Episteme* and Imprint Academic's monograph series, *British Idealist Studies*. He has been commissioned to write Oakeshott's official Life and Works, and is currently editing the proceedings of the Oakeshott centenary conference held at the London

School of Economics in 2001. His two forthcoming collections are *Imagined Meanings* and *The Liberal Idea*.

Evan Harris is MP for Oxford West and Abingdon, and Liberal Democrat spokesperson for Health. He was born in Sheffield in 1965 and studied medicine at Wadham College, Oxford, where he was President of Oxford Medical Students. He qualified as a doctor in 1991, and became an active trade unionist, acting as British Medical Association negotiator. He was elected to the BMA regional council and sits on its Medical Ethics committee. Dr Harris joined the Liberal Democrats in 1985. He entered the House of Commons in 1997, and before the last election he was frontbench spokesman on Science, Women's issues and Higher Education, and a member of the House of Commons Select Committee on Education. He is currently Liberal Democrat Shadow Health Secretary.

Diana Mabbutt lives in E. Sussex. She did her teacher-training at Homerton College, Cambridge, and subsequently taught in inner London schools. She later qualified as a special needs teacher in Sussex – a range of experience encompassing schools in inner-city problem areas, suburban, and rural contexts. She has been education editor of several books for primary and secondary school assemblies, and for teachers concerned with religious education. Articles by her have appeared in *Child Education*, *The Dalesman*, *The Lady*, and the *Guardian*, and she has taken part in programmes for Radio 4 and Radio Leeds.

Stephen Prickett was until recently Regius Professor of English at the University of Glasgow and now teaches at Duke University, in North Carolina, USA. He took his BA at Cambridge (Trinity Hall) and subsequently a Dip. Ed. in Oxford (University College), teaching English in a secondary school before returning to Cambridge to take his Ph.D. in 1968. Previous appointments include the Chair of English at the Australian National University in Canberra (1983-89), and teaching posts at the Universities of Sussex (England) (1967-82), Minnesota (1979-80), and Smith College, Massachusetts (U.S.A.) (1970-71), Aarhus University, Denmark (1997) and Singapore (1999). He is a Fellow of the Australian Academy of the Humanities, President of the George MacDonald Society, and is a former Chairman of the U.K. Higher Education Foundation, and President of the European Society for the Study of Literature and Theology. He has published one novel, fifteen monographs and edited volumes, and over eighty articles on Romanticism, Victorian Studies and related topics, especially on literature and theology. His most recent book, *Narrative, Religion and Science*, was published by Cambridge University Press in 2002.

Libby Purves is a novelist, broadcaster and journalist. As a diplomatic child she was educated in short bursts in Bangkok, Walberswick, France, Johannesburg and Tunbridge Wells, sampling convent, state, private and boarding-schools before reading English at St Annes College, Oxford. She has written three widely translated books on childcare and family life, and eight novels. She is a main columnist for *The Times* (London) and presents a talk programme, *Midweek*, on BBC Radio 4, as well as the education magazine *The Learning Curve* on the same network. She has two children, a son and a daughter aged nineteen and eighteen, who began their education at Knodishall village school and completed it at the Royal Hospital School, Holbrook.

Desmond Ryan read Modern History at Magdalen College, Oxford, before moving to Sussex University for his doctoral research, a participant observer study of teacher training in the University of Naples. As well as further work on universities in England and South America, he has been a research consultant for the EU on school — family links in Italy. He also evaluated basic nurse training in Scotland and the functioning of Catholic parishes in the West Midlands (*The Catholic Parish*, Sheed and Ward, 1996). In the field of health, while Director of Healthcare Education Research at the University of Dundee, he enquired into the incorporation of complementary/alternative approaches into the Cuban medical profession since 1990, and in 1999 compiled an in-depth report on teenage pregnancy in Dundee from a social medicine perspective. He is currently researching spirituality in the Scottish NHS as Senior Research Fellow, Nursing Studies Department, University of Edinburgh.

Roger Scruton was until 1990 professor of aesthetics at Birkbeck College, London, and subsequently professor of Philosophy and University Professor at Boston University, Massachusetts. He now lives with his wife and two small children in rural Wiltshire, where he and his wife run a small post-modern farm and public affairs consultancy. He has published over twenty books, including works of philosophy, literature and fiction, and his writings have been translated into most major languages. He is also well known as a broadcaster and journalist. His most recent book is *England: an Elegy*, published by Chatto and he is currently writing a study of Wagner's *Tristan und Isolde*.

Margaret Sutcliffe lives in Harrogate, North Yorkshire. She was born in Guernsey in the Channel Islands and subsequently educated in Aberdeen, Guernsey and Buckinghamshire, followed by teacher training college in Hertfordshire. She initially taught in Junior and Infant schools in Exeter followed by a time in Leeds and Harrogate, having married in 1960. She left teaching to have her two children and then set up a playgroup in her own home. During this time she became involved with the playgroup movement and was for some time Chairman of the local branch of the Pre-school Playgroup Association. She has lectured to teenage students and adults on the importance of play. She eventually set up and opened an independent Preparatory school in 1977 and was headteacher until her recent retirement twenty four years later, in 2001. During her time as head the school achieved success in a number of areas, both academically and in the field of music and drama. On two separate occasions the school won through to the Barclays Youth Music Theatre Awards, which were presented at the Queen Elizabeth Hall in London. Her particular interest is in children and the performing arts and she is proud to claim that she has taught every age group from nursery through to adulthood.

Rowan Williams has been Archbishop of Wales since 1999. He was born near Swansea and was educated at Dynevor School, Swansea, and Christ College, Cambridge. After lecturing in Theology at the College of the Resurrection, Mirfield, he was ordained in 1978. He became Dean of Clare College, Cambridge and, subsequently, Lady Margaret Professor of Divinity in Oxford. In 1992 he became Bishop of Monmouth in the Church in Wales. Dr Williams has wide ranging interests in Christian theology and spirituality, was elected a Fellow of the British Academy in 1990, and is Chairman of the Trialogue Conference, which brings together professionals from the worlds of spirituality, psychotherapy and literature. He is particularly interested in the relationship between Christianity and the arts. His publications include nine monographs as well as collections of essays and sermons, edited and co-authored books, and two volumes of poetry.

Stephen Prickett

Introduction

In March 2001, together with several thousand of my colleagues, I received a letter from a recruitment agency asking if, as a full-time university teacher, I might like to spend some of my 'spare-time' school-teaching. As an added incentive, I would also be paid £100 per person for anyone else I could find willing to do more than two days' teaching. No questions as to teaching qualifications or class-room experience were raised. Considering that a recent survey by the Association of University Teachers suggests its average member works more than a sixty-hour week, and that under the latest time-management survey (called, naturally, a 'transparency review'), everyone at my university has to complete a detailed form stating exactly how long they devote per week to 'teaching', 'administration', and 'research', the whole exercise smacked of fantasy — or desperation. Or both.[1]

Meanwhile teachers are recruited from Europe, from New Zealand, from Australia — from anywhere. Since prestige, pay, conditions, and facilities for teachers in many of those countries are generally far superior to those in the U.K. we can guess at the likely quality of such recruits. Those prepared to work in London are offered an extra £10,000 per year. British graduates prepared to train as teachers are offered a 'golden handshake' of £6,000. Meanwhile Scotland strikes out on its own, offering teachers a 20% rise over three years. Each new measure, even as it is announced, subtly reinforces the opposite message: that teaching is a low-status profession, prepared to take almost anyone prepared to stand in front of a class. How did Britain, well into the second term of a government that in 1997 proclaimed its priorities as 'Education! Education! Education!', come to this extraordinary pass?

One clue may be found in the strident insistence of those exclamation marks. Such stridency rarely implies a laissez-faire attitude; exclamation marks usually denote moral indignation and its close companion, more control. Charges of poor teaching, low standards,

---

[1] The fact that I did not complete it, and the absence of my return was apparently unnoticed, only reinforces my impression of the pointlessness of the exercise.

and complacency in schools, coupled with accusations of poor research records and publishing 'output' in universities have been met by a manic belief that the answer lies in ever more elaborate tests, regulations, and evaluations of every part of the system. The regular testing of pupils and of teachers, begun by Kenneth Baker and perpetuated by Chris Woodhead, has now become an institutional fetish of state education in the U.K., dominating the horizon not merely of schools, but of colleges and universities. Originally devised with the wholly admirable aim of measuring the attainments of pupils and the performance of their teachers and schools, the result has been a series of disastrous unintended consequences. Schools now regularly devote huge proportions of time and resources to preparing for inspection.

In higher education, a succession of bodies dedicated to subject assessments and whole-institution audits have now been brought together in the Quality Assurance Agency. Week after week *The Times Higher* records the attempts and the frustrations of the higher education system and individual institutions to influence for the better the operating procedures of the QAA, whose cost, in bureaucracy, time and the erosion of institutional autonomy and professional concerns has made it unquestionably the fastest-growing section of education. Universities now have teams of professional staff seconded on a permanent basis simply to study the data for Research Assessment Exercises and Total Quality Assurance (i.e. how well they are seen to teach), and to monitor their own progress (not to mention studying the success or failure of rival institutions). For a growing body of academics, insecure about their own scholarly futures, inspection has created a whole new career path, with power and influence within the institution undreamed of by most of its professorate. A recent conservative estimate of the annual cost of quality control, audit, accountability and research assessment systems in higher education in England alone puts the figure at £250 million — enough to pay the fees of 250,000 students; the annual cost of five universities, or the salaries of 10,000 lecturers. Scotland, Wales and Northern Ireland spend proportionately the same.[2] Even this astonishing figure (based on detailed studies of the two Universities in Leeds) is probably an underestimate of the time taken by university teaching staff in 'accounting' for their activities to their own internal audit systems, if only because the staff concerned can-

---

[2]   Figures cited by Roderick Floud (Provost of London Guildhall University), in 'Universities are Sinking Under Inspection Load,' *Times Higher Education Supplement*, March 23, 2001. p. 16.

not quite believe how much of their own time is being spent in this way. According to its own figures, recently published by the Quality Assurance Department of another major university (apparently as a proud mark of its own diligence), the entire staff of that university now spends more time in 'administration', mostly of their own research and teaching, than they do in either research or in teaching itself.

Given the greater size of the primary and secondary school systems in the UK, the real costs to those sectors are unlikely to be less than this figure, and are probably much more. The difference, of course, is that schools do not have the same auditing and accounting systems as universities, and thus the time so costed comes directly from the teachers' own time. In other words, in addition to the irritation and frustration caused by the quality assurance system, at least £250 million of teachers' time has been taken away from teaching children to be devoted to *auditing* that teaching. The fact that much of that time would be 'out-of-school' time is irrelevant. This is precisely the time that the good teacher would otherwise be using for marking, preparation, and organizing new projects. Anecdotal evidence suggests that it is these good teachers who are the most frustrated by the loss of this time, and who have been leaving the profession in the greatest numbers.

As a result, at its most basic level, education in state schools has been systematically reduced to those things which can be measured by so-called 'objective' tests. Diana Mabbutt tells of the pressures on teachers and pupils as young as five in state primary schools, not merely to assess children's performances, but to *predict* them. What head teacher, after all, is going to give much time to 'subjective' activities, such as music, drama, and art, when his or her personal reputation, that of the school, or even the educational authority hangs on the result of tests in mathematics and English grammar? As a recent real-life case has demonstrated, the chances of Billy Elliott (in the film of that name) getting state assistance to go to ballet school have gone down, not up, in the past four years. Yet, curiously enough, those very things that cannot be measured by objective testing are apparently the very things that our society seems to value most highly outside the school context. The measure of success and public esteem for wealthy individuals or cities is in concert halls, theatres, and art galleries. How many municipalities have built statues to accountants or grammarians? Outside the classroom we celebrate our authors, composers, musicians, playwrights, actors and painters.

If you want a child to excel in these fields, there *are* schools that teach them, and they teach them well, but (despite their name) they are not state, but 'public' (i.e. private) schools. Those who choose to send their children to fee-paying schools are, in effect, choosing to pay *twice over* for education: once through taxes, and again through school fees. It is interesting to ask, therefore, what they believe they are getting by paying (more than) double ? While we should never underestimate the forces of snobbery and ignorance in any social choices, the bulk of such parents are at least as well-informed as those who by principle or inertia send their children to state schools — and probably better.

The significant thing is that *what* parents are choosing is, increasingly, *not* a more high-powered or academic version of the local comprehensive, but institutions with quite different, and ever-more diverging, aims and ethos. Perhaps for the first time in modern British history, there now seems to be a significant and growing *ideological* difference between private and state education. Until a few years ago, it was possible to argue that the prime difference between (the best) private schools and the state sector was primarily one of resources. Given the money and facilities, it was assumed that the state schools would choose similar options to the private in their educational policy: smaller classes, plenty of sport, effective teaching of a range of modern (and classical) languages — backed by visits to other countries to understand them better, and use those languages in context — plenty of drama, music and art. If, at the end of the day, good public exam results and university entrance were also assumed, they were rarely seen as the sole purpose of the school.

Clearly there *are* state schools that still deliver all these things, but they are decreasing, not increasing in number. My own children's school did when they were there — but now does so less and less. The point is that those schools that still persist in trying to provide a rounded liberal education are, increasingly, doing so in the teeth of government opposition, rather than with its help. Similarly, not all private schools are centres of excellence by any means, but almost without exception they *claim* to offer qualities like community, moral values, and individual attention, as well as aesthetic and physical education. Such schools are commercial enterprises: they would hardly be likely do so if that did not represent what most caring parents actually wanted for their children. As we all know, it is these subjective and untestable qualities, together with activities like art, drama and music that nourish the growth and development of the individual.

If education is not built on the growth of the individual, it is based upon the instruction and training of an economic unit. It is quite clear that under the Blunkett regime, state schools were being actively and deliberately turned away from this liberal and creative ideal and being made into skill-centres. There is little evidence so far that Estelle Morris takes a different view. Yet, though that is something management may desire for others, it is not something we ever want for ourselves — or, more to the point, our own children. The Independent Schools Information Service (ISIS) shows that the number of children attending independent schools has been rising steadily since 1995, and now stands at astonishing 601,000 (2001 figures). In the same period the number of two to four year-olds has risen by 12% to nearly 71,000. Libby Purves' contribution examines the dilemma of those parents who care about the arts, aesthetic and moral education — and can afford the fees. Led by Tony Blair himself, whose children attend the Roman Catholic London Oratory School,[3] such parents are increasingly sending their children to independent schools — and that sector is booming as never before.

At the other end of the scale, something equally odd is happening. Not merely have the arts been sacrificed to testing, so has sport. The sale of school playing-fields during the 1990s was symptomatic of a wider neglect of sporting facilities. Britain's sporting record at the top level is, of course, closely related to expenditure by the sponsors — public and private. But the athletic base of participating teenagers has declined relentlessly. Fewer children take part in organized sports than for generations. There are more obese children than ever before. Mention of school sports days brings out anecdotes of overweight children lumbering round courses supervised by teachers frightened to urge them on for fear of promoting heart-attacks. One teacher tells of a child whose daily lunch consisted of five chocolate cup-cakes. By 15 years old, 17.3% of girls are obese and 28.2% overweight. The corresponding figures for boys are 16.4% obese, and 32.9% overweight. In other words, in 2001 roughly half the fifteen year-olds in the UK are obese or overweight.[4] Over 70% of girls claim to be dissatisfied with their body-images — and with good reason.

At the same time, government-driven stress on competitive performance in a narrow core curriculum has reinforced the tacit

---

[3]   Brompton Oratory School is, of course, a voluntary aided school, without fees as such (though parents such as the Blairs with two children in the school are asked to pay £45.00 per month (£540.00 p.a.). It has, however, many characteristics of the private sector, with fiercely competitive entry, and twenty places a year being reserved for musically gifted pupils.

[4]   *The Times*, Section 2, p. 4.. April 5, 2001.

assumption that the aims of state education, at every level, are primarily to be judged in economic terms (both personal and national) rather than in terms of individual development. This Gradgrind utilitarianism has the added advantage of justifying student loans, and will eventually, no doubt, justify top-up fees for universities. Few seem to have commented on the consequence that all students are tacitly encouraged to think of their education in commercial terms and values. Though this justifies making students pay for more of their education, it has had the unintended side-effect of progressively squeezing the poorest section of the community out of higher education, and relegating it, financially and cognitively, to an underclass from which it is more and more difficult to escape.

Nevertheless, taking their cue from governmental rhetoric, some institutions have begun to market themselves as providing a primarily economic service. A few years ago Glasgow Caledonian University launched a recruiting drive with the logo of a big 'C', and the slogan 'where Careers come first', evidently to distinguish itself from the two older-established universities in the city, who, it was implied, had a less business-like approach to learning. Like most advertising slogans in the field, it meant little — the most recent table of graduate employment put it level with Glasgow University (93), and slightly behind Strathclyde (95). But no one could accuse the management of Glasgow Caledonian of failing to practise what it preached. Shortly afterwards its Principal was suspended by the Governors for alleged malpractice, nepotism, and misuse of funds. After a lengthy and complex court case, he was subsequently reinstated, immediately sacked once again, and finally given a golden handshake running to hundreds of thousands of pounds.

If the process of testing in schools and universities has distorted both the curriculum and the educational ethos, it has also, contrariwise, had the opposite effect of distorting the prime instrument of testing — the public examinations system itself. Pressure to show improvement has led to a continual whittling-down of the actual standards of assessment. The fall in standards of GCSE English has gone beyond the anecdotal level. At the other end of the system, in universities, there has been a similar distortion of the actual degree-granting process. Among the criteria of 'quality' used in the tables now regularly published by the *Times Higher*, or the *Sunday Times Good Universities Guide*, is the number of upper seconds and first-class degrees awarded by institutions. Hardly surprisingly, this has not gone unnoticed by the institutions themselves, which have placed continual pressure on exam boards to award ever-greater numbers of firsts. It is noticeable that many of the 'new universities', recruiting at the lower end of the range of qualified applicants, award more firsts and upper seconds than well-established members of the Russell Group. Grade inflation is not merely an irresistible temptation in a competitive climate; it is, in effect, now built into the system.

In a parallel development, the Research Assessment Exercise in universities was set up to encourage and reward excellence in research. The measure of 'excellence' originally proposed was that of quantity. When a similarly misconceived scheme was originally pioneered in Australia in the 1980s, the first proposal from the Department of Education and Training in Canberra was to measure every academic's quality simply by the quantity of written 'output' page by page, or even word-by-word. The present British RAE scheme, though it gestures towards some notion of 'quality' by 'peer review', is only marginally more subtle. One proposal, to produce a 'citation index', reflecting how often a particular researcher's works were cited by others in the same field, was immediately countered by groups of friends or colleagues with a common interest in boosting their ratings, who simply cited each other in every possible publication. However many of the increasingly convoluted and time-consuming methods of assessment were tried, the result has been to encourage the predictable and the mediocre. Academics who publish outside their recognized 'field' lose credit — and therefore, increasingly, chances of promotion. One wonders how John Nash, the hero of the recent film 'A Beautiful Mind' would have fared in a QAA review. The consequence, unintended but equally predictable, has been a huge number of uninteresting and unread publications. A recent survey of library borrowings suggests that the readership for the average article in an academic journal is no more than two people.

Even the entirely laudable desire for higher education among young people has inevitably produced distortions of its own in a chronically underfunded system. The mass expansion of higher education has had the paradoxical effect of actually increasing, rather than diminishing, the hierarchy of academic institutions. Overcrowded classes, poor facilities, and lack of contact with teachers in many of the recently established universities has only served to enhance the attraction of Oxbridge for the brightest and best schooled. In his discussion of the Laura Spence case, Anthony Smith shows how even the best A Level grades are no longer guarantee of entry to the most sought-after institutions: and the cynical intervention of Gordon Brown for his own political purposes makes the government's lack of interest in real improvement all too clear.

As we have seen, recent history has fully vindicated those predicting that present policies would lead to a fall in standards of those entering teaching, and a massive shortage of teachers in schools (and eventually universities). The policy of 'naming and shaming' those schools, colleges and universities which perform badly in league tables, rather than leading to greater 'openness' or 'transparency' has become a source of corruption. Similarly the widespread criticism of teachers which was so characteristic of the Woodhead years, was, we must charitably suppose, intended to improve standards, but the effect was to make teaching an increasingly low-status profession. Even the idea of performance-related pay, one of the bones of contention between Woodhead and Blunkett, which was intended to reward 'good' teachers, again used a crudely managerial criteria of 'performance', taking little account of context. The cumulative effect of these ill-designed measures has been to lower teaching morale, with the predictable consequence that increasing numbers of well-qualified teachers, who can equally well do other, better-paid jobs, vote with their feet, and leave to do so. Those who remain are dispirited and demoralized. Thousands have left; there is increasing difficulty in recruiting new teachers. Many schools cannot attract any applications at all for the unenviable post of head teacher.

The novelist Louis de Bernières has described his own experience in an inner city London school. 'I was threatened with a bottle, a knife and a baseball bat and I was once attacked with a chair... It is quite usual to be told to f*** off several times a day.' He describes teachers swamped with paperwork, plagued by an 'anti-culture, anti-education ethos among the white working-class', and tormented by 'village Hitlers' in the ideological battleground' of the staff room.[5] De Bernières' experience was no doubt extreme, but numerous other anecdotal accounts make it clear it was not exceptional. Moreover, at that stage of his life he seems to have seen himself (however briefly!) not as novelist needing extra money, but as a possible career teacher.

The catalogue is a depressing one. There is widespread agreement about the low standards of many schools. Yet every attempt to 'improve' them, either by the Woodhead 'right' or the Blunkett 'left' (when, as rarely, non-partisans can see blue water between their two positions) simply makes matters worse. And here lies our problem.

---

[5] *Sunday Times*, April 8, 2001. p. 15.

Both sides are in broad agreement with the goals. The means must therefore be simply be a matter of better management — of people, of resources, of time. The latest production of the Campaign for Learning, *Schools in the Learning Age*, which has drawn such wrath from Woodhead is yet another example of the belief that what actually goes on — in or out of the classroom can be transformed by new managerial structures. This, in short, is what we have designated 'managerial ethics': the belief (indeed, the *dogma*) that the problems in our educational system are primarily those of management and control, and that reformation of teaching, the rooting out of bad or lazy teachers, the introduction of national curricula, are all part of what is, or should be, essentially a *moral* crusade. It is the contention of the contributors to this book that the explosive new mixture of control and moralism, has done more to damage our educational system than any of the original problems they set out to cure.

As always in such cases the observer must ask *cui bono*? 'who stands to gain?' If we look beyond the rhetoric to where new money is being spent, where new jobs are being created, the answer is depressingly clear. As we have seen, the extra money — if we count schools and universities, over half a billion pounds of it — is going not into teaching, not into libraries or better resources, nor even into student support, but into more government control, supported by an ever-expanding bureaucracy.

In short, as we shall see, the managerial ethics, the dogmatism, crude managerialism, and narrow economic objectives of the Woodhead culture were never appropriate for the needs of the UK in the late twentieth century. During the 1990s they have become progressively less so, and current rhetoric fails to conceal a massive crisis — of which the present exodus of teachers from the profession, and the attempt to replace them from around the world by those who cannot get jobs there, is only the first symptom. The essays in this volume represent an attempt to survey some of the problems described here. They are not written from any concerted political angle, but seek to identify and analyse the mistaken thinking, the loose rhetoric, the unctuous moralizing and the personal empire-building that have led to the present situation and its unintended consequences. In writing them, the contributors make a case for urgently-needed and radical reform that can only begin with a clear understanding of the catastrophe that has befallen our educational system. In the final section, we shall try to analyze that catastrophe in greater detail, and suggest a few, relatively simple, remedies.

Part I

The Mismanagement
of Universities

Bruce G. Charlton

Audit, Accountability, Quality and All That

The Growth of Managerial Technologies in UK Universities

Although independent corporations, UK universities are heavily dependent on state funding, and have become increasingly subject to government influence. Recent government policy is working towards the transformation of undergraduate university teaching into a continuation of the school system which will offer an extended intellectual training to around half of the age cohort.[1] The implementation of this strategy has led to a massive expansion in the use of managerial technologies as governments have struggled to gain control of all major aspects of university activity: student numbers, admissions policy, teaching, research, employment contracts etc.

Since UK managerial culture is dominated by the discipline of accountancy, the characteristic nature of government influence has been dictated by audit-based technologies of regulation with a particular role for concepts such as 'accountability' and 'quality'. Audit technologies have proved to be subtle and effective ideologies, since they form self-reinforcing rhetorical systems. The criterion that all organizational practices should be auditable has been a potent stimulator of structural changes in universities. These changes have shifted power from academics to managers, whose activities are more amenable to external monitoring and regulation.

Education for Economic Growth

State involvement in education tends to be taken for granted nowadays, although the magnitude of support may be hotly debated — but this is a comparatively recent matter in most countries. State sup-

---

[1]   B.G. Charlton, 'Shape of things coming', *Oxford Magazine*, 182, 2000, pp. 1-3.

port for education was historically linked to the need for a literate and numerate governing bureaucracy. For instance, the mediaeval church provided the (relatively small) bureaucracy, consequently the church ran the educational system. Only after the industrial revolution led to increased demand for a substantial secular intellectual workforce was there an expansion of state-funded education.[2] A major role of the state in *higher* education was pioneered by Germany in the nineteenth century with the emergence of Germany as a great power.[3] Germany's lead was followed by governments of all major industrial countries.

The large scale involvement of all modern states in education arises because of the need to guarantee an intellectual workforce to generate and sustain economic growth.[4] Governments of developed, non-militaristic states realize that growth is crucial to their survival, because continual wealth expansion allows governments to exert control by 'bribing' emerging powerful interest groups without the need to confiscate wealth from existing powerful interests. Growth allows the emergence of non-zero sum economics from which all can benefit, in principle.[5] States that fail to achieve continuous growth must usually resort to greater use of an expensive apparatus of propaganda, coercion and repression, which inflicts further damage on the economy.

Continual economic growth further implies continual cognitive growth in order to generate continual improvements in productivity. Productivity enhancement of course requires a (relatively small) number of highly trained creative and innovative specialists — engineers, computer scientists etc. But more importantly, cognitive growth requires ever greater division and specialization of labour, which implies information exchange on an ever increasing scale.[6] It is this massively increased information exchange that generates the need for a mass of non-specialist, flexible, generically literate and numerate intellectual workers who can retrain and re-skill in response to economic developments.

The main function of state supported higher education is therefore the 'mass production' of this class of generic literate, numerate,

[2]   E. Gellner, *Nations and Nationalism*, Blackwell: Oxford, 1983.

[3]   C.E. McClelland, *State, Society, and University in Germany 1700-1914*, Cambridge University Press: Cambridge, 1980.

[4]   Gellner, *Nations and Nationalism*.

[5]   R. Wright, *Nonzero: The Logic of Human Destiny*, Pantheon: New York, 2000.

[6]   *Ibid.*

intellectual workers.[7] Such education was — until recently — done largely in schools rather than colleges or universities. In the past, the mass-produced intellectual worker was 'the clerk': a clerk being a person with basic reading, writing and arithmetic skills. Throughout the early industrial revolution, clerks comprised a large and expanding proportion of the workforce that eventually comprised around half of the age cohort. It was the main function of grammar schools to produce 'clerks' in large numbers — which is why many grammar school places were funded by the state.

Grammar schools needed teachers, and the adequate provision of state grammar school teachers became the principal function of state-funding to universities — beginning with the civic (or 'redbrick') universities, which were enormously expanded from the inter-war period onward, being joined by new technical and 'plateglass' universities from the 1940s.[8]

The Future for State-funded Universities

But this is now set to change. In order to continue to generate economic growth in competition with other countries, it is now considered necessary that the mass produced generic intellectual workers should be educated to a higher level than in the past — the old style 'clerk' having become deskilled or superseded by the advent of widespread computerization. And since education to the necessary level appears to be impossible within 18 years in the UK state school system (impossible, at any rate, in the state school system as it currently exists) it is therefore the aim of current policy to extend the period of intellectual educational experience to include several more years at an institution of higher education.

In principle, the policy to extend the education of roughly half of the age cohort by several years might have been attained without affecting standards by a massive expansion of diploma level qualifications at further education or technical colleges. Instead, the decision was made to devalue the standards of universities and honours degree qualifications. Presumably the title of 'university' and the 'degree' certification were intended as a bribe, effective at least in the short term until inflation catches up, to encourage more people to stay in the educational system for longer. So instead of leaving school at age 16–18 with O-levels, GCSEs or A-levels, the idea is that the intellectual workers of the future will stay in the state educa-

[7]   Gellner, *Nations and Nationalism*.

[8]   W.H.G. Armytage, *Civic universities — Aspects of a British Tradition*, Ernest Benn: London, 1955.

tional system until age 21–22 and leave with an honours degree. Hence state universities will come to perform a similar economic function to the grammar schools of the past, and state university lecturers will become *de facto* grammar school teachers for grownups.

A university degree up to around, say, 1980 functioned essentially as a professional qualification — whether for teaching, the civil service, engineering, surveying, medicine, or whatever. By contrast, the educational level attained by the bulk of new-style university graduates will be somewhat above the usual level of skills of reading, writing and arithmetic which were attained at grammar schools (after all, the individual student will have stayed in the system for three to five extra years of learning and maturing) — and professional certification will presumably move up to postgraduate level.

In a nutshell, we could summarize the change as a shift from the mass production of clerks by grammar schools, to the mass production of 'middle managers' by universities. The new-style graduate will have abilities appropriate to the needs of modern commerce: accessing information sources, writing reports, using computer spreadsheets and word-processors, participating in structured arguments etc. The hope is that these mass-produced intellectual workers will prove able to do more than just clerical work acting under instruction, but will also be capable of participating in planning, auditing, sales, researching and other characteristic activities of contemporary economic life.

Given the nature of this policy shift for state education, the problem confronting government has been how to impose this new model on universities which would be highly resistant to the process since it involves institutional subordination, de-skilling, reduced pay and lowering of academic standards. So the problem facing government was how to *manage* the universities into switching their function.

Managerialism

Complex and differentiated modern economies require large numbers of managers whose economic function is essentially the coordination of the activities of specialized workers. The nature of managerialism seems to vary between countries according to the dominant disciplinary background of managers. For instance, in Germany, engineers form the most dominant school of managers, and engineering concepts seem to dominate managerial ideologies. However in the UK the dominant style of managerialism is derived from accountancy (managerial consultancy is dominated by the big accountancy firms) consequently audit-derived concepts and technologies dominate UK managerialism.

The concepts of 'accountability' and 'quality', which form the subject of this essay, can be taken as representative of UK managerial discourse. The word 'accountability' originally meant having the duty to present auditable accounts. In its technical meaning, accountability envisages a situation in which the business of the auditee was subordinated to the informational requirements of the auditor — and in a sense that is exactly what accountability still means, underneath all the managerial rhetoric. For instance, the Quality Assurance Agency (QAA) for higher education demands not only a set of 'accounts' of a particular form, but that university teaching be conducted in accordance with the demands of its auditing process so that these 'accounts' will be a valid reflection of organizational activity.

The current managerial use of 'quality' (as in QAA) was developed and adapted to the needs of managerialism during the nineteen eighties and nineties. What has emerged is a generic, audit-based version of quality control usually termed 'quality assurance' (QA). Quality Assurance has transformed 'quality' into an abstract requirement for a particular kind of regulatory system. Quality Assurance now refers to auditable systems, not to guaranteed excellence.

Accountability

Two Definitions of Accountability

Our era has been described as the 'audit society', because corporate life is increasingly dominated by accountancy-derived concepts and technologies.[9] Accountability is one of these concepts — as its name implies. The desirability of 'increased accountability' has become ubiquitous in political, managerial and even journalistic discourse. Accountability is assumed to be an intrinsically desirable goal, and nobody ever claims that one can have 'too much' accountability — the pressure is always for more.   Yet accountability is a slippery rhetorical term with two largely distinct meanings: a sharply-defined technical managerial meaning, and a looser, more general or 'popular' meaning.[10] This opens the way for accountability to be

[9]   M. Power, *The Audit Society; Rituals of Verification*, Oxford University Press: Oxford, 1997; B.G. Charlton, Essay Review of *The Audit Society* by Michael Power, *Journal of Evaluation in Clinical Practice* 4, 1998, pp. 249-53.

[10] B.G. Charlton, The ideology of 'accountability', *Journal of the Royal College of Physicians of London* 33, 1999, pp. 33-5.

used in a rhetorically manipulative fashion — by shifting back and forth between technical and general meanings. In general discourse, accountable means something similar to 'responsible', and carries connotations of 'being answerable-to'. Conversely, to be unaccountable may be used synonymously with 'irresponsible' and 'out of control'. Since responsible behavior is universally approved, then calls to increase 'accountability' sound self-evidently desirable.

The technical meaning of accountability in managerial discourse refers narrowly to the duty to present auditable accounts. Originally, this referred to financial documentation that was adequate in terms of completeness and self-consistency — such that it is amenable to the process of cross-checking which constitutes the basis of audit (see below). The current managerial use of accountability is a direct extension of this financial usage — an accountable organization is one that has the duty to present auditable accounts of its *activities* — in other words an accountable organization is one that will provide comprehensive and self-consistent documentation of whatever it does.

Only insofar as it is legitimate to assume that the provision of auditable documentation is synonymous with responsible behaviour is there any overlap between the technical and general concepts of accountability. But the rhetoric of accountability operates on the basis of a 'quick switch' between the two. Any individual or organizational problem which can be connected to irresponsible behavior can be termed unaccountable in the general sense — and then the discourse can be switched over to a technical level in which the solution to unaccountable behavior is to set up regular audit cycles that require comprehensive and self-consistent documentation of that behavior. Behavior may be rendered technically 'accountable' even when the real world behavioral problems that led to the introduction of audit are unchanged or exacerbated.

Unaccountable means un-managed

Now that this model of accountability has become habitual, it is able to *generate* problems of technically 'unaccountable' behavior, even when there is no evidence that actual behaviour has been irresponsible. There is a profound circularity about this reasoning. Accountability involves an assumed model of how organizations ought to operate, and how individual judgment should be regulated within these organizations. For behavior to be accountable means that it must be embedded within an auditable system of formally-related elements.

Accountability in its technical sense carries almost the opposite meaning to those democratic, egalitarian, radical and 'empowering' values that are associated with the term in general usage.[11] The drive for increased accountability may operate as an excuse to justify managerial takeover. Behavior is labelled as unaccountable (hence unacceptable) simply because it is not subject to managerial control, and this is taken (by managers and politicians who wish to control this behavior) to imply a need to introduce audit systems. Audit systems may then be set up to advance the interests of those who have introduced them.

For instance, many university academics retain significant autonomy in their work, exercising independent judgment over such matters as hour-by-hour time-allocation, teaching style and content, and the subject matter of personal research. Such autonomy has — over many years and in many cultures — proved to be the only way to generate and maintain high academic standards. However, this autonomy poses a serious threat to political control, since there is no formal mechanism by which academic behaviours can be managed. The concept of accountability provides the answer.

If typical academic behaviour can be labelled as technically 'unaccountable', and if 'unaccountable' is regarded as unacceptable by definition, then there is a perfect rationale for introducing a formal system of monitoring and control. One might be a brilliant and popular university teacher, a first-rate researcher of international reputation, a diligent administrator, and employed by a prestigious university — but technically such a person is 'unaccountable' when there are no formal institutional mechanisms for monitoring, documenting and regulating behaviour.

Autonomy is re-packaged as irresponsibility while subordination of employees by top-down and hierarchical control mechanisms is restated in terms of 'increased accountability'.

Quality

The proliferation of 'quality initiatives', 'quality units' and the ever-more-frequent use of the term 'quality' in institutional discourse is evidence that state control over universities will substantially be achieved by some version of 'Quality Assurance' (QA) auditing. As with accountability, the effectiveness of this form of managerial discourse depends upon the rhetorical device of switching between general and technical meanings of the word.

---

[11] *Ibid.*

Quality Assurance

Quality Assurance (QA) is a technical managerial term for that type of auditing which is concentrated upon *systems and processes* rather than outcomes.[12] QA is built on the assumption that any properly-constituted organization should be based around a system of auditing systems and processes.

Quality Assurance auditing has become closely identified with older managerial approaches including the word 'Quality' – such as Total Quality Management (TQM) ,and the awarding of quality assurance systems of organizations with 'UK Standards' and 'International Standards'.[13] Quality Assurance auditing therefore has close evolutionary links to 'quality enhancement' strategies, based upon creating a 'culture' centred on 'quality' which usually means reorganizing production around reliable processes and systems of checking and feedback.

The idea of Total Quality Management is usually credited to the late W. Edward Deming, who was held to be responsible for generating the Japanese economic miracle of the post-1945 era. TQM stands in contrast to traditional assembly line quality *control* inspections which focus upon testing the completed product and rejecting faulty items. According to TQM, the best strategy to achieve excellent products was an indirect one: to concentrate attention on the system and the ethos of the company, rather than being narrowly focused upon the product. But, as is natural in an engineering context, the final arbiter of success for the Deming-style TQM would remain the excellence of the product. For instance, the international sales success of Japanese cars and motorcycles was based upon the value-for-money and reliability of the product, not upon approval for the managerial systems by which they were made.

But Quality Assurance auditing was developed by accountants, not engineers – hence QA is an abstract activity that focuses upon systems and processes almost to the exclusion of the excellence of the product. Quality Assurance actually defines 'quality' in terms of systems – specifically in terms of auditable systems. A 'quality assured' product is one produced by an auditable system. The prod-

---

[12] B.G. Charlton, Clinical Governance: a Quality Assurance audit system for regulating clinical practice, in *Clinical Governance: Encouraging Excellence or Imposing Control?* ed. Andrew Miles et al., Aesculaepius Medical Press, London (in press).

[13] A.V. Feigenbaum, *Total Quality Control*: 3rd edition, McGraw Hill: NY, 1983; M. Perigord, *Achieving Total Quality Management*. Productivity Press: Cambridge, MA, 1990; TQM International, BS 5750/ IOS 9000 Handbook, TQM International: Frodsham, 1992.

uct of a QA system is therefore quality assured *by definition* — without necessarily guaranteeing its excellence or fitness for use.[14]

When 'quality' has thus been re-defined in terms of auditable systems and processes, rather than excellent outcomes, this has the effect of liberating 'quality enhancement' initiatives from the need to *define* desirable outcomes or best practice. This is of particular relevance to education, since it has proved impossible to agree upon valid and reliable definitions of the real-world 'quality' (ie. excellence) of teaching. However, with the advent of QA, politicians and managers have no need to worry about whether they are measuring real-world quality.

Educational debate has been shifted away from the contested territory of outcome measures towards obtaining agreement to a standard *system* of practice — and this must be a fully explicit Quality Assurance system in which all essential elements can be planned, documented, monitored and audited. Such a deft act of redefinition has the effect of rendering teaching *at last* amenable to quasi-objective quantitative measurement, to external monitoring, and to external control.

Transparent organizations

In other words, with the introduction of QA applied to teaching, *proper* teaching is conceptualized only as those activities and systems which are transparent to auditing. To be 'transparent' to auditing means to be amenable to comprehensive and self-consistent documentation — it is the existence of this documentation that renders all significant organizational activities visible to external gaze.

Since the rise of the 'Audit Society' and the dominance of managerial discourse over practice, for an organization to be 'opaque' to auditing, to include significant activities that are not documented, is regarded as intrinsically deficient and probably dishonest.[15] Yet although transparency has become a term of approbation among managers and politicians, it is merely a technical term that refers to auditability. And auditability does not legitimately carry any necessary implications of responsibility to the public or of excellent or desirable practice, especially when auditing is implemented and evaluated by government officials.

The conflation of 'transparency' with probity has arisen because modern managers equate a properly constituted organization with a

---

[14] Power, *The Audit Society.*

[15] *Ibid.*

fully auditable organization. And this equation is endorsed because, in the accountancy-dominated world of UK managerialism, managers exert control by means of auditing. Transparent organizations are auditable, and auditable organizations are manageable — and *vice versa*. Therefore, organizations *must be made auditable* — at any price. And the price can be high. In a market system, there is a brake on excessive auditing — in a monopoly public sector activity such as the UK universities, audit can grow even when its growth is exerting significant damage on performance and efficiency.

By its concentrations upon systems and procedures, QA provides a mechanism for quantifying almost any aspect of organizational performance that can be given an operational definition — 'quality', 'excellence', 'equity', 'access' or whatever the current buzzword happens to be. Any aspects of measured organizational performance may be attached to these terms with no more justification than face plausibility, then these can be quantified 'objectively' and judged against pre-established 'performance' criteria.

The magic of Quality Assurance is that what was un-measurable has been rendered measurable — so long as one does not inquire too carefully into what words like 'quality' actually mean in operational terms. Although in the real world we are no nearer to measuring the excellence of teaching than ever we were, by the enchantment of QA, numerical values have been attached to quantified aspects of individual and institutional performance, marks have been awarded, league tables prepared, performance criteria monitored, differential funding allocated. In short the system has been rendered manageable.

The example of QAA

Criteria to measure the real-world excellence or 'quality' of university teaching have proved impossible to agree upon. Instead, the 'quality' of teaching has been re-defined by the QAA (Quality Assurance Agency for higher education) in terms of documented compliance with an approved Quality Assurance system.[16]

The most fundamental attribute of a QAA approved system of teaching is that it is auditable — in other words that it can be comprehensively and self-consistently documented. 'High quality' teaching is therefore an explicit system characterized by Mission Statements, aims and objectives, flow-charts, monitoring, feedback and formal procedures for all imaginable contingencies. Only that

---

[16]   B.G. Charlton, QAA: why we should not collaborate, *Oxford Magazine* 169, 1999, pp. 8-10; B.G. Charlton, QAA: 'light touch' auditing is not an option, *Oxford Magazine* 176, 2000, pp. 12-13.

which is documented, hence auditable, is deemed to count as legitimate teaching activity. (Unfortunately this eliminates everything that people mean by 'high quality' teaching in normal everyday discourse — however, this regrettable fact has not prevented the widespread equation of QAA score with teaching excellence.)

The QAA inspection of my own medium-sized university department (approximately 15 academic staff) generated considerably more than ten thousand pieces of paper housed in dozens of box-files that filled a room; and the inspection lasted four full days. The logistics of preparation took many months including full- and part-time secondment of several academic and secretarial staff, countless hours of meetings and 'away days' involving dozens of staff, and temporary employment of extra secretarial help. While the QAA central bureaucracy is itself a relatively small organization, and relatively inexpensive for the government, the heavy cost of inspection is borne by the department being audited. It has been estimated by a group of economics professors that the QAA Subject Review exercise has probably costs the university system approximately a hundred million pounds per year.[17]

No attempt was ever made to prove that the QAA method of organizing and evaluating teaching tends to lead to 'high quality' teaching, nor that this method of teaching was superior to previously practiced methods of teaching. The QA-approved system was assumed to be higher quality by definition, because the pre-existing systems were undocumented, hence unaccountable and lacking in transparency, hence 'low quality'. Indeed, evidence and rationality suggest that QA-driven university teaching will be inferior to traditional methods. Certainly the QA system is completely unproven. There has never, at any time or in any place, been a university of acknowledged real-world excellence in teaching (or anything else) that was run in this fashion. Excellent universities have taught their students in many different ways — but never in a fashion which would meet with QAA approval.

It would perhaps be an exaggeration to state categorically that excellent teaching is *impossible* under a comprehensive QA system — after all human ingenuity can achieve the most surprising things under the most adverse conditions. Nevertheless, especially in an underfunded system, QA causes a shift in resources away from teaching and towards auditing, a shift from 'doing' towards documenting, and a shift in power away from teachers and student

---

[17] M. Harrison, B. Lockwood, M. Miller, A. Oswald, M. Stewart and I. Walker, Trial by ordeal, *Guardian* (Education) January 30 2001, pp. 12-13.

towards managers, auditors and the politicians who set the audit agenda.

A substantial decline in the real-world quality of university teaching and the standard of honours degrees over the past decade is as certain as anything can be in so large and complex a system. That this decline has been disguised by the QA-generated mass of pseudo-objective measurements is no accident. But then QAA inspections do not, even in theory, measure real-world teaching quality — indeed they make no attempt to observe real world teaching. Instead 'teaching quality' is defined as that which is measured by the QAA audit.

The Nature of Auditing

Cross-checking for Consistency

To this point, auditing has been described in very general terms. But so dominant an activity demands closer examination — scrutiny in particular of the way in which auditing seems inevitably to be associated with vast exercises in 'bureaucratic' documentation. Quality Assurance auditing derives from financial auditing, and the principal purpose of financial auditing is to detect and deter incompetence and dishonesty in the handling of money. Incompetence is relatively straightforward to discover — but it is the claim of audit to detect dishonest dealing which requires further examination.[18]

There is an apparent paradox involved in auditing. At first sight, it might seem that checking *the books* fails to solve the problem of dishonesty. After all, if a practitioner is not trusted to do their job honestly, then why should they keep the books honestly? The answer is that audit detects fraud through *cross-checking for inconsistencies*. It could be said that the essence of audit is the search for discrepancies in documentation.[19] Fraud is detected when 'the books don't balance'. Cross-checking in financial auditing works when the accounts contain independent sources of evidence, making-up a web of money flows that constitute the operations of the organization. Each strand of the web should be consistent with each other strand when checked every-which-way. A large organization has so many strands that the number of potential cross-checks is almost infinite. Anyone wishing to 'cook the books' has a great deal to fake if they are to ensure that every possible inconsistency between independent sources has been ironed out.

[18]   Charlton, Shape of things to come.

[19]   Perigord, *Achieving Total Quality Management.*

Fraud is therefore usually apparent to an auditor — especially when the volume and inter-connectedness of organizational activity is unmanageably large, and when information input involves many people. In effect the auditor is like a detective who takes a statement from each witness to a crime, then checks that each witness's 'story' is consistent with all the others. For example, in his 'how to do it' manual of quality auditing, Mills describes the ways in which an auditor can use cross-questioning and observation to catch the auditee in various types of discrepancy.[20] It is a basic assumption that inconsistency is evidence either of incompetence or dishonesty. Discrepancies are assumed to constitute attempts to cover up fraud.

Financial accounting (usually) works in its job of deterring and detecting fraud because it is (usually) easier, cheaper and more efficient to be honest than it is to prepare internally consistent fake accounts which can stand up to skilled cross-checking. In other words, true accounts automatically balance when cross-checked because they are a reflection of reality, while it takes a great deal of work to create audit-proof false accounts.

Quality Assurance auditing — information instead of money

QA auditing has many analogies with financial auditing. But instead of monitoring money flows to detect financial fraud, a quality assurance system monitors compliance to a quality assurance system — it monitors that such a system is in place, and is functioning. Instead of money, the 'currency' is information.

QAA audits university teachers on their compliance to a particular, audit-compatible model of teaching, and this model must be explicit, factual and (so far as possible) quantitative. The specific content of the model does not much matter — what is vital is that there *are* explicit procedures, and that they are complied with. The ideal QA system would be one in which, ultimately, every significant aspect of teaching is formally and explicitly planned and monitored. What is not documented does not count as significant, because it cannot be part of the QA system, hence cannot be audited, hence cannot be 'quality assured'. Good teaching is defined by QAA in terms of an explicit information flow system; and whatever is implicit, or outside of the system, does not count as good practice.

A QA-compatible system will be expressible in terms of flow diagrams: these diagrams define the relationship of information sources, and the legitimate range of cross-checking between infor-

---

[20]   D. Mills, *Quality Auditing*, Chapman and Hall: London, 1993.

mation flows. Armed with these diagrams of what is supposed to happen, QAA inspectors behave very much like financial auditors in their search for inconsistencies in documentation. And as with financial auditing, inconsistency implies incompetence or fraud. A QA system audits teaching documentation firstly for completeness, and secondly for internal consistency — each item of documentation must be consistent with all other items of documentation when cross-checked. Undocumented practice is *prima facie* evidence of bad practice — and the nature and level of documentation will be defined by managerial demands, not by teaching need.

As the QA system becomes more comprehensive, so the potential for cross-checking will increase. Each specific item of information from each person must also be consistent with the documentation from each other person. Teaching must also be consistent with the Mission Statements, aims and objectives of the organization; and documentation must be provided to demonstrate this consistency. Internal information can be checked for consistency with external policies, such as relevant government or Department of Education policies. All this cross-checking inevitably requires vast documentation, hence vast bureaucracy, hence substantial cost.[21] And this is the essential reason why QA systems have an irresistible tendency to become highly bureaucratic and expensive. Escalation of documentation is built in, even when this is not the initial intention and when the early phases are relatively modest and sensible.

The fact that auditors could not conceivably read all the vast documentation, let alone perform the almost infinite number of potential cross-checks, does not matter. The point is that the auditors *might* want to know anything. And failure of either comprehensiveness of documentation or consistency in cross-checking in *any one respect* is taken as evidence of generalized fraud. If the auditee has failed to stick to recommended procedure (failure to 'stick to guidelines'), then the auditee is culpable.

Interestingly, the first round of QAA inspections was not sufficiently documentation-intensive to prevent fraud. So far as the pre-1992 universities were concerned, the documentation provided to QAA was a bogus facade — a Potemkin village successfully concealing the reality of a non-auditable teaching system.[22] For QAA to prevent 'fraud', it will be driven into making the demands for documentation so comprehensive that fakery is easily established by the vast number of potential cross-checks, and so heavily labour inten-

---

[21]   Charlton, QAA.

[22]   *Ibid.*

sive and multidisciplinary that fake accounting will not be an option. It must be made easier to comply with the letter of the audit than it is to cook the books. In practice, QA systems will always generate a demand for truly vast quantities of documentation — whatever the hopes or promises of its advocates.

Advantages of audit-based management

In old-fashioned 'command' systems of management, the managers must directly 'order' the workers to perform certain tasks. This raises the problem of enforcing obedience. Orders will either need to be face-to-face, via an intermediary (eg a foreman), or by written instructions ('memo'). But however it is done, this style of command management involves an element of confrontation, of one person directly asserting their will over another person, and achieving dominance.

When managers are more skilled, better-educated, of higher status and more confident than the workers, attaining dominance is not usually a problem. Indeed, imposing dominance on others, bending them to your will, is enjoyable for some people. But when the workers include people more skilled, better educated, of higher status and more confident than the managers who are supposed to command them — this makes command style management difficult and unpleasant at best, and impossible at worst.[23] More indirect methods of control have therefore evolved.

As audit technologies have evolved away from outcomes and towards systems and processes, difficult policy decisions and unpleasant personal confrontations have been *exported* outside the organization's executive — away from the corporate management and onto *third-party* groups.[24] Managerial consultants or government agencies are used to generate standards, guidelines and protocols (for example the National Curriculum for schools), and enforcement of these standards has been devolved to external agency auditors (such as OFSTED). A manager's role can be presented merely as ensuring compliance with these external standards and enforcement agencies.

Quality Assurance therefore appears to be an evolution of managerial technology, a style of management which (from the managers' perspective) is *superior* to previous styles of management, such as a direct command system. Superior not in the sense of necessarily

---

[23] Charlton, Clinical governance.

[24] Power, *The Audit Society*.

improving the performance or efficiency of the *organization*, but superior in the sense that QA works more effectively to promote the interests of *managers*.[25] In particular, audit enables managers of low-level expertise and modest individual dominance to impose their will upon a more expert and dominant intellectual workforce.

The Future of Audit in UK Universities

The past decade has seen the untrammelled expansion of auditing in the UK universities as governments have used funding restrictions to gain control of research, teaching, student numbers and academic standards. But this is probably a transitional phase. The very success of audit technologies has created the conditions of its own destruction by triggering the breakup of the unified monopoly state university system.

Auditing has generated such a heavy administrative load that resources have been drained from teaching and costs are much higher than they need to be for universities to do their job effectively. As things stand, private universities could almost certainly out-compete the state sector, by undercutting costs and/or providing a better service. For example, the situation is ripe for prestigious universities to opt out of state control, and raise more income than they lose by charging market level fees (presumably these would be at least as high as private school fees — which are running at about five to ten thousand pounds per year). Such an institution could save on the 'transactional costs' imposed by a bloated bureaucracy, and attract the best academic staff (who naturally seek greater autonomy and a lower administrative load — as well as higher salaries).

It may be predicted that the UK state university system will soon begin to break up, as institutions realize that the state asks too much in return for too little. Under pressure of a resurgent private sector, the 'audit society' in universities will be rolled back. With luck, we shall see 'accountability' to officials replaced by responsibility to students, and teaching 'quality assurance' replaced by genuine educational excellence.

---

[25] Charlton, Clinical governance.

Anthony Smith

The Laura Spence Affair and the Contemporary Political Mind

New Labour came to power with a hostile *idée fixe* about Oxbridge, the Oxford half in particular, though their disgruntlement spread gradually to encompass all of the 'elite' universities. Among the first measures announced by New Labour after the publication of the Dearing Report was the removal of the Oxbridge college fee but this, after much acrimonious parliamentary debate, was transmuted, face-savingly, into an Oxbridge 'premium' i.e. the additional money was paid to the university to pass on to the colleges. Then came the strange 'MIT affair', when Gordon Brown, having deprived the Oxford colleges of several millions a year, suddenly thrust tens of millions of UK public money into MIT (Massachusetts Institute of Technology) in order that it might form some sort of joint institution with Cambridge University, the purpose of which was to encourage the energetic commercial exploitation of the UK's academic scientific discoveries (something which was already going rather well, in fact, unaided). Then came a series of ministerial speeches attacking the survival of privilege in the UK (all down to Oxbridge); the Foreign Secretary said there were too many Oxbridgians in the FCO. The Leader of the House of Lords (sic) even went all the way to Washington DC to proclaim to a somewhat puzzled audience of American Oxonians her discovery of an 'Oxford problem'. The attacks appeared gratuitous, under-informed and uniformly vindictive. To Americans they were incomprehensible: no US President would consider it appropriate to wander around the world slagging off Harvard or Princeton or pouring cash into the LSE to help Yale sort itself out.

But of course it was the issue of Oxbridge undergraduate admissions (and to some extent admissions to all of the dozen or so UK research universities) that provided the animus for the complaining and which, in May 2000, caught the political tide. The issue was

highlighted by the Chancellor of the Exchequer's intervention, made
at a TUC gathering, about the case of a young woman who had happened — six months earlier — not to have been selected for a place at
an Oxford college. This part of his speech spatchcocked into a discourse which was actually about something else, had been handed
out to the media and took fire. The row it detonated rumbled on for
over a year and led to much more information than ever before coming to be known about the Oxbridge admissions processes (most of it
to the credit of those universities and their component colleges).

So many of New Labour's aspirations can be seen glimmering
through the Laura Spence Affair, but also much of its inability to
handle issues of class and to cope with questions of 'excellence' and
'elitism'. New Labour's approach to change is illuminated by the
affair, its automatic belief that anyone not toeing the line must be
malign or incompetent. More worrying is its recourse to goading
and humiliating people when a trend does not appear to be moving
in the direction the government desires. It was probably inevitable
that a UK party of the left which had given up the traditional coer-
cive instrumentations of the left would turn to education as the
available means for bringing about desired social change. The education system presented itself as the ideal means by which to transform the attitudes and habits which had long held back economic
development in the UK. Moreover, putting education at the commanding height of policy commended itself simultaneously to egalitarians, managerialists and modernizers. For all those involved in
the New Labour project education was — and is — the most suitable
social institution on which to demonstrate the ethics, the techniques
and the commitment to political professionalism of New Labour.

Political discourse, especially the statements of senior ministers, is
usually conducted in generalisations, in principles rather than cases.
If, on Budget Day, the Chancellor's speech were to begin "Mr. & Mrs.
Jones of Number 7, Acacia Avenue, Tunbridge Wells, you are smok-
ing too much — and I therefore intend to sort you out by trebling the
tax on cigarettes", we would all feel that some sort of transgression
had occurred, a category error. Politicians are supposed to stay
inside their own compound, as it were. When, therefore, Gordon
Brown, in May 2000, startlingly opened up a jihad against 'elitism' in
the UK by singling out one named failed applicant to a single Oxford
college and proclaimed this failure to be proof of the socially biased
selection procedures of the college and of Oxford as a whole, widespread indignation was inevitable. The Chancellor of the Exchequer
had come at us. During the 1980s people often reported dreams in

which Mrs. Thatcher had come to inspect their washing or run her fingers through the layers of dust on their mantlepiece. Well, the Laura Spence Affair was that kind of thing. It was more than a breach of manners or of political manner, it was an attempt to insult and outrage. And if that was the intention, it did not fail.

Had someone from the Chancellor's staff used the telephone and asked for the facts it would not have taken more than a few minutes to correct the various misapprehensions entailed in the Brown speech. His 'facts' about Laura Spence had simply been lifted from the tabloids. His assertion that the College was biased against women, ethnic communities and state schools could have been easily corrected. The students we had taken in our tiny annual permitted intake of medics, plus others we helped to find places in other colleges, were also largely female, largely from the ethnic communities and from state schools. The selection procedures had been conscientious and impeccable, the records meticulous, the results precisely of the kind that New Labour claimed it wanted to see. The applicants had been interviewed not in daunting versions of nineteenth century men's clubs (as Mr. Brown had sneeringly averred) but in professional mode, by understanding adults (male, female, ethnic) who shared a passionate concern for social equality. We had five places available. We chose five young people and got two more equally good applicants into other colleges. Miss Spence did not happen to be close enough to the top of the list, very good though she is. Brown had said that she had five A-grade A-Levels, but she had not even sat the exams and one of her subjects was in any case one of the general subjects which are treated as 'extras' rather than as the core subjects in which an aspiring doctor needs to excel. The places are given in competition and all the competitors have very high academic achievements.

To insert that corrective material impression into the minds of the people who had been influenced by Brown's intervention was a difficult problem. His statement had been couched in a satisfying overlay of revengeful egalitarianism. It is very hard for facts to fight their way through demagogue material, especially when that material emanates from a source of high prestige. It took many weeks of media grind, of harnessing the help of increasingly helpful journalists in all the media, before we felt that the record had been straightened out. About a hundred and fifty articles and interviews appeared. Even now people refer in the press to the Laura Spence Affair as if it stood for Oxbridge bias against state school students. What an examination of the facts reveals is rather different: it shows the almost obsessive concern (attested by many state school staff) to find suitable candidates from state schools who might go on to win places in open competition. (But in a letter to a member of the public, a copy of which has been sent to me, Baroness Blackstone, the Minister responsible for higher education, a year later, in April 2001, acknowledges that the Chancellor's remarks in the Laura Spence Affair are felt in certain quarters to be "controversial". That is as close to a decent withdrawal as New Labour has yet reached).

The 'affair' had served to conceal from public view the actual condition of the schools in the state sector whose students Oxbridge colleges attempt to persuade to compete for college places. But a jibe had been born — out of untruth, begotten of political opportunism. In the urgent necessity to rebut the Chancellor's assertions, much that needed to be said was omitted, and many aftermath questions were left to be addressed. One Labour MP keeps saying, somewhat hopefully, that the affair 'energised' the debate about admission to elite universities. In fact it drew attention away from the deeper issues. An emphasis on the number of state school students 'taken' by Oxbridge draws attention from the failure of schools in providing and encouraging suitable candidates.

The Laura Spence Affair focused the debate on the admissions practices of Oxford colleges and away from the harshly unequal distribution of actual academic achievement among schoolchildren in this country. That is something more important than comparative university admission figures between state and private sectors for it is in our secondary schools that children are educated to the level at which they may choose to compete for a place at a major university. The affair also drew attention away from the sad British phenomenon of social disincentive, that bias against aspiration, which runs through large sections of British society and disfigures our education system. Yet ministers still find it easier to blame the institutions which try to reverse the fault.

Consider the following facts. All the universities in the UK which demand high qualifications among their admission cohorts are looking at the group which gets high grades in the school-leaving examinations. But one third of all the children who achieve three A grades in the Advanced Level examinations have been educated at private schools even though these schools cater for only 7% of the total school population. If you look further into this statistic you discern an even gloomier situation. Strip out all those whose A-grades were in the less respected subjects (i.e. General Studies, Media Studies, Business Studies), which the more demanding universities look upon as useful 'extras' rather than as evidences of high level educability, and you see this bias more starkly. In Physics 40% of all the A-grades go to children at private schools, while in Chemistry the figure is 45%. In the main modern language taught in the UK, French, 51% of the A-graders go to private schools, seven times more than you would expect if educational achievement were evenly spread between state and private sectors. In classics — though this result is less surprising since only a handful of state schools continues to teach Greek and not many have remained loyal to Latin — over 80% of all the A-Graders went to private schools. This is the position confronted by all of the dozen universities which demand the highest qualifications among the students they admit, the so-called 'elite' universities of the Russell Group. Private fee-paying schools are helping their pupils to reach much higher levels; they are also, in some cases, recruiting their pupils selectively.

Educational provision in the UK between rich and poor is grossly unequal. It is generally thought that about one third of the UK's schoolchildren live in the poorer areas of the country and yet if you look at the entire cohort of UK children who get into the top universities, you find that only 6% of them come from these poorer areas. The 'elite' universities recruit their students mainly from relatively well-to-do families and the more upmarket neighbourhoods (whether the students were sent to state or private schools). Whatever measures you use these ugly inequalities glare at you from the pages of statistics. Of all the children who achieve 5 GCSE passes at grades A, B and C, only one fifth have parents who are unskilled manual workers; two thirds of this higher-achieving group have parents whose occupations are professional and managerial.

So the children who have in fact been to state schools and who have managed to reach the high grades expected by the elite universities mainly have parents whose occupations and life-styles are very similar to those who sent their children to private schools. For people who believe that this country requires a large highly educated workforce the picture is depressing indeed. But forget the needs of the economy and just think of the millions of lives involved, all those young people who know inside themselves that they are brainy, yet who never get to first base. Surely, *all* young people should be equipped to reach for the things which give joy and stimulus throughout life, the great products of our culture. They *all* deserve to go to schools that give them access to literature, science, music, history, theatre; they *all* need to relate to teachers of high quality, whom they can treat as role models. They need contact with good, living, human examples of what it is to be educated. That is far more important than which university they get into. It is also the key to the issue of admission to the elite universities.

There is a further and more sinister way in which the Laura Spence affair drew attention away from rather than directing it towards the really telling issues. Government is unwilling to criticize the people whose unreconstructed attitudes, whose belief system, causes the lack of educational aspiration among many of the able young. Brown hit out at the two ancient universities for not 'taking' enough state schoolchildren, but was silent in respect of the schools, the families, the whole ideological infrastructure, which deliberately inhibits young people from reaching out for the highest they might achieve. Why the ministerial silence about the school-teacher who told a parent that she will never see her child again if the child goes to Oxford or Cambridge, who told able pupils that only class traitors apply to Oxbridge? Why is it a 'scandal' if a young woman fails to get a place in a fair competition and not a 'scandal' if she has been told by teachers not to try? (There is surely some scope here for politicians with a predilection for 'naming and shaming').

There is also a delicate question of ethnic politics to be faced by politicians who participate in this debate. For there appears to be a higher propensity among middle class parents of ethnic origin to send their children to fee-paying schools than among other middle class parents of similar financial means. Why should a middle class white pupil at a local state school be thought to be more virtuous, than, for example, a brown pupil at a local private school? Why should professional parents whose disposable income has been invested in their children's education be stigmatized at the expense of parents with the same means who choose to spend their income in other ways? What we appear not to be able to acknowledge in this country is that aspiration is the *sine qua non* of excellence. There are many possible variants and manifestations of aspiration and it is not really the business of politicians to allocate degrees of virtue among them. We are being politically inhibited in this country from discussing the needs of children who simply want to get on in life and New Labour has not entered into these issues with the subtlety of understanding the issues require. There are of course no easy answers but one thing is certain: politicians who play out the ancient class war rituals will get nowhere near the answers.

The affair also naturally increased the concentration paid by the Oxbridge colleges to all the admissions issues. My own college now invests considerably more energy in the whole process and considerably more cash. We are currently spending nearly £2,000 per student chosen; the cash goes on the whole business of selection, on open days, sending students out to 'target' schools, entertaining the candidates, entertaining teachers, on ferrying candidates from college to college in taxis (that's mainly to protect them against predatory reporters), organising two separate interviews for every candidate, accommodation and parties, and hiring squads of students to entertain the hundreds of candidates. Very few applicants are turned away without receiving the complete treatment. It is gratifying to note that many candidates are making a point of saying thank you before they leave, adding that, whichever way the selection goes they have just spent three of the most socially and intellectually satisfying days of their lives. But the proportion of state school students who are admitted to places rises only very slowly indeed.

The fact is that, despite all of this activity of persuading and recruiting candidates, the percentage of state school children admitted to the University remains roughly in the same proportion as among the applicants. The state school numbers are indeed rising — unevenly year by year — but never far from the proportion of the total applying from state schools. There is no point in applying political pressure on Oxford and Cambridge to 'take' more in the name of social justice, for the competition is not (I trust) ever going to be fixed. The young people must first apply and then win their places and no-one, least of all the would-be Oxbridge students, would have it otherwise. One should remember that only thirty years ago the proportion coming from state schools to Oxbridge was much higher, close to 70%. The proportion came down as soon as the grammar schools disappeared, the schools that positively encouraged their products to have a shot at Oxford and prepared them properly. It is neither snobbery nor social discrimination which has reduced this proportion in the years since 1970 — it is the quality of schooling and the increased level of social *discouragement.*

Governments have long tended to look at universities as instruments rather than as institutions that are ends in themselves. Universities are being presented with the task of creating social change at a moment when other levers of egalitarianism have largely been abandoned as ineffective or undesirable. Governments of right and left have seen universities as the means to create a nation that is future-oriented, or science-oriented or business-oriented, or Euro-oriented or motivated in some other beneficial direction. As a result we have lost sight of the role of the university as a learned and learning community, indeed as a model of a community. The modern terminology of 'skilling' and of 'excellence' are words with salience to individuals rather than collectivities but these terms are bringing about a displacement of the traditional purposes of universities as the designated carriers of national cultures. The new political terminology, added to the other pressures now weighing upon the academy, is subverting the whole nature of universities, just at a time when governments are saying they want at least half of the entire population to have the chance of going to them.

The only way in which universities can satisfy the new political demands is gradually to abandon education in favour of training, to switch to web-based courses, modularised, distance-based, globalized, computerized. Governments must somehow be made to understand that goading and harassing the academy will undermine and never achieve their highly laudable aims. If the majority of the population are to be educated into and beyond adulthood, it is necessary to proceed slowly and with every form of encouragement which government can supply. That means more money but much more than that. The attack on the elite universities is just one glimpse of the misplaced governmental zeal to get quick results, and to send in the tumbrils if the education system is not democratized between general elections. It can't be. It won't be if the university institution is to continue as a seat of research, culture and scholarship.

Some participants in the current debate over Oxbridge admissions have even fallen into the temptation of suggesting that the tests should be those of chance. Take the 'top' student from every state school in the country, cried one. Draw lots, has suggested another (seriously, I think). Some want to institute selection techniques based upon tests of perfect fairness, applicable irrespective of the quality of education that an individual has received in the twelve years preceding his or her university application. Does anyone really believe that such tests can be devised, as *substitutes* for the assessment of actual knowledge? Certainly, there might be supplementary tests for detecting innate ability which has been distorted by bad teaching. But in the US SAT's are clearly discredited as tests of academic ability and there appears to exist no 'elite' US university with a better social mix than Oxbridge already has. Are we just trying to measure the wind?

So what measures would make a difference and help bring about the great upswing in educated talent that the country requires? First, the recognition by government that the task is immense, entailing the reversal of whole tides of history. Fiddling about with Oxbridge admissions procedures will do little more than, perhaps, getting a few middle class children from state schools to replace a few middle class children from private schools. Very able working class children will come forward in larger numbers when the level of encouragement provided by family and school improves, i.e.when the cycle of low expectations and poor achievement is broken. Educational deficiency has much more to do with family than with school and begins before the children even reach school. So, improve the cities and streets where children live, ensure that their fathers have jobs, reduce the huge disparities of income in the UK, restore the quality of television, deal with the supply of drugs and reduce the level of social violence. All that would help to transform our universities.

Evan Harris

Higher Education:
A Question of Access

Gordon Brown's misdirected outburst about the case of Laura Spence and Magdalen College, Oxford, of 25 May 2000 propelled the issue of university access into the limelight. In the wake of the Chancellor's comments the Education and Employment Select Committee decided to conduct an enquiry into access at the more selective universities and in higher education generally. What emerged in February 2001 from the (Labour) majority of the Select Committee was a failure, or rather a refusal, to draw any conclusions about the appropriateness or otherwise of Gordon Brown's attack on Oxford. In fact, a mild criticism was deleted from the report at the last minute. It also failed to deal in any way with the controversial question of student financial support — the Government had been widely criticised for abolition of grants for poor students. I described it at the time in my minority report as 'one of the most craven acts of Government back bench fawning ever witnessed'. The enquiry evidence entirely contradicts Gordon Brown's allegation that the admissions and interview process at Oxford is biased or based on the 'old school tie'. When subjected to rational analysis, there is no basis at all for the view that the number of students entering Oxford University is not in direct proportion to the oft-quoted '93 percent of school pupils educated in the state sector', nor is there any evidence of discrimination on application.

In dealing with access we need to consider the application process in stages: the eligible cohort, the rate of application and the success rate of application. 93 percent is not the correct baseline — this figure is affected by staying-on rates, performance at 'A' level and the 'deterrence' factor in applying to Oxford University, which all serve to reduce the number of applications made to Oxford University from the maintained sector to just fifty percent.

The Eligible Cohort

Firstly, staying-on rates reduce this figure, since only 80 percent of sixth formers are being educated in the maintained sector. (Curiously, the Government has identified the role that financial hardship plays in reducing staying-on rates by introducing Educational Maintenance Allowances for sixth formers, although it fails to identify this as a deterrent for those considering university). Secondly, only 66 percent of those who achieve between 28 and 30 points (two As and one B or three As) at 'A' level — the requirement for entrance into Oxford University — are from the state sector. The major responsibility for dealing with these staying-on rates and performance lies with the Government.

The Rate of Application

Thirdly, there is still a significant battle to be won against Oxford's 'old boy' image, which deters some potential students from making the initial application. Oxford acknowledges the existence of this image and numerous programmes are in place to widen access: some, indeed, have been in place for over fifty years. These include:

- The Higher Education Summer School (128 year-11 students from Excellence in Cities areas in the North West visiting Oxford)

- Sutton Trust in-service week for teachers (up to 125 places for a programme in July 2001)

- Sutton Trust Summer School (250 students in 2000 and 2001)

- Target Schools Scheme, run by Oxford University Students' Union. Undergraduates visit state schools during the Easter vacation, plus open days in Oxford and tours of particular regions.

- Oxford Access Scheme — to encourage students from inner city areas, particularly those from ethnic minorities, to enter higher education in general and Oxford in particular.

- Access Cymru — focusing on Welsh applicants, with a Welsh Open Day hosted by Oriel College.

Success Rate

The Oxford entrance examination was removed for the 1997 applicants. It was seen as providing an unfair advantage to independent schools which, unlike the maintained sector, had the resources to coach pupils for the exam. Following this, the interview process has gone some way to closing the gap between maintained and independent sector pupils. An analysis of what happens at the post-application stage provides no evidence of unfair discrimination, direct or indirect, on offers of places made to applicants. As the table below shows, the proportion of students from comprehensive schools, grammar schools and independent schools achieving first and third class degrees is practically identical.

Class of Degree by School Type
 (3 and 4 year courses graduating May 2000) [1]

	First	2.1	2.2	3	Total Classified
Independent	291 (20.9%)	847 (60.7%)	229 (16.4%)	28 (2.0%)	1395
Comprehensive	120 (20.9%)	327 (56.9%)	112 (19.5%)	16 (2.8%)	575
Other maintained	126 (19.8%)	397 (62.3%)	100 (15.7%)	14 (2.2%)	637
Other	49 (15.9%)	189 (61.2%)	68 (22.0%)	3 (1.0%)	309

The implication of this is that the independent school entrants in 1997 were not, on average, even marginally of a lesser standard than the comprehensive school entrants. This is despite the fact that in 1997 the success rate was not equal.

 Success Rate by School Type (%)

Year	Maintained	Independent	Others	Total	Ratio success rate Independent vs Maintained
1996-1997	37.4	46.1	20.7	37.9	1:2

The assumption was that the unequal success rate meant that fewer good independent school students are being admitted at the expense of better comprehensive school students (or the converse, that the comprehensive school students who were admitted were on average better — even slightly — than the independent school students

[1]   Entry cohort mainly 1997.

who gained places). These figures suggest that Oxford's admissions procedure is appropriate, and that, even with more power to make decisions over admissions, the university does not discriminate against state schools.

Missing the Grades

Although more offers are made than there are places at Oxford (120 offers for every 100 places), only 80 students achieve the requested grades. The remaining 20 places are then offered to those candidates — among the 40 remaining — who are selected by the university. Whittling down 40 applicants for 20 places is where Oxford tutors are able to exercise the most discretion. Professor A.H. Halsey and Dr. N.G. McCrum of the University of Oxford described this as a 'black art' in their evidence to the Select Committee[2] This was then seized upon by Gordon Brown's acolytes to suggest the doing down of the hard-working, horny-handed sons of toil like Ms. Spence. Dr. McCrum has explained that this term 'black art' implies, for him, 'an art of the night', one executed in darkness. He bases this description on the fact that 'entirely independent decision centres, in one or two days, rationalise dozens of entry subject lists right in the middle of the long vacation, when many tutors are away'.[3] In fact, evidence shows that they are doing anything <u>but</u> discriminating against maintained sector students. Figures obtained from Oxford University and the Universities and College Admissions Service (UCAS) show that for those applicants who do not meet their required grades (almost universally three As), for the first time Oxford University is positively discriminating in favour of students from comprehensive schools compared to independent school students and grammar school students from the maintained sector. 23 percent of comprehensive pupils gained admission without getting three As, as opposed to 18.5 percent for grammar schools and 17.2 for independent schools. While the vast majority of those students who were admitted with fewer than three As achieved 28 points (two As and a B), one third got in with an even lower score. Of these, comprehensive school students accounted for twice as great a proportion of entrants (6.7 percent), compared to independent school pupils (3.3 percent). Thus, somewhat more consideration is given to comprehensive school students who failed to meet their grades than to their independent sector counterparts. In other words, it is felt likely that,

[2]   Education and Employment Committee: Fourth Report, Higher Education: Access, Jan 2001, p. 196.
[3]   McCrum, personal communication, 3 April, 2001.

all other things being equal, those who get an A and two Bs from Sunderland comprehensive are more likely to do well in their degree than those who, with all the benefits of an Eton education, still 'only' get an A and two Bs. The steps we are suggesting mean putting a stop to unfair discrimination rather than filling quotas in order to be 'politically correct'.

The Benefits of the Interview Process

It appears that the more discretion admission tutors have in deciding who to admit, rather than basing their choice solely on A level performance, the more likely one is to have a fair outcome which takes into account the difficult educational background of some state school entrants. It is now accepted that independent schools were able to provide the resources to help students prepare for the entrance exam in a way that comprehensive schools — who do not have a critical mass of students taking these exams, nor small class sizes — are not able to do. I fear a similar situation arising with the extended 'A' level test. If these are factored into the entrance requirement they would have a negative impact on the ability of comprehensive school students to compete on a level playing field. Alternative means of differentiating, such as the interview, would be increasingly relied upon when everyone is getting three As. Indeed, it is far easier to train interviewers to spot potential and make allowances for the educational backgrounds of students, than it is to persuade them somehow to 'overlook' the stark results of extended A level examinations.

The more selective universities or departments are the most challenged by the increasingly widespread achievement of 3 As by more and more students. For most other universities and courses A levels still provide adequate differentiation between applicants. Nevertheless, while a few universities or courses still have the interview process and can thus be more selective in grade offers, other universities rely purely on 'A' level grades. Institutions in this latter category are far more likely to discriminate *against* students from the state sector, as they cannot possibly take into account each student's background. Since the interview has replaced the exam at Oxford, the figures set out above show that tutors are evidently exercising their discretion both equitably and fairly.

Alternative Methods of Differentiation

There is evidence to show that an association does exist between 'A' level point score and academic background. Robert McNabb, Sarmistha Pal and Peter Sloane found that among 60,000 students who graduated[4] from the old universities in 1992, those from maintained schools were one-fifth more likely to have been awarded a first class degree.[5] Universities need to undertake further research on this relationship and then offer accordingly differential tariffs. More work needs to be done to ascertain whether for a certain A level points score comprehensive school students do better in their degrees than those from the independent sector, and if so, by what margin.. This will give Universities the confidence they need openly to impose a differential tariff to take into account the students' educational background until the state sector is improved. This will end any allegations that Oxford University's admission procedure is a 'black art'. Following this research there are several steps which may be taken in an attempt to introduce more equality into the application process.

1.   UCAS deadlines for applications

The Select Committee recommended moving the Oxford and Cambridge UCAS deadline to January to 'simplify or de-mystify' the entrance procedure.[6] The Oxbridge universities said they would be willing to do this. However, there could be serious consequences for the interview procedure, which would then have to take place in the midst of intensive preparation for the imminent A level exams.

2.   Post-qualification application

This has been supported both by UCAS and the Select Committee on Higher Education.[7] One of its advantages is that it encourages people who might otherwise not think their academic performance was of the required quality for university (or, in the case of the more able, for the more selective institutions) to submit an application in the

---

[4]   Excluding medicine and dentistry.

[5]   University of Aberdeen Department of Economics, *Gender Differences in Student Attainment: The Case of the University Students in the UK.* Discussion paper 98-10, 1998 as cited in Education and Employment Committee, Fourth Report, Higher Education: Access, p.xxviii, January 2001.

[6]   Education and Employment Committee, Fourth Report, Higher Education: Access, p. xxxvi, January 2001.

[7]   Education and Employment Committee, Sixth Report, Higher Education: Student Retention, p. xxxvii, March 2001.

cold light of 'A' level results. A drawback, however, is that it presupposes an overt selection from applicants with published 'A' level results, making it problematic for any university which seeks to make allowances in the tariff to take account of educational background. If the differential tariff quoted above is implemented, it would ensure tutors still had some discretion, although this would be much more explicit than presenting a differential tariff in a conditional offer.

3. Aptitude Tests

Such differential tariffs should be combined with aptitude tests. Obviously, there could still be some preparation for these tests, leading to a possible extension of the current practice to one in which those who can afford a preparation course for a form of SAT are advantaged over those who cannot. Indeed, the Select Committee, when investigating access to Higher Education, was very struck by comments heard in America to the effect that 100 or so points were routinely added to an SAT score upon payment of $600. Many people keep retaking the test, too, to try to boost their overall score — although this is less successful than the boost obtained by initial preparation. Jane Mellanby and John Stein at Oxford are doing some innovative work looking at real aptitude tests which do not allow preparation and we await their results. Interestingly, it was John Stein, medical tutor at Magdalen College, Oxford, who was berated by Gordon Brown!

4. Allow Universities access to GCSE and AS results of prospective applicants

The Select Committee recommended that Universities should be able to contact students with good GCSE or 'AS' results from traditionally under-represented schools which they are trying to target, either before those students come to apply or before they reject the option of applying to a higher education institution.[8] This system already operates in America and would most likely increase application rates and foster a sense of healthy competition.

---

[8]   Education and Employment Committee, Fourth Report, Higher Education: Access, p xxxiv, January 2001.

*5.   US scheme of 'guaranteeing' the top performing group of
students from each school a place at university*

The Government might commission further research into the effectiveness of US schemes of guaranteeing the top 5-10 percent of students from all schools a university place, regardless of their actual
results. These schemes are aimed at improving access to students
from under-represented backgrounds and raising standards in
schools through competition.

Retaining Students

Once the students have entered the Higher Education institution,
there is an increasing problem of how to retain them. I would recommend a reform to access funding. The Government prefers to have
available separate pots of money for which each University then
puts in a competitive bid. This is directional, it is gimmicky and it
tends to reward those universities which have performed badly. A
better solution would be to increase the 'access premium' — currently five percent extra funding given for students from postcode
areas of deprivation — by a significant amount. This 5 percent is supposed to reflect the higher cost of teaching pupils from these areas,
and universities get it when the student is admitted. The money is
kept even if the student is subsequently lost, however, and we know
that retention rates from these areas are particularly poor. There
ought therefore to be some form of incentive to encourage universities to make a concerted effort to keep such students. One alternative
approach might be, say, to triple these funds and ensure that one
third of the total amount is held back until the student successfully
completes his or her course. The additional funding would have to
be such that the final graduation 'pay-off' is effectively profit and
can be re-invested in other university work. Given the right returns,
universities will be sensible to invest in seeking more applications
from these under-represented students, to work at retaining them
and then to target yet more from similar 'problem' educational backgrounds. Healthy competition is thus set up. These monies would
provide access funds for the universities, who would, in turn, have a
vested interest in making sure that students do not drop out because
of financial hardship. In addition, funds go to those universities
already doing well rather than exclusively to those who are less successful.

Tony Blair's stated goal, that fifty percent of all British pupils
should participate in some form of higher education by the year

2004, will not be achieved unless there are changes to the admissions process and some desperately needed funding. Oxford continues to adapt in order to improve access to the university and alter the false assumptions surrounding it, assumptions which Gordon Brown has managed very adroitly to reinforce and perpetuate. However, unless we see dramatic changes not only in the application process, but also in the secondary state sector, the situation is going to get steadily worse. Further, as the editor of this volume has pointed out, the mass expansion of higher education will increase rather than diminish the hierarchy of academic institutions. Overcrowded classrooms, poor facilities and larger class sizes will only enhance the attraction of Oxbridge for the brightest and best-schooled. It seems apt, considering that I started off this chapter quoting Gordon Brown, to end it with the words of my fellow contributor to this volume, Anthony Smith, President of Magdalen College, Oxford: 'the Government should stop attacking élite universities for failing to recruit more state school pupils and focus instead on the failings of state education.'[9]

---

[9]   *Daily Telegraph*, 25 April, 2001 (see also Smith, this volume).

Robert Grant

Education, Utility and
the Universities

The first version of this essay was written in 1989, well before Mr
Kenneth Clarke's Further and Higher Education Act of 1992 was put
into effect by Mr John Major's government. Virtually unannounced,
the Act granted university status to all polytechnics, thus doubling
the number of UK universities to something like 100. It also abol-
ished the Universities Funding Council (previously the University
Grants Commission), establishing in its place four regional Higher
Education Funding Councils, with responsibility for both funding
and the external, so-called 'quality assessment' exercises on which
each institution's funding has crucially come to depend.[1]

Accordingly, what follows here will doubtless be condemned as
'out of date' by those — utilitarians, managerialists and almost all
contemporary British politicians — hostile to its theoretical assumptions, even though they are underpinned by argument. And it must
be admitted that its practical recommendations, though perfectly
feasible given the political will, face greater obstacles to their adop-
tion than they did in 1989, despite coming much cheaper, at least to
the taxpayer, than present arrangements.

On the other hand, the underlying principles still seem to me
valid, so that updating has involved little more than changing
tenses. Even in the present deeply inimical climate, those principles
visibly continue to be exemplified in the best university teaching
and research, and will undoubtedly resurge once the world returns,
as it must, to sanity. More than seventy years of communism in the
Soviet Union, and over forty in Eastern Europe, showed that despite
decades of repression — and even of terror and murder — liberal,
civilized habits of thought are remarkably hard to eradicate. Historically contingent they may be, but their existence for more than

---

[1]   The future of QA is currently (2002) in doubt, but it will almost certainly be back
in some guise or other. Too many people now depend on its existence for their
jobs and their self-importance for its permanent abolition to be a genuine
possibility. I make some further observations on it at the end of this essay.

two millennia surely refutes all shallow historicist and materialist attempts to 'deconstruct' them — usually as being an epiphenomenon of 'bourgeois' economic power (which they long pre-dated, which communism actually did succeed in eradicating, and which they nevertheless survived).

* * *

It may seem odd that universities in a free society should require a justification, when so much else, of far more dubious benefit — the popular music and junk food industries, for example — consumes hugely greater resources. But the answer to that is obvious: rubbishy though they are, those industries are part of that free society, while the universities, which ought to be, are not.[2] When the excuse for universities is generally thought to be their 'utility', it is particularly important to defend the education which only they can provide. But let us first distinguish education from other forms of instruction.

Human beings differ from other animals in virtue of the very much smaller and more indirect role which their fundamental genetic or instinctual equipment plays in their behaviour. The role of learning is correspondingly greater. No doubt we learn much spontaneously, or from experience; but by far the greater part of our learning results from deliberate instruction, imitation, and initiation. To survive we must learn, not merely to shun danger, but to seek our subsistence, and also, in all but very primitive societies, to produce it. That requires not raw experience, undergone anew by each generation, but experience concentrated, ordered, and transmitted as knowledge and method — in other words, taught.

Of course, our need for instruction goes far beyond the satisfaction of material needs; but unless certain minimum material requirements are met, our 'spiritual' potential avails us nothing. There is nothing materialistic in asserting that material needs are primary, so long as we mean only that they must be satisfied first. Materialism is the doctrine either that we have no needs other than the purely animal, or that our other, 'spiritual' needs are merely offshoots or disguised forms of those animal needs. It follows (for the materialist) that to devote resources to our so-called spiritual needs is justified only so far as it also serves the needs of production.

In this light 'culture' (by which I mean merely the non-material realm) can be seen as 'useful'. It becomes either a rehearsal for pro-

[2] Exactly why not, and how, I shall show in due course; but the chief reason lies in the combination of government funding with governments' increasing reluctance to let the universities themselves decide how best to spend it.

duction, as kittens learn to hunt by first stalking leaves, or recreation, in which we recuperate our energies for the next bout of production. Mill in his *Autobiography* attributes some such function to poetry and 'the very culture of the feelings'. Bentham rules in the 'real' (sc. productive) world, but (he says) we also need Wordsworth and Coleridge to save us from its desiccating side-effects.

This view is connected with another, advanced in Mill's *Utilitarianism*, which assimilates culture to 'pleasure'. No doubt it is a 'higher' pleasure (whatever that means, since pleasure is essentially a quantitative conception), but it is still, like all pleasures, implicitly an object of self-centred consumption. The truth of the matter, however, is the reverse, to the effect that culture, or the spiritual side of humanity, is the goal of our existence, whereas production is merely an indispensable precondition of it, and thence derives its importance. That view of the matter, of course, stems from Aristotle, who used the word *scholē* or leisure — whence 'school' — to express what I mean here by 'culture'.

Things may be otherwise in educational theory, but in educational policy and administration no serious distinction is made between education and training. Both, after all, are forms of instruction, both in some sense equip people for 'life', and both involve expense, since at the very least teachers and learners must be freed from immediately productive labour. But the distinction is nevertheless important, and is this: education is a matter of ends, while training is a matter of means.

One is always trained *for* something. That 'something' may be education, or it may be production. Both a shopkeeper and a pure mathematician need to have learnt simple arithmetic. But there seems to be no conception of education proper in which it can be seen instrumentally, as a means to some end beyond itself, and even though (in our society) it may confer some non-educational advantages on those who have it.[3] There is no answer to the question, 'Why should I be educated?', except this: 'It is your nature, destiny and fulfilment to be so, to whatever the degree is of which you are capable.'

Those who speak of 'education for democracy', or of the indispensability of educated people to a desirable society, and so on, either misconceive the nature of education (and are thus really talk-

---

[3]   Those are now almost certainly outweighed by the disadvantages. It is, for example, almost impossible for a genuinely educated young person, whatever his or her social origins, to get a job at (say) the BBC, as it was not even twenty years ago. Such a person will be perceived as 'posh', and as an affront to the official ethos of 'inclusiveness', despite belonging to a genuinely discriminated-against minority. (Posh 'ethnics', though, are still acceptable.)

ing about something else, e.g. a form of training) or are using a kind of shorthand to express the (correct) intuition that a desirable society is one composed of educated people. (I shall come later to what is meant by 'an educated person', merely observing here that it is not limited to the academically accomplished.) Education is not an *ingredient* of the good society; education, or a state of general educatedness, is what the good society actually consists in. Education is intrinsically conducive to the social bond, not merely because it is socially acquired, through the transmission of skill and knowledge from person to person, and generation to generation, but also because, tacitly or overtly, it is social in aim.

Each generation hopes by educating the next not merely to equip its successor to fend for itself, but also to endow it with its own interests and values and the means to hand them on to succeeding generations. In educating our children we intend, not merely to train them for survival, but to give them something that will make their survival meaningful and them tolerable companions for ourselves so long as we survive. We aim, in short, at perpetuating the things which most matter to us, even beyond the point when we will no longer be there to enjoy them. A Robinson Crusoe marooned in childhood with nothing but basic literacy and numeracy, a store of books, and sufficient intelligence to have developed his mind, had he remained in society, to the highest degree, would by himself acquire no education to speak of; and even if, by some miracle, he were to do so, it would avail him little. For the end of education (if momentarily, for argument's sake, we treat it as a means) is nothing other than educated intercourse with people of like mind, in other words, educatedness. And that is merely to repeat that although education has a beginning and a middle, it has no end but itself.

Education is not all of the same kind or degree, and, so long as people differ in intelligence, background and motivation, not everyone can be raised to its highest level. Even if things were otherwise, there would still always be an educational élite, though it consisted only of those engaged in instruction. For the whole notion of education as a process, and as something acquired, is inevitably inegalitarian, simply because teaching *eo ipso* presupposes ignorance in some and knowledge in others. On the other hand, the very same feature gives education an equalizing tendency, and more, since its object is to raise learners as nearly as possible to the level of their teachers' attainments and to encourage them, if they can, to surpass them.

It seems unlikely that within the normal ranges of intelligence and emotional complexion there could be anyone completely ineducable. Observing the *de facto* division of labour, Plato supposed that there must be an appropriate niche in society for everyone, and that each individual, if steered to it, would find therein the greatest fulfilment of which his or her nature was capable. We need not agree with Plato's authoritarian *dirigisme*, or indeed with his very implausible assumption that niches and people will automatically match each other in both number and quality, to agree with his general point that fulfilment, of some kind, is desirable for as many as possible. For neither pleasure, nor utility, nor production is the point of education, but the rational fulfilment of the recipient ('rational', because such fulfilment constitutes a real reason for the individual to be educated). A society whose members are fulfilled will be what Plato was centrally preoccupied with devising, a society at peace with itself, even if it does not much resemble his ideal republic.

Only that instruction can properly be called education, which treats the learner and what is learnt as ends in themselves, no matter what secondary advantages in utility or material productiveness attach to the latter. Education rests on Kant's second categorical imperative — the injunction never to treat anyone as a means only, but always also as an end in himself. Obviously, however, a society dependent on producers — a stage we have yet to outgrow — will do well to ensure that enough of the education it provides happens also to be useful in production, and also that as little production as possible takes the form of alienated, mechanical drudgery for those engaged in it.

In proportion as a task engages the performer's talents, to that extent training him or her for it approximates to education, and the more so the more the task requires the development of those talents. It follows that what is an education for you might amount to a mere training for me, if my talents lie in another direction, and are thus ill-matched to the task in question. That is perhaps one reason why training and education are easily confused; another is that to train people merely to secure their subsistence is nevertheless to direct one's attention to their welfare, albeit only of a material — or if you like, 'selfish' — kind. The only case in which it is surely impossible ever to confuse training with education is when the subject's welfare, talents and inclinations are left altogether out of account, and the training is undertaken exclusively for the benefit of something or someone else (an obvious example is slavery).

It is not hard, however, to show that education is more than a mere training in selfishness, and that it has a naturally altruistic tendency. It is perfectly true that self-fulfilment, self-realization and the rest have long been the buzz-words of a peculiar cult of egocentricity much in vogue on the Pacific coast of the United States (one amusingly commemorated, a quarter of a century ago, in Cyra McFadden's *The Serial*). But egocentricity, or self-gratification, is just the opposite of self-fulfilment. The 'self' which is gratified is as different from the 'self' which is fulfilled, as selfishness is from self-respect.

Education capitalizes not upon the first, but upon the second. It harnesses the learner's self-respect to his or her natural curiosity, so that truth, like truthfulness, becomes a matter of honour. Scorning lies, one scorns even more to lie to oneself. Curiosity seeks to experience the world as it is in itself, undistorted by subjective fantasy or will. It gives us a certain pleasure for once to restrain our impulse to interfere, and to contemplate things in their independence of ourselves. In them we perceive, so to speak, the mirror-image of our own freedom. This, perhaps, is the primary scientific impulse, to which we owe our knowledge of the natural world, a knowledge truly amazing by comparison with what prevailed in the era of magic, when the immediate impulse was to bend nature to human purposes. It is evident that such an epistemology contains the seeds of a moral attitude, and thus that an education in scientific inquiry is also indirectly a moral education. (And that is true even if, as a result of our understanding, we find the long-sought-after mastery of nature within our grasp.)

The same altruistic impulse lies behind the desire to understand, rather than manipulate, the human world. It is significant that the Sophists, who, like their latter-day champion Nietzsche, were sceptical about the possibility of truth, were also professional teachers of rhetoric. For them truth was what, by fair means or foul, people could be persuaded to believe, and they peddled the techniques of its manufacture in democratic Athens, where power hung upon the ability to convince. But a genuine education in the humanities is different, even though 'truth' there is inevitably something less factual and clear-cut than in science. Of course in science 'truth' is provisional, in the sense that it is always corrigible in the light of new interpretation and evidence; but in the humanities what matters is less the absolute truth (for that will always remain elusive) than the observer's will to approximate to it, in other words his objectivity.

Objectivity means something different in the humanities from what it means in the sciences, since the observer actually belongs to the world described. (He also belongs to the natural world, but only physically, not *qua* observer.) In order to describe it accurately —

that is, objectively — the observer must take into account, or even share (though not uncritically), the intimations of value it contains. The scientist's task, by contrast, is precisely to rule out such considerations and to see his world as far as possible from a non-human perspective. To see the human world from the scientific angle, therefore, is not to see it at all, since, though no less open to inquiry in its own way than nature, it is not a scientific object. All educated inquiry presupposes a perspective appropriate to the particular object or field under study. Both science and the humanities demand a certain judgment, taste or *Taktgefühl* in the inquirer, who will thus instinctively know which assumptions or procedures are or are not legitimate (that is, likely to be fruitful). And that, of course, is something one can only learn as a member of a self-conscious community of inquirers, as the heir and contributor to a tradition.

The drive to objectivity is a feature not merely of academic studies. People properly educated — and I mean educated — in bricklaying, gardening, cabinet-making or motor mechanics have learnt no less than academics an appropriate scrupulousness in procedure, respect for their materials, the ability to follow up a hunch, and a love of their art and their fellow-practitioners. All these are really a form of respect for things as they exist independently, not necessarily of human will altogether, but of one's own purely subjective will. To have acquired them is to have forsaken the childish illusion that the world (and its other inhabitants) can or should be made to yield to one's own desires. Self-knowledge, self-control and self-direction supplant the fantasy of control over nature and others.

In education as I have characterized it we have not only a compelling motive for voluntary association, but also the germ both of a virtue (call it disinterestedness) and of political order in a free society (call it fairness or justice). Similarly, in those resistant to education — again as I have characterized it — we have the model of despotism, which is self-will reinforced by power. In totalitarian societies, accordingly, genuine education is scarce in many fields and forbidden in some, while so-called political education (which of course is no such thing) occupies a major part of the curriculum. In free societies, by contrast, we have in ordinary education almost all the political education that citizens need, unless they also intend to make politics their study or career.

All education throws political shadows, but university education does so particularly, partly because (incredible though it may seem) the political élite is overwhelmingly drawn from the educational élite, and partly because (in the UK) the universities are still government-funded to the point of virtual monopsony. This mattered less when the University Grants Committee was simply given the money by government and told to get on with it, than it does now, when the Higher Education Funding Councils are, in Lenin's phrase, 'transmission belts' for central government policy.

A university consists of two things: first, a permanent community of scholars engaged in various kinds of inquiry; second, a transitory population of students who hope to learn something from them. It might seem perfectly possible to defend high-level free inquiry, whilst regarding the upkeep and tuition of those who were themselves never going to participate in it as a waste of time and money. For it is obvious that the subjects traditionally studied in universities have (at least in the form in which they are studied) no immediate, tangible application. The average student of French is not going to teach it, set up as a translator, or do business in it (and there are specialist courses elsewhere in commercial French). And even in the sciences, some have no application at all, while others are read only to be abandoned on graduation.

Of what value, it may consequently be asked, is the education of those who never actually use the particular skills they have acquired? And why concentrate so many diverse studies in a single location? What is the university student supposed to gain that could not equally be gained in a liberal arts college, a language institute, a college of technology, or in a professional or other apprenticeship? In other words, what makes a university education a *university* education?

The history of universities, though not an infallible index of their nature and function, is not without interest. The mediaeval curriculum consisted of the seven liberal arts: a lower or basic division, the *trivium* (grammar, logic, rhetoric), and of a higher, the *quadrivium* (arithmetic, geometry, astronomy, music). The whole had both a practical and a theoretical character, though in each individual subject the two aspects are not always, if they ever were, easily distinguishable. The study of music was not meant to equip graduates to seek their living as composers or performers, nor astronomy to meet the needs of navigation; and something similar might be said of grammar and logic. But arithmetic and geometry are simultaneously abstract and applicable (indeed architecture, in which they are essential, had been reckoned among the liberal arts by the Romans), while rhetoric provided training in public speaking partly through exposure to literature.

Furthermore, though university faculties had an unmistakably vocational aspect, being divided into law, divinity and medicine, it was evidently thought that one could not practise a chosen vocation in a proper manner unless one's education had also contained what, from a narrowly pragmatic point of view, were irrelevancies. Thus it was that such vocations enjoyed the title of the 'liberal' professions, meaning those that the *liber* or 'free' man might practise, i.e. one who, though he might earn his living by them, was not constrained by necessity to do so.

In translating that idea into modern terms we need not assume with Aristotle that such a person must be of independent means and in that sense 'leisured'. For so long as he or she can make a living by practising a profession, he or she *is* financially independent, in the relevant sense. What matters is what is left over from the immediate exchange value of these services. That will be something that affords food for disinterested reflection, and (consequently) has a moral dimension. Moreover, it plays an essential part in all professional activities. For what is required in the professional, and is also paid for by the client, is this same quality of disinterestedness.

In Chapter 2 of *The Wealth of Nations*, Adam Smith said that we secure others' services by appealing not to their benevolence, but to their self-interest. This may be true of much economic activity, but it is not strictly true of the professions. The ideal structure of a professional relationship is this: I need your skills as a lawyer (doctor, priest). In asking you to act for me, I ask you to set aside the normal motives to which I might appeal if I required something simpler or more material (meat, bread, candlesticks). I ask you to consult not your interests, but mine. To enable you to do so without thereby imperilling your interests, I propose, along with your other clients, to take immediate material considerations off your hands. You will then be free to devote yourself to my concerns, and I understand, indeed, that in setting yourself up as a professional governed not by straightforward financial considerations, but by an ethic enforced by your professional corporation, this is precisely what you undertake to do. What I am doing is not 'paying for your services', but conferring financial independence on you so that you may, so to speak, provide your services *gratis*.

This is much less fantastic than it may sound. It is self-evidently the paradigm of the pedagogical relationship (which is one reason why education, like medicine, has a strong historic association with charity), though it is of course likely to appear idealistic in the light of much current practice in the professions, particularly in the United

States, where professionals have largely become tradesmen or entrepreneurs working on commission. The consequences are visible in
the vastly inflated damages secured by successful litigants from
those who, at similarly vast expense, have insured themselves
against it, and in the destruction of trust between doctor and patient
by constant malpractice suits.

Some people are doing well out of this grotesque lottery, but the
cultural impoverishment is enormous. Indeed, the whole slide into
materialistic anarchy may well have begun in the American education system, in which, by the very fact of their being taught and
examined side-by-side in the same institutions, little distinction is
made between academic, professional and business studies, and the
whole baggage of potentially ephemeral skills (and even non-
existent ones) from tourism and golf course management to
aromatherapy. (Which is not to say that non-academic things cannot
be taught in institutions, though they are often better taught on the
job. The question is simply, *if* in institutions, then in which?)

The professions are an obvious, natural and long-established
bridge between the academic and the 'outside' worlds. But, as just
noted, the modern university increasingly includes subjects which
have little or no theoretical, 'liberal' or philosophical component.
Economics is nowadays rightly reckoned to be a proper university
subject: it is difficult, abstract and possessed of an intrinsic intellectual fascination. Further (some say), it contains elements which
involve serious reflection on the nature and ends of human life,
which, even if useless to financiers (for example) in their day-to-day
dealings, would still be of value and interest to them as rational
beings. But, if there is any value in a university's having a school of
accountancy, it will lie only in whatever 'liberal' values budding
accountants imbibe from their environment, since accountancy is in
itself a wholly utilitarian discipline, whose theoretical content is
completely consumed in its own exercise.

I am emphatically not saying that vocational or utilitarian subjects
necessarily lack the moral dimension of traditional academic subjects, nor that, having commercial value, they must somehow be
inappropriately 'materialistic'. As in the manual crafts I instanced
earlier, there is moral discipline, and hence educational value, contained in the very effort to master them. Moreover, in a student who
has a genuine talent for them, they will conduce to what I have called
his rational fulfilment. What they lack, however, is the ability to generate disinterested theoretical reflection. (If anyone needed persuading that accountancy was not an especially fruitful standpoint from

which to reflect upon life, he need only consider the Benthamite legacy.)

Some subjects, though worthy and useful so long as an external demand for them exists, open no windows on to anything else. If they are grouped together in a single institution, that is simply for the sake of convenience. They may share their usefulness, they may share techniques, resources and facilities, they may even team up to solve some newly-perceived problem or to pursue some potentially profitable research, but they have nothing fundamentally to say to each other, because, strictly speaking, they have nothing to *say* at all. Everything at bottom is doing, and when the doing ceases (just as when a trade or a technique becomes obsolete) then so does the subject. Such subjects may have educational value, but are surely inappropriate in a university.

In implying that 'real' university subjects have something to say about the world I do not mean that they have anything directly to contribute to the solution of its practical problems, though they may have, and even today employers value a liberal education for its so-called 'transferable skills'. The 'world' on to which 'real' university subjects open a cognitive window is not the everyday practical world, nor a purely ideal world such as Plato imagined, but a world from which time, and thus the immediate motives to action, have been mentally bracketed out. So much is obvious from the study of history or theoretical physics, since we are powerless to affect the past, or the laws of nature. It is a world, in short, without urgency, and hence without the parochiality naturally consequent upon an exclusive preoccupation with the immediate. A man with his nose held perpetually to the grindstone will take his grindstone for the world; and he will be wrong.

For these general reasons, although an academic may also be, and frequently is, an intellectual, the academic and the intellectual are different species. Both seek theoretical understanding, but the intellectual generally does so as a prelude to action. And action, like material subsistence, is always necessary, though intellectuals are frequently the least reliable of guides as to what it should be, and are seldom to be entrusted directly with power. Nevertheless, they may perhaps be thought disinterested enough to be worth listening to when, as I am doing here, they call for action to preserve an ethos to which they cannot *qua* intellectuals belong. For the liberal university is worth preserving as a major, if historically emergent, part of our distinctively human world. In it, we appear as pre-eminently creatures of culture, who do more than just eat, drink, squabble and reproduce like the animals we also are.

Each traditional university subject offers an escape — though only the utilitarian will think that 'escapist' — from whatever purely practical concerns it also happens to serve. What distinguishes it from other forms of higher education is that in it contemplation is of the essence, and not merely a possible by-product. Moreover, its immediate focus is not the self-fulfilment and self-realization of the student (the eliciting and development of his particular talents), but the good of the subject. It is true, of course, that undergraduates have nothing much to contribute to their subject. But it is of the greatest importance that they be taught by those who do have something to contribute, so that they get from them some idea of what it is to pursue a line of inquiry for its own sake.[4] Their fulfilment is achieved precisely by its being subordinated it to their subject, even though they will not usually persevere with their subject after graduation.

There is another, and difficult, point to be made about university subjects. How can they conduce to the breadth of mind and the synoptic overview which we associate with liberal education, when their intrinsic differences, and the freedom of inquiry essential to each, leads them off in wholly divergent and unpredictable directions? Have they not a centrifugal tendency that must ultimately destroy all communication between them, and hence the whole point of their being brought together in a university?

Some thinkers, such as the literary critic F.R. Leavis, seem to have found this a worrying possibility, and have wished to promote certain so-called 'central' disciplines (his own, in Leavis's case) to pride of place in the university curriculum. But to regard one particular subject as 'central' is to misconstrue the whole academic enterprise. So far from arresting the disintegration of the university, it would accelerate it, by marginalizing less privileged (but equally 'real') academic subjects. Secondly, to subordinate any discipline to another — just as to subject it, like the academy as a whole, to any

---

[4]   This is not to approve the current uncritical fad for 'research-led' undergraduate teaching. This merely blinds the student with science, focuses his mind prematurely on minutiae incomprehensible without the broader picture, prevents him from meeting his teacher on a basis of potential equality, and consequently bestows on the teacher a means (not seldom exercised by those so disposed) of permanent, humiliating domination. Without substantial trust in his teachers a student will learn nothing. Yet almost no trust is more easily abused. It is, in fact, good for a student to be taught by someone of greater knowledge and experience who, simply through not having mugged it up last week, is less immediately familiar than himself with their common topic. (It is good for the teacher too.)

external, non-academic authority — is to constrain its free development, and thus, by cutting off its academic life-blood, to extinguish
it. There are reasons, which I have already given, for excluding perfectly genuine but non-academic subjects from university study, but
none for introducing an inequality between those that remain.
Thirdly, the motive for privileging some university subjects is not
academic, but political, whereas their supreme political value lies
precisely in their *not* being available for immediate political consumption. In their self-motivated, corporate independence they are
a public advertisement for the Aristotelian truth that the ends of the
polis are no more narrowly political, than the ends of life are material.

What university disciplines have in common is not their sub-
stance, but their spirit. Their joint message to the world, which justifies their incorporation into a single institution, is no more than an
affirmation of the value of free inquiry as such, undertaken in a spirit
of mutual tolerance, which sets limits to the pretensions of each to
trespass on its neighbours' territory and to pronounce the final word
on the constitution of things.

As Matthew Arnold and Cardinal Newman stressed, there is here
a spillover into culture at large. As we should, we still send people to
universities for a liberal education, even in scientific subjects. An
induction into the academic ethos was thought to have a beneficial
effect on the character, and such a character to have a beneficial effect
on the world, once its owner had returned to it. By an educated person we mean more than merely one who is intellectually skilled, possessed of a given type and quality of information, and so on. We
attribute to such people a certain conversability, a readiness to listen
to anything decently presented and not manifestly absurd, various
types of quasi-moral restraint, and the like.

Such a character displays what may be called liberality of mind, a
thing barely separable from high culture. It presupposes an ironic
catholicity of outlook, a reluctance to be always claiming the moral
high ground, and a general distrust of partisanship. All this leaves it
ill-equipped to survive in a straight battle against fanaticism,
unscrupulousness, ignorance, intolerance and sanctimoniousness,
in short against the spirit of 21st-century British democracy. That
antagonism alone is a good argument for preserving liberal education. For what else in our society ranges itself against that unholy,
fortuitous, implausible, yet all-too-real alliance of the *Sun* on the one
hand and the *Guardian* on the other?

I suggested earlier that there might be some value in exposing students of utilitarian subjects to a university environment. This was

recognized, indeed, in the traditional stipulation that students at polytechnics (when they existed) and even at Colleges of Further Education should attend classes in 'liberal studies'. (Though no-one who has seen a sensitive woman, or man for that matter, attempting to initiate an unwilling class of 17-year-old plasterers into the delights of *Adam Bede* will reckon the time or the tears well spent.) But there are difficulties involved.

One is, that the benefits of any 'liberal' discipline are likely to come only from full-time immersion in it. The aptitude for contemplation is not universal, nor is the kind and degree of intelligence it demands. If, under external pressure, and possibly hoping thereby to preserve its liberal core, a university admits significant numbers to read wholly utilitarian subjects, it will find that core dwindling into a rump, especially when the teachers of such subjects — who in private may be as 'liberal' as you please, but who also have their professional interests to protect — are admitted to university government.[5] The same is more obviously true of institutions designed to be hybrid from the start.

Alternatively, universities might admit 'vocational' students, of sufficient motivation and intellectual calibre, to read 'liberal' subjects for some proportion of their higher educational career. That way the student would benefit, while the university remained uncompromised in its fundamental aim. But then something like this has always happened anyway, only in reverse order, as when university graduates in maths or English go on to train as accountants, business executives and so on.

But speculation on such minor logistical details is futile, when it is simply the external pressure on universities — in short, their dependence on government — that creates most of their difficulties. Higher education needs what, until lately, secondary education had within its grasp,[6] namely independence. Government funding of all

---

[5] Given that university teachers are no longer admitted *ex officio* to university government (as that activity is now understood), this consideration no longer applies, though the result, from the viewpoint of 'liberal' academia, is the same. The genuinely liberal academy is either self-governing, or nothing. It is under no threat from utilitarian or vocational education (or training) whatever, so long as it is not forced to co-exist with those things (which are also necessary) in a single institution, and thus be dominated by them. Or, one might add, to compete with them for resources from the same pot of tax revenues.

[6] The grant-maintained, quasi-independent state schools, encouraged by the present government's Conservative predecessor to 'opt out' of LEA control, no longer exist. Most have now chosen 'foundation school' status, under which, whilst once more funded by their LEA, they supposedly retain the freedom to spend their allocations as they see fit. It is doubtful whether they can any longer be seen as a precedent for 'opting-out' or fully independent universities, since it

utilitarian education should (and could) cease forthwith. There might just be a case for retaining it in liberal education, but only until such time as private, personal and charitable initiatives can take over. Those who think their education requires some liberal component will then be at liberty to seek it from whatever institutions are prepared to admit them, for whatever period.

Nothing is odder than the modern belief that government support should be concentrated on the utilitarian sector, for it is precisely those subjects which could safely be abandoned to the market. High-level practical skills are no different, economically speaking, from any other factors of production. So let employers pay for them directly, either by funding their employees' education as it proceeds, or by paying fully-qualified staff an appropriately enhanced salary on recruitment, so that they can finance their own education by borrowing against their prospects. Employers will be well able to afford either option, once repossessed of whatever proportion of their revenue is currently being expensively re-routed through government to precisely the same end.

Producers are surely better judges than governments of what they themselves require. And so are universities of what universities require. As a result of governments' favouring utilitarian or (what they take to be the same thing) scientific subjects, some universities, even before 1992, were without a department of classics, or a department of philosophy, despite the piddling sums required to keep such minority disciplines alive. I should say that an institution which lacked either, let alone both, scarcely deserved the name of a university.

Such an institution, however, typically has good departments in utilitarian subjects, and thus still discharges a valuable educational function. The answer is not only to allow, but to encourage it to do so. Humanities or pure science departments could be wound up and their staff reallocated to whichever universities were prepared to take them. Their students and their salaries would follow them. If it should be thought invidious to reintroduce the term 'polytechnic' for what remained (though it has never bothered our French neighbours), something else (e.g. 'technical university') could doubtless be found. At all events, the reality is that for so long as we continue to entrust vocational training and education to higher educational institutions rather than (as previously) to articles and apprenticeships, most of those will be polytechnics, whatever else we choose to

---

is likely that LEAs, deprived of direct administrative control, will endeavour to exercise control indirectly, by squeezing such schools' budgets.

call them. The important thing is that universities proper, and the liberal education which they alone can provide, should survive, as they will not if they are simply rolled up along with technical education into comprehensive 'multiversities' (to use a once fashionable term).

All this amounts, of course, to reversing Robbins whilst retaining an expanded higher education sector.[7] Robbins was concerned less with university education than with utilitarian education dressed up to look like it. What was needed was as many polytechnics as employers and employees required, together with an expansion of established universities consonant with preserving the true academic ethos. Both would have come about spontaneously anyway, given the enormous post-war increase in wealth. There might have been a few new universities, but with each made large enough to sustain flourishing minority departments, and perhaps beginning as affiliates or extension colleges of established universities, with the latter awarding the degrees (the relation in which Newcastle once stood to Durham, and Dundee to St Andrews).

The outer limit of university expansion, as Enoch Powell once remarked, should have been set by the availability of suitably-qualified staff, and precisely that would have been ensured by the expansion of existing departments. For which of them would readily have admitted inferior colleagues to share in their decisions? Yet we all know what happened in many of the new 'Robbins' universities, and where, in combination with early tenure, it led. One especially serious consequence was that, with 'Sixties mediocrities clogging the pipeline (and running departments and appointments committees), it became desperately difficult for first-rate graduates to find university employment at all. That situation has definitely not improved, and if anything has got worse.

If only in the short run, any universities in the strict sense which survive the current trend towards 'comprehensive' higher educa-

---

[7]   In October 1963 the committee headed by the former LSE economist Lord Robbins published its report on higher education. The main proposals were that six new universities be created, that the ten Colleges of Advanced Technology be upgraded to universities, and that the existing universities should expand. All this would more than double the university intake, and do so (said the Report) without compromising academic standards. Some critics (e.g. the authors of the unofficial 'Black Papers') contested the latter claim, but many (myself included) would say that, as things turned out, the charge was not proven. The reason, I take it, was that many people of quite sufficient ability to profit from a university education were then just not getting one. But there is every reason to suppose that that pool of previously untapped academic talent is long exhausted.

tion will continue to need some government support, simply because so much of what they do by definition lies outside the market. (And they should get it through some buffer institution on the lines of the UGC, in order to minimize direct political interference.)[8] With utilitarian education off their hands, governments should be well able to afford it. In the long run, however, there is no reason to think that universities cannot flourish as they once did, on a combination of economic tuition fees and charitable endowments. The latter, which also lie outside the market, have traditionally been motivated either by the donor's vanity or by a disinterested regard for learning. Both are potent incentives, especially when stimulated by tax breaks.

As for economic fees, those could be charged straight away, with the student subsidized where necessary from public funds. We are constantly told of the enormous (utilitarian) demand for graduates in applied science. (If it is true, though, why are scientists so ill-paid?) Industry therefore has only to put its money where its mouth is. And I see no evidence to suggest that graduates in humanities or pure science are any less in demand than formerly, and much to suggest the opposite. It has been observed at least since the twelfth century that a liberal education enables one to turn one's hand to almost anything. There is therefore no reason to think that students in less immediately 'useful' subjects will find funds any harder to come by than others. And economic fees of course also ensure funds for those very few students who wish to make their careers within the university.

In the long run, I believe, a successful enterprise culture — which, despite everything, and whether or not we also like it, is what we now have — ought to have no difficulty in generating the wealth necessary to put universities back on their feet (much of it, after all, would come simply from its redistribution back from government to the public), and in re-establishing the habit of philanthropy. Desirable though endowments are, however, they are unnecessary to the universities' day-to-day subsistence. Simply by putting their services on the market at their true cost, universities would almost cer-

---

[8]   The HEFCs are supposed to be such buffer institutions, but the criteria under which they operate, though not political in the everyday sense, are perceived by most of the institutions subject to them as being virtually indistinguishable, at least in point of their oppressiveness, from political interference. This is especially so in the case of the Research Assessment Exercise, which has led, not only to the farcical situation described later in the main text, but also to the establishment by universities of journals specially designed to notch up a few extra RAE points by taking in each others' dirty washing.

tainly recoup the maintenance of their other, central activities, which, lying outside the market, are literally priceless.

What stands in the way of these recommendations is not so much the current, post-1992 situation in itself (for that can be changed) as the political interests which brought it about and mean to preserve it. None of our last three Prime Ministers has had any time for universities in the traditional, liberal sense. Oxford notoriously fell foul of Mrs Thatcher by refusing her the regular PM's honorary degree, on the well-worn, ritualistic grounds of 'Tory cuts' (so it was claimed by the leftist dons who engineered this childish discourtesy), when in fact her government spent proportionately more on education as a whole than any of its predecessors. But it is also true that, in her Philistine, good-housekeeping, muck-and-brass, get-up-and-go perspective (tonic though it was for a paralysed economy), liberal education and its associated values and attitudes could figure only as an unintelligible, quasi-aristocratic luxury. She was no friend either to the professions, seeing them, as no traditional Tory could possibly see them, as well-fed bastions of unaccountable monopoly power, mere middle-class trade unions.[9]

Though more pacific, Mr Major was reportedly so chippy about his own educational deficiencies (which were not, in fact, glaringly obvious) that nothing could stay his abolition of their visible reminder. None of his Cabinet, so far as I know, and well educated (largely at Cambridge) though many of them were, raised even the slightest protest at the 1992 Act. And we now have a Prime Minister for whom one of the best and most expensive educations in the world (Fettes and St John's, Oxford) appears to have done nothing except freeze his self-complacency into a permanent schoolboy smirk. (Just imagine how the gorge of Hardy's Jude the Obscure would have risen at the spectacle.)

Despite his own immense privilege, Mr Blair's limited notions of education seem never to have risen above the level — not in itself to be despised, of course — of 'qualifications'. Worse still, he has opportunistically dragged his (and our, and your) government into the illiberal, value-inverted, looking-glass world of the tabloids, so that ministers of the Crown now go toadying to witless footballers,

---

[9]   Here is an occasion to observe that one of the (perhaps *the*) deepest and most unbridgeable of all class divisions is a vertical one, between the professional and the commercial or managerial middle class. (E.M. Forster's Schlegels and Wilcoxes respectively.) For the most part, and roughly speaking, the first has the education and status, the second the power and wealth. (So much for Marxism, which sees them, implausibly, *en bloc*.) Since the division is natural and inevitable, there is no point in deploring it. It might even be a good thing.

soap stars and 'yoof' icons, only to be insulted for their condescension (and rightly so) by loutish Mancunian pop singers.

Like every tyranny from antiquity to the present, what the modern democratic politician especially fears is public criticism, especially when that comes from an informed, independent source, whose authority is only reinforced by its lack of formal power. Mr Blair's nervous reluctance, despite his enormous majority, to answer to, vote in, or even appear in the House of Commons was publicly censured by its last Speaker (who had previously sat for his own party). Almost his first act in government was to cut Prime Minister's Questions by half, and his second to abolish as many as he could of the hereditary House of Lords, notwithstanding that the Lords were powerless to delay any measure longer than a twelvemonth, and that for half a century the so-called Salisbury convention, that the Lords oppose nothing in the Government's election manifesto, had been faithfully observed. It is hardly surprising, then, that the Prime Minister is not anxious to defend, or to continue recruiting, a liberally educated class, at least some of whom will be accustomed to appraise each measure (as also our politicians) disinterestedly, on its merits, rather than by simple partisan reflexes or the otherwise safely predictable promptings of their wallets.

As Stephen Prickett points out in his introduction to the present volume, nearly every government-inspired or government-enforced educational measure of late years has been counterproductive. This is unsurprising, given the combination of trendiness, populism and (at least in higher education) resentment which provoked such measures, and the sheer ignorance and incompetence which went into their contriving. In principle, access to post-16 education can be 'broadened' until the teachers are as ignorant as their students (a terminal point which could only be reached under public provision, since self-financing pupils would long since have saved their money for something more worthwhile). What is not possible, whoever pays, is to give everyone a traditional university education, for reasons already made clear: a shortage of both suitable students and suitable teachers. If standards and syllabuses are to be made sufficiently 'inclusive' to accommodate everybody, or even (as in the US) only half the population, then the result, whatever you choose to call it, will not be a university education.[10]

---

[10] I once appeared on the *Today* programme with the 'progressive' education guru Professor Ted Wragg, who said he wanted every young person to have the benefit of a university education. I forget my answer, but it surely ought to have been that any education from which *every* young person could benefit would hardly, in the nature of things, be a university education. (There is no way that

As I have said, this would not matter, except that real, and not merely nominal, universities are being conscripted wholesale into the task, so that their unique role, ethos and educational outcome will be squeezed out of existence if they continue to collaborate in successive governments' work of destruction. But this will not happen, because they will not do so. As Dr Bruce Charlton shows, the market alone — by which I mean not the competitive pursuit of material gains, but merely the range of choices, economically profitable or not, open to the citizens of a modern democracy — ensures that at least some 'real' universities will survive by going private. Just before the 2001 general election the Leader of the Opposition said that his party if elected would enable them to do so; not that this gained him any votes from academics, who seem constitutionally blind to their best interests.

It is just a pity that such universities will probably be fewer than they were in the golden age, from (say) the mid-Fifties to the early Nineties. My own Department at Glasgow University held regular, one-to-one, Oxbridge-style Honours tutorials until 1993, when the sheer weight of student numbers made it impossible to continue. Unusually, despite the increased intake, there was no fall-off in quality, because entrance had become much more competitive. This was for reasons which, as at Manchester, had nothing to do with education, and everything to do with the host city's burgeoning reputation for style, but so what?

The most spectacularly counter-productive piece of governmental folly to afflict the universities has been so-called Quality Assurance, about which other contributors to this volume have spoken. It is true that, as this book goes to press, the future of QA is uncertain; nevertheless, I shall still say this: quality assurance, in all its forms, is the direct enemy of quality. Its real object, as nearly everyone now knows, is to force higher education, against the wishes of those who conduct it, into the government's preferred mould. This is bad enough in the vocational sector, since (as I have already observed) governments know no better than anyone else what future patterns

---

great-aunt Gladys is going to graduate from a racing drivers' academy with distinction, but not even egalitarians seem to mind that.) As Paul Fussell long ago remarked in his myth-buster *Class*, the difference between the US and the UK was not that 48% of young Americans went to university while only 13% of young Britons did. The proportion actually going to *university* was about the same in each country. The rest (in America) simply went to places *called* universities. It is impolite to say so, but that is also what has now happened, or rather been made to happen, here. As I have already said, it need not matter, just so long as we do not allow the change of nomenclature to mislead us in the way that it was evidently designed to do.

of demand and employment will be. But it is nothing short of disastrous in the academic sector, whose health, just like that of the individual disciplines of which it is composed, is crucially dependent on its self-government.

In pursuit of the government's homogenizing goals, the distinctive character of universities, together with their right to genuine (i.e. collegial, corporate or 'bottom-up') self-management, has all but been destroyed. Only the most unworldly dons have yet to realize that they are now employees rather than (what they once were) senior members of their institutions. Those are no longer run by academics, but by 'management groups', many of whose members (even according to their own university websites) can point to no record of serious publication or scholarship. An analogous pattern has long been familiar within the NHS, and is bitterly resented by the medical profession.

Add to this the vast recent proliferation within the universities of totally superfluous bureaux (staff development, teaching methods, sexual harassment, ethnic monitoring, equal opportunities, etc.) whose real aim is not quality but surveillance; the insane quantity of time, paperwork and documentation (much of that perforce faked, and known to be so) required for teaching quality assessment, when the best, most stimulating teaching has always been spontaneous and unpredictable; and the disgusting farce of the Research Assessment Exercise, which has led merely to the slaughter of entire forests, subsequently transformed into mountains of unread and unreadable books and journals; and you will see why most academics deeply loathe and despise the boring, oppressive and meaningless routines to which they are now being subjected, and which seriously detract from the time and attention they know they should be devoting to teaching and research. If they only knew that they were an overwhelming majority, and that nothing could be done if all refused to comply with the nonsense demanded of them, they would carry the day.

The London School of Economics unilaterally announced in 2001 that it would no longer participate in QA. It would have been interesting to see what, if any, disciplinary measures were taken against it had it withdrawn, and had QA not (only temporarily, you may be sure) been suspended. It would not be surprising to discover that the LSE is already preparing to go private. Among the reasons it gave was the sheer, staggering size and cost of the administration necessary to comply with HEFC (which is to say, government) directives. Over half, and in some cases well over half, of every university's budget today goes on administration, which is nice if you happen to be an ethnicity monitor or an unequal opportunities witch-finder, but an outright atrocity if you are a student, teacher or researcher trying against increasing odds to pursue your career or do your job properly.

Our masters made one huge mistake in their calculations. The pretext for all this interference, which is reinforced by the natural propensity of bureaucracies to expand unchecked, is the government's funding of the universities. But though more money than ever is being spent (and wasted) on the universities and higher education generally, less is being spent per student, and more is being raised from students themselves, from alumni, and from other, external charitable sources. (Forget about commercially-funded research, which is by the way.) In other words, in requiring more contributions from non-government agencies, the government has actually relinquished some of its monopoly power.

Those agencies — the student body, alumni, and charitable donors and organizations — all have a direct interest, as government does not, in seeing that their money is spent on education, rather than on strangling it to death. Alumni in particular like to feel that a new generation is being inducted into values and a way of life from which they benefited, and which they naturally wish to see preserved. If all these people knew what was already happening in the universities, they would either withhold their money or, if they could, take themselves and it elsewhere.

Two things follow. First, we should tell them the truth. Dr Charlton and others, at great risk to their careers, are already doing a magnificent job in the press. Secondly, as I have already said, as many universities as possible should go private, not least so that the disaffected have somewhere to go. This idea is less utopian than it looks; at all events, I have heard of its being seriously discussed by vice-chancellors and others who presumably know something about its feasibility. For the rest, we can only entertain a plan of concerted criticism and non-co-operation, in which Dr Charlton has already led the way. (You can forget the Association of University Teachers, whose functionary mentality ensures that all its sympathies naturally lie with the *nomenklatura*.)

The awful thing is that all this was foreseen in the 1920s, after the University Grants Commission was set up (1919). Those who opposed it did so on the grounds that to take the government's shilling was to compromise the universities' independence, without which they would be unable to continue fulfilling their unique task.

It is true that the UGC worked well enough for half a century. But as Lord Melbourne is supposed to have said about some worthy measure whose undesired consequences eventually brought it to grief: 'All the bloody fools were against it at the time; but it turns out that the bloody fools were right.'

Roger Scruton[1]

The Idea of a University

In their recent book *The New Idea of a University*,[2] Duke Maskell and Ian Robinson describe the hot air of official Philistinism which has caused the inflation, expansion, explosion and collapse of British universities. Their sobering reflections remind us of the fact that the traditional university was not a routine part of the state educational system but an autonomous society, and a self-regulating organ of a Christian culture. In the wake of Maskell and Robinson, it is worth revisiting the writer who inspired them, and whose ideal of the autonomous university society had not altogether vanished from the Cambridge of my youth.

John Henry (later Cardinal) Newman delivered his lectures on *The Idea of a University* at a time (1852) when the brief period of social power the universities had enjoyed since the end of the Napoleonic Wars was (as he saw it) profoundly threatened. The Royal Commissions that were to end the Anglican hold on Oxford and Cambridge, abolish the Test Acts and the celibacy of the college Fellows, and introduce new scientific studies to the universities, had already begun their work. In a peculiarly English manner, Newman's was an innovative rearguard action to try to preserve in the new Catholic University of Ireland what he knew was about to be swept away in his own country. As a programme for what was to become the University College of Dublin it was a total non-starter. But it was a classic statement of the nature and purpose of universities, underlining their private and domestic role, in addition to their public function as repositories of knowledge. Time and again, discussions of the subject have found themselves returning to Newman's apparently impractical and useless ideal.

For Newman a university moulds the character of those who attend it. By immersing its students in a collegiate environment, and impressing upon them an ideal of the educated mind, it helps to turn raw human beings into gentlemen. And this, he implied, is its true

[1]   An earlier version of this essay was published in *The Salisbury Review*, **20** (1), Autumn 2001, pp. 4-8.

[2]   Haven Books, 2001; paperback: Imprint Academic, 2002.

social function. Within the college walls the adolescent is granted a vision of the ends of life; and he takes from the university the one thing that the world does not provide, which is a conception of intrinsic value. And that is why the university is so important in an age of commerce and industry, when the utilitarian temptation besieges us on every side, and when we are in danger of making every purpose a material one — in other words, in danger of allowing the means to swallow the ends

Much has changed since Newman's day. To suggest that universities are engaged in producing gentlemen is faintly ridiculous in an age when most students are women. Newman's ideal university was modelled on the actual universities of Oxford, Cambridge, and Trinity College, Dublin, which at the time admitted only men, did not permit their resident scholars to marry, and were maintained as quasi-religious institutions within the fold of the Anglican Church. Their undergraduates were recruited largely from the public schools, and their curriculum was solidly based in Latin, Greek, theology and mathematics. Their domestic life revolved around the college, where dons and undergraduates had their living quarters, and where they dined together each evening in hall, robed in their academic gowns.

In Oxbridge this uniquely British form of celibate domesticity has survived into our era, sustained by an army of porters, servants, 'scouts' and bedmakers, and, while all undergraduates were required to sit examinations, only a small proportion of those who attended university in Newman's day regarded study as the real purpose of being 'up' at the *alma mater*. Some were there to row or play rugby; some were biding time before inheriting a title; some were on their way to commissions in the army, and were meanwhile rioting with their chums. Almost all were members of a social elite that had hit on this unique way of perpetuating itself, by coating its power with a veneer of elegant knowledge. And in this protected and beautiful environment you could also take knowledge seriously, as an end in itself. With money in the bank and time on your hands, the 'renunciation of purpose' was not so very hard.

Even in Newman's own time, however, this state of affairs had come under strong criticism from some of his own closest former allies. In 1840 the saintly John Keble had called for reform of Oxford by removing the aristocratic 'hearties' and instituting a national system of scholarships for poor but hard-working boys.[3] What Keble

[3]   See Stephen Prickett, 'Church and University in the Life of John Keble,' *The English Religious Tradition and the Genius of Anglicanism*, ed. Geoffrey Rowell,

did not envisage was any change in the curriculum, which in Scotland had already been considerably extended. From the end of the eighteenth century, that country, which had twice as many ancient universities as the vastly larger England, had developed what were then recognised as the finest universities in the world. When he left Eton, just after the Napoleonic Wars, the young Lord Palmerston (later to be Prime Minister) was sent by his father first to the University of Edinburgh for three years, to gain an education, and then to Cambridge, for one year, to meet the right people.

Today's university is different from Newman's in almost every respect. It recruits from all classes of society, is open equally to men and to women, and is very often financed and provisioned by the state. Little if anything remains of that delicate and poised domestic life that had shaped the soul of Newman, and the curriculum centres not on sublime and purposeless subjects like Greek, in which there hovers the entrancing vision of a life beyond commerce, but on sciences, vocational disciplines and the now ubiquitous 'business studies' through which students supposedly learn the ways of the world. Success lay behind the student of Newman's day — in the form of a bank account, a title, or a country estate. Success lies in front of his equivalent today — in the form of a career that will justify this otherwise quite useless knowledge.

Moreover, universities have expanded to offer their services to an ever-increasing proportion of the population, and to absorb an ever-growing amount of the national budget. In the state of Massachussetts university education has the largest financial turnover of any industry; there is at least one university in every major British or American city, and American state universities may contain, at any one time, upwards of 50,000 students. Higher education is offered as a right to all who pass the French *baccalauréat*, and European politicians often speak as though the work of educational reform will not be complete until every child is able in due time to become a graduate. The university is no longer in the business of creating a social elite, but in the rival business of ensuring that elites are a thing of the past. As for the social life of the university, who can deny that the celibate idyll that appealed to Newman and his contemporaries has disappeared? Already satirized by Evelyn Waugh in *Decline and Fall*, and subsequently mourned by the same author in *Brideshead Revisited*, the world of posturing aestheticism and rowdy impudence, of refined scholarship and pederastic longing, which had produced geniuses as diverse as Coleridge and Pater, Russell

Wantage: Ikon Press, 1992, pp. 195-210.

and Keynes, did not survive the egalitarian revolution. Indeed, its last authentic product — the circle of communist spies that radiated from the collegiate precincts of Cambridge — was testimony to its willing suicide, as it turned on the culture that had nurtured it, and betrayed it to the enemy.

In all these changes, however, one thing has supposedly remained constant, which is the over-riding aim of the university — the enhancement, perpetuation and transmission of knowledge. The social function of the university may have changed, we are told, but its internal purpose has not. Knowledge was once the exclusive property of a ruling class; now it is accessible to everyone. But it is still knowledge, and just as valuable to those who are now acquiring it as it was to those who previously reserved it for their own exclusive use. The connection between knowledge and the collegiate way of life was a mere accident, a consequence of the fact that the traditional curriculum, and the traditional ways of teaching it, were formed at a period when education was a Church monopoly.

There is sense in that view. After, all, mediaeval colleges were primarily schools for the clergy, and only secondarily places for the disinterested pursuit of learning. And they acquired this second function without losing the vestiges of their ecclesiastical discipline. It is arguable that, from the intellectual point of view, the crucial point in the development of the modern university was not the emergence of the mediaeval college, with all its trappings of domesticity, celibacy, religious routine and social rivalry. It was the Enlightenment, which established in Germany and in Scotland a new ideal of higher learning, without the mediaeval fetters that had bound scholarship in the dogmas of theology. In the Königsberg of Kant or the Glasgow of Adam Smith, the mediaeval garments begin to hang loosely from strong Renaissance shoulders: the muscular life of the intellect is beginning to show through the worn-out rags of faith. And when the new man stepped forth to lay claim to the field of knowledge, this brought about a massive expansion of the curriculum, to embrace natural sciences, literature and history, so placing human reason in the place that had been occupied by faith. Newman's gentle attempt to refurbish the collegiate idea for modern uses can be seen as a late reaction to the unbrookable flood of Enlightenment sentiment which had swept through the German universities and which had entirely displaced theology from its central place in the curriculum.

American universities were strongly influenced by the German example. Their method of teaching follows the German model, with professors devising their own courses and also examining them. The scientific world-view tells us that the greatest enemies of knowledge are two: faith, which makes things unquestionable, and censorship, which forbids the question. If a university is really to be a repository of knowledge, therefore, it must be a place of continuous questioning and experiment. American pragmatism fuelled the urge for innovation, and it is a long-established custom that, in an American university, professors can teach whatever interests them, so that the curriculum is in a constant state of flux. The pressure towards innovation has been fuelled by the democratic spirit, which is naturally suspicious of any attempt to prescribe what can and cannot be taught, and which will always ask who is doing the prescribing, and why?

Little by little the American approach has invaded the British curriculum, with degrees now regularly put together out of modules, often examined by the person who invents and teaches them. And often these modules form part of some new subject — sports studies, media studies, animal welfare science — designed to correspond to the interests and careers of the new intake of undergraduates.

All in all then an optimist might say, things have improved since Newman's day. Under the pretence of providing a 'purpose beyond purpose', the university extolled by Newman was really a rite of initiation, designed to protect the privileges of an existing elite, and to place obstacles before the advance of its competitors. It imparted futile skills, which were esteemed precisely for their futility, since this made them into a badge of membership. And far from advancing the fund of knowledge, it existed to safeguard the sacred myths: it placed a protective wall of enchantment around the religion, the social values and the culture of the past, and pretended that the recondite skills required to enjoy this enchantment — Latin and Greek for example — were the highest forms of knowledge. In short, the Newmanite university was an instrument for the perpetuation of a Mandarin class.

Now, by contrast, we have universities dedicated to the growth of knowledge, which are not merely non-elitist but anti-elitist in their social structure. They make no discrimination on grounds of sex, race or class, and have so firmly justified their claim to be a public good as to call forth large amounts of government funding. They are places of open-minded research and questioning, places without dogmatic commitments, whose purpose is to advance knowledge through a spirit of free enquiry. This spirit is imparted to their students, who have the widest possible choice of curriculum, and acquire knowledge that is not merely firmly grounded but eminently useful in their future life: business studies, for example, hotel management, or international relations. In short the universities have evolved from socially exclusive clubs for the study of precious futilities, to socially inclusive data-banks, for the propagation of necessary skills.

So the optimist will say, at any rate. But is this an example of what Schopenhauer called 'unscrupulous optimism'? We should at least look at the facts. Out of the German university formed by the Enlightenment there emerged in the early nineteenth century those wonderful free, poetic and polymathic minds that transformed Western culture: Schopenhauer, Hegel, Herder, Hölderlin, Humboldt, Ranke. For a while it seemed as though the regime of censorship that had protected theology from the encroachment of the sciences was forever banished, and that free enquiry would prevail. Revolution and counterrevolution brought this period quickly to an end, and, looking back on the history of the German university we can only conclude that the periods of intellectual freedom have been the exception, not the rule.

Pressures towards ideological conformity did not always issue from above. In the Nazi period, and again in 1968, it was the student body that laid down the law and told the professors what could and could not be said on the campus. Meanwhile the old collegiate universities of Oxford and Cambridge, with their fusty rituals and obligatory religious routines, had offered shelter to dissenters of every kind, while remaining places of refuge, where fascist and communist, conservative and labourite, atheist and Roman Catholic, would discuss Racine versus Shakespeare or Brahms versus Wagner over port.

Nor is it only the German universities that have fared badly since Hegel's day. A visitor to the American university today is more likely to be struck by the indigenous varieties of censorship, than by any atmosphere of free enquiry. It is true that Americans live in a tolerant society. But they also breed vigilant guardians, keen to detect and extirpate the first signs of intolerance among the young. And these guardians have an innate tendency to gravitate to the universities, where the very freedom of the curriculum, and its openness to innovation, provides them with an opportunity to exercise their censorious passions. Books are put on or struck off the curriculum on grounds purely of their political correctness; speech codes and counselling services police the language and conduct of both students and teachers; courses are designed to impart ideological conformity, and students are often penalized for having drawn some heretical conclusion about the leading issues of the day. In sensitive areas, such as the study of race and sex, censorship is overtly directed not only at students but also at any teacher, however impartial and scrupulous, who comes up with the wrong conclusions. 'Racism awareness courses' on the American campus frequently resemble the Chinese communists' compulsory 're-education' (i.e. brainwashing) programmes'.

There are also whole subjects which announce, through their titles, the ideological position that students are expected to adopt: feminist studies, for example, gay studies, gender studies. When these subjects were first proposed university authorities were reluctant to oppose them, for fear of offending against the spirit of free enquiry. But how would they have reacted, one wonders, to a proposed course of Nazi studies (taught exclusively by Nazis), or even a course of conservative studies designed to form the next intake of the Republican Party?

This is not to say that you could not envisage a course of women's studies, say, which offered a fair-minded assessment of women and their place in society, of the works of women artists and writers and the vision of women in Western literature. But it would not be a course exclusively focused on, taught by or addressed to women, nor would it lay down the law as to what students of such a complicated subject matter should think. It would leave room for such conclusions as that women's lot was happier in the traditional family than it is today; that feminism has undermined the self-confidence and the hopes of ordinary women; that if women have not been great artists, mathematicians or composers this is not the fault of men; and so on.

Once you allow such conclusions to be entertained, however, you will quickly come to see that the whole subject of women's studies as a genuine discipline is thrown into doubt. The questions that it considers simply cannot be settled by an exclusive study of women, nor can they be usefully addressed with the intellectual equipment acquired from an undergraduate course devoted only to such questions. A postgraduate with a grounding in biology, sociology, history and musicology might conceivably be able to advance human knowledge in the matter of the missing women composers. But, all too often, it is clear from the outset what conclusions have to be reached, and that they will not be favourable to the male sex.

This raises an interesting question concerning the relation of the modern university to the acquisition and propagation of knowledge. Let us stay for a moment with our example of women's studies. There are deep questions about the nature of sex and gender, which certainly can be and ought to be studied in a university. But new subjects have been designed precisely to make it difficult to ask them. Women's studies is there to inoculate the student against the desire to question feminism. This process of inoculation occurs even in those subjects which have not been invented to provide it.

A constant theme which runs through the humanities as they are regularly taught in many American and British universities is that of the illegitimacy of Western civilization, and of the artificial nature of the distinctions on which it has been based. All distinctions are 'cultural', therefore 'constructed', and therefore 'ideological', in the sense defined by Marx — manufactured by the ruling elite in order to serve its interests and bolster its power. Western civilisation is simply the record of that oppressive process, and the only purpose of studying it is to deconstruct its claim to our membership. This is the core belief that many students of the humanities are required to ingest, preferably before they have the intellectual discipline to question it, or to set it against the literature which shows it to be false.

To put the point in another way: the Enlightenment displaced theology from the heart of the curriculum in order to put the disinterested pursuit of truth in place of it. Within a very short time, however, we find the university threatened by theology of another kind — a godless theology, to be sure, but no less insistent upon unquestioning submission to doctrine, and no less ardent in its pursuit of heretics, sceptics and debunkers. Of course, people are no longer burned at the stake for their views: they may simply fail to get tenure, or, if they are students, flunk the course.

If we are to understand this phenomenon we should recognize how precarious is the status of truth in human affairs. Aristotle told us that all human beings desire to know; but he failed to point out that they do so only when first reassured that knowledge will not be dangerous. People turn from uncomfortable truths, and construct walls that will make them unperceivable. It is difficult to construct such a wall on your own; but, in partnership with others, and protected by a well-endowed institution, you can participate in the joyous work of falsehood, and add your own block of adamantine prose to the ramparts. The purpose is not to tell lies, but to create an acceptable public doctrine. And a public doctrine is acceptable if it provides the foundation for a stable and internally secure human community.

The need for such a community is especially apparent in a university, where professors are suitors for the approval of young people, who in turn are searching for the rite of passage that will confer membership of the adult world. The doctrines of the new theology are therefore community-forming beliefs. If ever we came to think that the distinction between men and women is not 'culturally constructed' but natural; if ever we came to believe that Western civilisation is not just an arbitrary ideological device, but one of the highest achievements of mankind, and one which contains the moral knowledge that young people need; if ever we came to think that the purpose of education is not equality but distinction — if ever any of these heresies took root in us, we should become a danger to the kind of community with which the current unholy collusion of relativism and managerialism seeks to replace the traditional idea of a university. For the modern university is trying to cater for students regardless of sex, race, or cultural background, even regardless of ability. It is to a great extent a creation of the state and is fully signed up to the statist idea of what a society should be — namely a society without distinction, all the members of which are potential recipients of welfare. It is therefore as dependent on the belief in equality as Newman's university was dependent on the belief in God. In order to include everyone, the new university invents subjects like hotel management and business studies, designed to accommodate those who have no interest in the intellectual life. The fact that these skills are better obtained in the real world is not relevant: for the purpose is to create a microcosm of the new society, just as Newman's college was a microcosm of the gentleman's world.

The dispassionate pursuit of truth is as much a threat to this new community as it was to the community that created the universities of mediaeval Europe. Hence, despite their innate aspiration towards membership, young people are told at university that they come from nowhere and belong to nothing: that all pre-existing forms of membership are null and void. They are offered a rite of passage into cultural nothingness, since this is the only way to achieve the egalitarian goal. In place of the old beliefs of a civilisation based on godliness, judgement and distinction, they are given the new beliefs of a society based on equality and inclusion, and are told that the judgement of other life-styles is a crime. If the purpose were merely to substitute one belief system for another it would be open to rational debate. But the purpose is to substitute one community for another.

It is tempting to liken humanity to a herd perambulating in some gloomy valley, where the warm smell of collective life provides a ref-

uge from anxiety. Every now and then the herd emerges on to a hill-
top, and is suddenly bathed in the rays of the sun. Cool breezes
scatter the scent of fellowship, but for a while the true nature of mankind is visible. A few individuals try to stay aloft, enjoying the light
and the knowledge that it brings. But the rest are troubled by the
breezes and the herd moves on, dragging everyone downhill into
darkness.

I went from my state grammar school to Cambridge. I did not
belong to Newman's elite. I was of humble origins, but not humble
enough to be a gentleman. I was uncomfortable in the celibate society of Jesus College but, thanks to life in college, I was forced to dine
each night with people who were my intellectual, cultural and social
superiors. By degrees, the rough edges were worn off my personality, and I learned to respect, even if I could not emulate, the elegant
manners and cultural competence of my privately educated contemporaries. I was condemned to live in the same courtyard as quiet
bachelor dons who resented every noise above a whisper. I was
made to wear academic dress in town, and forced to return each evening before eleven. And I was granted complete intellectual freedom. All that was required was the weekly essay, which I had to
defend before a 'supervisor' whose sole purpose was to find fault
with what I had written, and who never revealed to me his opinion
on any subject whatsoever. Courses were optional, and I could
attend lectures in any faculty and borrow books from any library.

One day, during national elections, I entered the weekly lecture on
the *Critique of Pure Reason*, to find that the professor was wearing a
'Vote Labour' sticker on his lapel. My astonishment was not so much
that he should vote for the Labour Party (had I been old enough, I
would have done the same), but that he should choose to announce
this fact, in a lecture devoted to the transcendental deduction of the
categories — a matter elevated far above the dim debates of party
politics. This was the sole occasion that I can remember, during my
undergraduate years, when I discovered the political opinions of
one of my tutors. Although I studied philosophy, attended lectures
in English, German and modern Greek, and was eager to engage my
professors in conversation on all matters of intellectual concern, the
disinterested pursuit of truth really did seem to regulate our mutual
discourse. No teacher was in the business of imposing ideological
conformity or recruiting students to the new community of equals.
We were invited to read Mill and Mary Wollstonecraft on the eman-
cipation of women, and to discuss this as we would any other matter
of intellectual interest. But we also read Henry James's *The Bosto-*

nians, Ruskin's *Sesame and Lilies*, and other works that are now on the feminist index. All this was simply part of understanding 'the best that had been thought and said', and learning to exercise our minds in a spirit of dispassionate enquiry.

That opportunity to pursue the life of the mind was undoubtedly made possible by the peculiar domestic society that we enjoyed: membership was being acquired in another way, through example, ritual and daily contact. In all our studies we could get on with the serious business of truth. And although many of our contemporaries were studying useful subjects like medicine, law and biology, Cambridge adhered rigidly to the distinction between knowledge – which was the business of the university – and skill – which belonged to the world outside. The most useful disciplines are those that focus the mind on disinterested scholarship, and have nothing to say about the world beyond the college walls. Hence they have an air of futility, and will be shunned by those who see education as the first step in a career. But the old curriculum, centred on those futile-seeming subjects, and, from the social, political and commercial point of view, obstinately 'irrelevant', had a purpose, the kind of purpose that only the avoidance of purpose can achieve. This purpose was to train the mind.

Advocates of the new university would insist that the expansion of the curriculum has made the university more useful to modern societies, and that the loss of that old, inward-looking collegiality is the loss of nothing worthwhile. The curriculum and the apprenticeship that shaped Roger Scruton are as anachronistic as Roger Scruton; the needs of society have changed and the university must change along with them if it is to supply what our societies now need. But none of that alters the fact that the university is as much today as it has ever been, a repository of knowledge.

Having come, in time, to accept the official view of myself as an anachronism, I left the university and explored the world of business. I did not apply myself to the matter whole-heartedly, since I wanted time to read and write. Nevertheless, having been all my life an item on other people's budgets, I now could put other people on mine. The consultancy that I established has forty employees in six different countries. Its work is extremely delicate, involving negotiations with politicians, civil servants, the media and the channels of public opinion. The most important discovery that I made, very early in the venture, was that the one person who should never be employed is the graduate in 'business studies'. For such a person has wasted the best years of life acquiring information which, precisely because of its status as 'useful knowledge', is entirely useless in the world outside. Indeed, to brand as knowledge this hotch-potch of flow-charts, book-keeping, ethical exhortations and stock-market tips is to misuse the word. In our business the qualities required are these: subtlety; the ability to communicate and to understand; the ability to make comparisons and to conceptualize difficult facts; the capacity to understand the historical and cultural formation of a person to whom one may be entirely antipathetic; and above all irony and the invulnerability that comes from it. None of those qualities can be nurtured by business studies, and all, I have discovered, are promoted by Greek, Latin, and philosophy. I have been lucky to find people who have spent their formative years in studying those useless things; for they alone have been useful.

It was this experience, more than my years as a university teacher, that made me side with Newman. Confine learning and teaching within a sacred precinct, shut it off from the world, so that it can move by its own inner force towards futile knowledge, and you will produce the whole and healthy mind, the mind able to adapt, to focus and to comprehend, in all the changing circumstances of the world outside. Let that outside world into the classroom, however, and the result is an ossification of the mental powers, a blind addiction to relevance, which renders the mind incapable of dealing with any situation that has not appeared in the pages of the textbook. Relevance is the enemy of knowledge, and when universities make relevance their standard, they betray their mission. Then nothing remains, save the new form of community to which they are devoted — the community of equals, which none of us wants.

Stephen Prickett

Polyphony, the Idea of Education, and Social Utility

I
Polyphony, Society and Education

A recent, and uncomfortably topical, book by the British scholar Bernard Lewis, Professor of Near Eastern studies at Princeton, is provocatively entitled *What Went Wrong? Western Impact and Middle Eastern Response.* For Lewis, a distinguishing characteristic of Western music is polyphony, which has left its mark in almost every area of life.

> This begins in its simplest form with the choir, in which matched voices sing different notes in a planned sequence to produce a combined effect; then comes the keyboard instrument, matching the ten fingers of the two hands, following different routes in a common purpose; and finally, the musical ensemble, from duets and trios to the full orchestra. Different performers play together, from different scores, producing a result that is greater than the sum of its parts.
> With a little imagination one may discern the same feature in other aspects of Western culture — in democratic politics and in team games, both of which require the cooperation, in harmony if not in unison, of different performers playing different parts in a common purpose. In parliamentary politics and team games, there is further cooperation in conflict — rival parties or teams, striving to defeat their opponents, but nevertheless acting under an agreed set of rules, and in an agreed interval of time.[1]

To judge from the quantity of publications on the subject, the very obvious problems of pluralism in our society have attracted more attention than the tacit conventions of polyphony.[2] Religious conflict and civil war ensured that by the second half of the seventeenth

[1]   Ch. 6, 'Time, Space and Modernity', in Bernard Lewis, *What Went Wrong? Western Impact and Middle Eastern Response,* Princeton University Press, 2002, pp. 128-9.

[2]   See, for instance, John Kekes, *The Morality of Pluralism,* Princeton University Press, 1993, or Charles Taylor, *Multiculturalism,* Princeton University Press, 1994, and the extensive bibliographies supplied by both books.

century England had become the world's first pluralistic society.[3] Others, such as the USA and France, were shortly to follow. Yet if pluralism evolved painfully from irreconcilable differences in all three countries, what Lewis calls polyphony has had a no less profound influence on our whole social awareness, and was, in turn, to shape subliminally our vision of such very different activities as politics, sports and science. The complaint that all three activities are 'over-dramatized' rests on the assumption that drama is alien to their proper nature or function, and somehow denies that it is actually intrinsic, even necessary to those activities as we have come to practise them.

Yet European politics, sport and science were as much shaped by its drama as was its literature. Chaucer and Rabelais are in their own ways as polyvalent as the Mediaeval Miracle Plays, Marlowe or Shakespeare. What brings their worlds alive is the multitude of conflicting, even dissenting, voices. Even seemingly uni-vocal writers like Dante or Milton, are, if we stop to examine their writings, no less dramatic and polyphonic.[4]

Polyphony, indeed, is such a basic quality of our modern society that it becomes almost invisible except by contrast with societies, such as those cited by Lewis, that conspicuously lack such pluralism and polyvalency. Lewis's thesis about the Middle East, however, here concerns us less than the ramifications of a polyphony within our own society and education so basic that we scarcely recognise its presence — let alone the historical sequence that created what one might call the polyphony of modernity. Certainly the argument that education is better thought of in dramatic and polyphonic terms makes more sense than the kind of essentialist analyses frequently heard today. To begin with, the word 'education' itself does not have, and, historically, never has had, an agreed definition. The Latin derivation from *educo*, to 'lead out', however much it may be held to stress the internal nature of true learning, begs the question of what is to be thus led. From the *trivium* and *quadrivium* of mediaeval Oxford, to the voluntary class system of A.S. Neil's Summerhill, Western education has always been 'polyphonic', providing a range of different subjects and disciplines to satisfy radically different purposes. Moreover, most educational theories have relied on some kind of 'balance', or variety of different subjects, as if

[3] See Peter Harrison, *Religion & Religions in the English Enlightenment*, Cambridge University Press, 1990.

[4] One has only to think of Beatrice's stinging rebuke to Dante at their first meeting, or Satan's parliamentary grandiloquence in *Paradise Lost*.

in recognition that not merely is the study of languages, mathematics, music, art, and science valuable in itself, but that there is an essential interplay between them that is itself also a source of intellectual and spiritual health. Whether conceived as Plato's 'music and games', the Latin *mens sana in corpore sano* ('a healthy mind/spirit in a healthy body'), mediaeval *trivia* and *quadrivia*, developing both right and left-hand lobes of the brain, or stressing the need for both education and training, educational theory seems always, tacitly or explicitly, to have reached after some kind of creative disciplinary interaction.

At a quite different level, polyphony is crucial to our education system because it is inherent in our language and culture. Indeed, as much recent debate has shown, it is impossible to make an unambiguous unequivocal and complete statement in modern English — in the sense that nothing further can be said about it.[5] As the philosopher Michael Polanyi has pointed out, it is the nature of living language that only those words whose meaning is stipulated in advance can have precise content. Thus, though we cannot so define that still mysterious and complex phenomenon we call 'electricity', we can, for instance, define our units of measurement of it, such as 'ohm', 'volt', or 'amp'. Like all words in the real world, 'electricity' has a history, a freight of associations, implications, misunderstandings. Not merely is it a word whose meaning has changed radically over the past two hundred years; it will almost certainly continue to change in the future. Even more to the point is the converse to Polanyi's dictum: 'only words of indeterminate meaning can have a bearing on reality.[6] The mentality that believed that one could encapsulate and define the 'aims and objectives' of any educational process is itself a profoundly uneducated one.

It is interesting, therefore, to see how often all this is forgotten or ignored when we come to debates over educational policy, which

[5]   One of the most rightly derided requirements in Quality Assurance documentation was that teachers should declare the 'aims and objectives' of their courses. What were they to put? 'To give a better understanding of changes in shipbuilding technique between 1485 and 1490?' 'To make students more aware of Shakespeare's lasting genius?' 'To make all who come to this class finer, broader, more sensitive members of the human race?' All three answers, of course, might be valid, but are totally incommensurable. If the first raises the question 'why is this knowledge important?' The second, at the least, raises questions concerning the nature of 'genius', and the third, questions about the nature of the good in our whole culture. It is a mark of the patent inadequacy of the whole operation, that only the first, one imagines, would be a satisfactory QAA answer.

[6]   *Personal Knowledge*, Routledge, 1958, p. 251.

often bristle with definitions and tacit assumptions of exclusive and essentialist meaning. Pronouncements by Ministers of Education are themselves revealing. Here, at one extreme, is George Tomlinson of the Attlee Labour government at the end of the Second World War — a man whose own formal education had begun and ended in Accrington Road Wesleyan Elementary School, at Rishton, in Lancashire:

> At a pinch you might do without Parliament. You could do without the Minister: you could certainly do without Civil Servants and almost as certainly without education authorities. Without any or all of these the world might not seem much worse. But if there were no teachers the world would be back in barbarism within two generations.[7]

> I am doing something I wanted to do more than anything else on earth. I am trying to translate Acts of Parliament into deeds of kindness for young people.[8]

Tomlinson, we note, was covering two traditional aims of British education: national utility, and personal development. Yet how startling is the tone compared with modern utterances on the same topic. Not surprisingly, in the wake of the Second World War, national utility is conceived first and foremost in terms of civilization versus barbarism rather than economic growth — as values, not wealth. Personal development is interpreted as 'kindness' to young people — a word whose roots rest in the Anglo-Saxon conception of kin and family. The implication is that the primary business of the state is to assist its members to be happy (within a system of family and communal relationships), through developing whatever potential talents they may have. Something of the same excitement and enthusiasm for the possibilities of education are still present in the setting up of the 'new universities' in the 1960s,[9] as well as in their primary-school equivalent, the Plowden Report.

Forty years later, on the other hand, for Correlli Barnett the stark economic needs of a war-ravaged Britain made the 1940s no time for such idealism.[10] Viewed from the prospective of the Thatcher years in the 1980s, the post-war education system had tragically failed to meet the agenda of national growth. For Barnett, the interests of the

[7]   F. Blackburn, *George Tomlinson*, London: Heinemann 1954, p. 173. I owe this, and the following reference, to Donald Tranter.

[8]   From *The Guardian*, January 7, 1985.

[9]   See David Daiches (ed) *The Idea of a New University: An Experiment in Sussex*, Deutsch, 1964; and Michael Beloff, *The Plateglass Universities*, Secker, 1968.

[10] Correlli Barrnett, *The Audit of War: the illusion and reality of Britain as a great nation*, Macmillan, 1986.

individuals would in the end have been better served by rising national living standards than by pursuing short-term personal goals. In apparent agreement, fifty years after Tomlinson, his Labour successor, David Blunkett, declared himself an out-and-out instrumentalist. For him 'the unique importance of the Department for Education and Employment's role stems from its responsibility for ensuring that the U.K. has a well-functioning labour market.' Tomlinson, Barnett and Blunkett would all presumably agree with the definition of education offered by Clark Kerr, of the University of California, that 'education was the prime investment in national purpose' — though whether the latter two would have been aware of its delicate ambiguities is open to question. Certainly, as Bruce Collins and Keith Robbins in *British Culture and Economic Decline* remind us, both Tomlinson and Barnett are part of a long-standing debate about the nature of education in Britain, and Barnett's critique belongs as much as Tomlinson's speeches to a particular moment in history.[11]

The point is that none of these are intrinsically illegitimate objectives. What is illegitimate is to suggest that education, any more than capitalism or industry, can have only one proper 'objective'. In a modern society, any enterprise of any size or complexity whatsoever is going to have multiple goals, values and objectives, whose relationship is, and may well remain, unclear and undefined. This is not a fault in the system, it is rather one of the conditions under which the system operates at all. Similarly, the polyphony of modern society is not necessarily a sign of its confusion or lack of coherent purpose, (though both may well also be true) but rather the normal and proper mechanism of modernity.

But if polyphony is an inevitable and, indeed, an essential part of any concept of education, that does not mean that all voices in this debate, all educational agendas, are equal — or equally important. We should heed Robert Grant's subtle but important point that though there is a clear distinction between education and training, it may vary from person to person.[12] Moreover, educational needs themselves change. But if, following Barnett, we ask ourselves if there was ever a time for the educational idealism of a Tomlinson we have a quick reply from writers like Libby Purves.[13] What we attack as irresponsible idealism in a minister of state, we are immediately

---

[11] *British Culture and Economic Decline*, ed. Bruce Collins and Keith Robbins, Weidenfeld & Nicolson, 1990.

[12] R. Grant, Education, utility and the universities (this volume).

[13] L. Purves, Against the grain (this volume).

prepared to pay large sums of money for when it comes to our own children. Yet the current instrumentalist dogma is that it is not the job of the state to provide happiness and well-rounded development for its children. Yet Tony Blair is an honourable man. (Perhaps we need a spin-doctor or three on this one...) The problem with the pursuit of wealth, national or personal, is always relative. Values, translated simply into economic goals, present an endless staircase which can only be measured by the treads above and below. If other, economic, objectives figured less in the educational rhetoric of the 1940s, does that mean they were altogether neglected? If education is indeed a 'prime investment in national purpose', how we organize our education is, in effect, a statement of the values of the nation.

But, as we have seen, 'national purpose' does not mean the same as 'government policy' — and has not meant the same since at least the seventeenth century. As Desmond Ryan shows, the British transition from an agrarian to an industrial society was achieved privately and piecemeal, often in the teeth of official opposition. For a government to seize control of the British education system and, and, after three centuries of polyphony, attempt to give it a single direction and focus is more reminiscent of Cromwell or the Stuarts than of a modern post-industrial society. Neither precedent is encouraging.

II
Maskell and Robinson, Newman, and the Utility of Education

In what we have here called 'managerial ethics' we have a confusion affecting and, we believe, damaging our entire educational system. Moreover, it is important to recognize, as several contributors to this volume have done, that this is not just a matter of tinkering with methods. We recall Paul Tillich's comment on the argument that a particular procedure was 'all right in theory, but did not work in practice': if it did not work in practice, he pointed out, what was wrong was the theory.

Though it is rarely spelled out as such, there is here an important point of educational principle. In a recent book, *The New Idea of a University*, which takes its title from Newman's *The Idea of a University* (with implied reference to David Daiches' *The Idea of a New University* (1963))[14] its authors, Duke Maskell and Ian Robinson, launch a powerful attack on the idea that a university should try to teach everything. For them the division between 'education' and 'training'

[14]　Daiches, *The Idea of a New University*.

(or 'skills') is sacrosanct. Both are clearly important, but it is 'education' — the discipline of learning to think straight, to exercise taste, discrimination and judgement — that properly belongs to a university. The rest, 'training', 'skills' etc. should be taught in the properly-named 'polytechnic'. They are comically scathing about the government's obsession with the notion that 'skills' are transferable (how does a study of bread-making enable you to be a better car mechanic? Would you want to know that the surgeon about to operate on you was using 'transferred' skills?).

They are, however, equally opposed to the idea of polyphony as an educational principle, deriding the idea of a 'polyversity' (or what the Americans called the 'multiversity'). However great the range of disciplines practised or studied, what should go on involves 'practice' by a community of scholars, not 'teaching' in the sense of a teacher telling students what to think. A 'university' must have a single intellectual focus — that of serious thought and independent judgement — and seek to apply the same standards of logic to whatever field of knowledge being studied. True at least to their own principles, they also take the logical next step of denying that true education, in their sense, has any commercial or even practical utility to the community at large. University education is valuable in itself, and it should only be for the minority who seek it as such.

For the widespread assumption that education is valuable and indeed useful in all spheres of life Maskell and Robinson have an unusual villain: John Henry Newman, author of the original *Idea of a University* — a series of lectures given at the foundation of the (Catholic) University College of Dublin, and later collected and revised as a book. At the centre of Newman's argument for the public and practical value of education is his vision of the wholeness of the human personality.

> ...as health ought to precede labour of the body, and as a man in health can do what an unhealthy man cannot do, and as of this health the properties are vigour, energy, agility, graceful carriage and action, manual dexterity, and endurance of fatigue, so in like manner general culture of the mind is the best aid to professional and scientific study, and educated men can do what the illiterate cannot; and the man who has learned to think and reason and to compare and to discriminate and to analyse, who has refined his taste, and formed his judgement and sharpened his mental vision, will not indeed at once be a lawyer, or a pleader, or an orator, or a statesman, or a physician, or a good landlord, or a man of business, or a soldier, or an engineer, or a chemist, or a geologist, or an antiquarian, but he will be placed in that state of intellect in which he can take up any one of the sciences or callings I have referred to or any other,

with an ease, a grace, a versatility, and a success, to which another is a stranger.[15]

For Maskell and Robinson this is 'a specious analogy' dependent upon a 'sophistry', whereby he slides from one meaning to another of words like 'mind… mental nature… character…intellectual powers' coming to rest, for them 'fatally', 'in the idea of mind as something which can not just be trained but trained scientifically'.[16] Here is the passage in question:

> We know, not by direct and simple vision, not at a glance, but, as it were, by piecemeal and accumulation, by a mental process, by going round an object, by the comparison, the combination, the mutual correction, the continual adaptation, of many partial notions, by the joint application and concentration upon it of many faculties and exercises of mind. Such a union and concert of the intellectual powers, such an enlargement and development, such a comprehensiveness, is necessarily a matter of training. And again, such a training is a matter of rule; it is not mere application, however exemplary, which introduces the mind to truth, nor the reading many books, nor the getting up many subjects, nor the witnessing many experiments, nor the attending many lectures. All this is short of enough; a man may have no power at all of advancing one step forward of himself, in consequence of what he has already acquired, no power of discriminating between truth and falsehood, of sifting out the grains of truth from the mass, of arranging things according to their real value, and, if I may use the phrase, of building up ideas. Such a power is the result of a scientific formation of mind…[17]

Unfortunately, though Maskell and Robinson are familiar with Newman's *Idea of a University*, and with his autobiography, the *Apologia*, they seem to be less so with his last, and in many ways his most interesting work, *A Grammar of Assent* (1870) — for which this argument is in many ways a rehearsal. The passage they quote anticipates, with uncanny accuracy, Newman's later, and more completely worked-out argument for the wholeness of the human personality.[18] This is, in effect, one of the earliest sketches for what, in the *Grammar*, he was to call the 'illative sense' — at its simplest and most basic, the instinctive power by which we turn the fragmentary

[15] Duke Maskell and Ian Robinson, *The New Idea of a University*, Thorverton: Imprint Academic, 2002, p. 31. ['The Idea of a University', in *Newman: Prose & Poetry*, sel. Geoffrey Tillotson, Reynard Library,1957, p. 505.]

[16] Maskell and Robinson, *The New Idea of a University*. pp. 30-31.

[17] Newman, *The Idea of a University. p. 497.*

[18] See Stephen Prickett, *Romanticism & Religion: the Tradition of Coleridge and Wordsworth in the Victorian Church*, Cambridge University Press, 1976, and 'Newman: the Physiognomy of Development', in *Narrative, Religion & Science: Fundamentalism versus Irony*, Cambridge University Press, 2002, pp. 170-79.

and partial evidence of the senses into a coherent and three-dimensional world.

Nothing for Newman, of course, remains at its simplest or most basic for long. What in the *Apologia* had been linked with personal integrity, by 1870 he had come to see as a fundamental law of the mind's operation. For Newman the human psyche was neither logical nor a-logical, but, as befitted a story-telling animal, possessed of 'super-logical' powers — capable of reaching beyond the limits of reason and proof to form conclusions from partial evidence that we nevertheless act upon as certainties.[19] So far from being the tabula rasa assumed by Locke, for Newman the human mind is active and assimilating, stepping beyond evidence to create for itself wholes that are greater than the constituent parts. It is so much an accepted characteristic of our normal behaviour, moreover, that it occurs at an unconscious level in every act of sense-perception, and even when it occurs at a conscious level we scarcely notice what it is that we are doing. Newman had read Hume as a teenager, and had been lastingly impressed by his so-called 'scepticism' — the demonstration of that yawning gulf between probabilities so strong that we stake every aspect of our lives upon them, and real 'proof'.

This, the central argument of the *Grammar of Assent*, has always seemed to me Newman's most powerful contribution not merely to philosophical theology, but to psychology. For him it was not the case that religious faith demanded a peculiar kind of existential leap, but rather that it represents the most extreme, and therefore the most clearly visible example of a process that is constantly going on in every part of our lives without our normally being aware of it. We do not perceive in terms of propositions; our schemata come from the life of the whole personality, and, beyond that, from the no less organic life of the cultural and linguistic community in which we live and move and have our being. The stress now is no longer on the truth or falsehood of specific propositions, but on the wholeness of our personal narrative. That wholeness of personal narrative is at once the mark of spiritual and mental development — in short, that of the fully educated human being.

Whether or not this changes the way in which we understand 'faith', it does, I think, make clear the way in which his idea of an educated mind should affect every aspect of an individual's life — in

[19] Religious assent is not therefore a peculiar and isolated phenomenon of human experience — of 'believing where we cannot prove' as Newman's contemporary, Tennyson suggests in *In Memoriam* — but only the extreme end of a spectrum that begins in simple sense-perception, and includes in its scope all our normal intercourse with the external world.

work, in human relationships, in living what the Greek philosophers called an 'examined life'. Newman's point is that the liberally 'educated' person is better fitted for any human activity than his narrowly 'trained' counterpart — which does not, of course, rule out the need for the 'educated' person also to receive appropriate training. Certainly, so far from being the 'sophistry' suspected by Maskell and Robinson, the analogy between physical and mental fitness has sufficiently impressed the British Army that it views officers who are physically unfit as *ipso facto* mentally unfit to be in command of its troops.

This vision of individual (and communal) wholeness was also, of course, the vision that, though then not fully articulated, underlay *The Idea of a University*. Newman's Dublin lectures are often treated as if they were the first modern statement of an (unreachable) ideal of university education. Yet his actual defence of disinterested scholarship was not that unusual for its time. John Stuart Mill's evidence to the Royal Commission on Oxford in 1852 is surprisingly similar in tone. Only a few years later, Mark Pattison described 'learning' as 'a peculiar compound of memory, imagination, scientific habit, accurate observation, all concentrated through a prolonged period, on the analysis of the remains of literature. The result of this sustained mental endeavour is not a book, but a man.' Nearer the end of the nineteenth century, A.E. Housman (apparently anticipating Maskell and Robinson) wrote that 'The desire of knowledge does not need, nor could it possibly possess, any higher or more authentic sanction than the happiness which attends its gratification.'[20]

Both are at once similar to Newman, but also fundamentally different. In a recent lecture to the British Academy, the historian Keith Thomas suggests why. 'Four hundred years ago,' he writes, 'scholars enjoyed much higher esteem than they do now. Monarchs competed for their services and their work was assumed to be of importance to everyone.'[21] The three major areas of scholarly enquiry were Christianity, classical antiquity, and the English past, all of which were of vital political value to the Tudor and Stuart dynasties of post-Reformation England. What followed from the sixteenth to the eighteenth centuries, argues Thomas, was a progressive undermining of those original objectives. 'For the more they discovered about the classical or mediaeval periods, the more exotically different did the past appear, and the harder it became to draw anal-

---

[20]   Cited by Keith Thomas, 'The Life of Learning: why scholarship still matters — or ought to', *Times Literary Supplement*, December 7, 2001, pp. 12-13.

[21]   *Ibid.* p. 12.

ogies with the contemporary world.' The end result of this great transformation of historical scholarship was the discovery that 'historical erudition had to be for its own sake, or not at all.'[22]

All the great nineteenth-century defences of disinterested learning, Newman, Mill, Pattison etc. can therefore be seen in terms of a rearguard defence of something that had once been regarded as socially valuable and productive, but now, almost for the first time, had to be presented as valuable in its own terms. As in all statements of deeply-held values, reasoned argument follows instinctive belief. The Victorian sages who defended purposeless scholarship knew that it had been important in their own lives, and therefore sought to articulate that importance in terms those who had not necessarily experienced it might be presumed to understand. The difference between Newman, and his secular colleagues, Mill, Pattison or Housman, is that whereas they, as agnostics or even atheists, were attempting to articulate their values in purely material terms, Newman's argument was openly grounded in his religious conviction.

His advantage was obvious. For Newman, as for the scholarly tradition of the previous two hundred years, human utility takes second place to what one might call the 'Christian oeconomy': the grand scheme of things whereby all learning is, as it were, a way of thinking God's thoughts after Him. In a divinely-centred universe, all true knowledge, whether of human history, literature, the arts or the works of nature, is, by definition, valuable, both because it contributes to our understanding of the universe, which is an end in itself, and also no less because the self-development of every individual is a worthwhile end, since all are of value in God's eyes. The humanist version of this suffers from the same disadvantages as that secular liberalism suffers in comparison with Christian liberalism. It is, in effect, simply a weaker and attenuated version of the same thing. 'Natural rights', 'inalienable human dignity', and similar United Nations clichés, whatever their current cross-cultural appeal, all stem from a similar source within a traditionally Christian Western civilization, whose values, however secular in phraseology, were originally derived from a transcendent authority. The French Catholic Chateaubriand once observed of the arch-sceptic and anti-clerical Voltaire that his values were unmistakably the product of the very Church he was attacking. Similarly the claim of the postmodernist American philosopher, Richard Rorty, that there is no such thing as 'truth' (itself, of course, a truth-claim) was neatly countered by the German theologian Jürgen Moltmann, who com-

[22] *Ibid.* p. 14.

mented that it relies on what he nicely calls a *nostalgie de la verité* — a 'nostalgia for the truth' that lingers in the air like a delicious scent long after its actual source has disappeared.

Much the same thing can be said of secular arguments for the value of disinterested scholarship. These, in effect, fall into three distinct categories:

1)   All knowledge, however arcane, should be pursued because one never knows what may turn out to be valuable. 'Useful' research has a distinctly patchy record, and such things as x-rays, penicillin, and lasers, were all the products of 'pure' rather than 'applied' research.

2)   Abstract thought and a training in logic may have no practical value in themselves, but they give the possessor a huge advantage and flexibility in dealing with unforeseen circumstances.

3)   It is simply a good in itself, and worth pursuing without any expectation whatsoever of practical pay-off.

It should be clear that these are not exclusive positions. I myself, for instance, happen to believe all three. My point is the purely logical and formal one that of these three, the first two are, of course, arguments not for the pursuit of disinterested knowledge, but for concealed utility. The third, which is the position of Maskell and Robinson — but not, of course, of Newman — is the only truly consistent version of the argument. The trouble is that it is manifestly incomplete. It is by no means clear that all disinterested enquiry for its own sake is of self-evident value, and ever since Swift's Gulliver encountered the Academy in the flying island of Laputa, it has been subjected to constant ridicule. Hence the extraordinary convolutions that many of those who genuinely and sincerely hold this austere and rigorous view have undergone to present their beliefs in the form of options 1 and 2, and to demonstrate from the history of 'pure' or disinterested research that it frequently has practical applications of enormous importance.

The fact that they are often right, and that, conversely, applied research (especially when directed by civil servants, bureaucrats and politicians who have no real knowledge of the subject) has a distinctly patchy record, does not alter the basic disingenuousness of this argument. What it does illustrate, however, is how difficult it is to sustain an argument for genuinely disinterested knowledge without recourse either to arguments for concealed utility, or to supernatural justifications. It constitutes a kind of uncomfortable middle ground between what are for its proponents two equally unacceptable poles.

I wish to propose that there are in fact very good reasons for this, and that the purely secular claim for the value of disinterested knowledge is in fact untenable for all but a small minority of particularly high-minded agnostics — which included, of course, people like Mill and Housman. It is certainly not one that is likely ever to appeal to politicians of any hue. Just as many mathematicians who publicly express purely instrumentalist views of their discipline turn out to be secret Platonists who believe that their ideas do indeed correspond to a greater abstract reality,[23] so a great many of those who argue for the third position turn out to be either practising Christians or fellow-travellers — such as those conservative proponents of the value of a non-utilitarian education who also invoke what one might call a 'secular religious' authority: more as a kind of social cement than as an ecstatic (and probably uncomfortably disruptive) inward experience. One of the less noticed features of our so-called secular society is that it is has historically much tougher and more durable metaphysical roots than most observers are willing to recognize.

There are two ways of expressing this phenomenon. The first is to note what Michael Polanyi has observed to be the 'instinctive reluctance' of Anglo-American society 'to pursue accepted philosophic premises to their ultimate conclusions' and 'to pretend that ethical principles could actually be scientifically demonstrated'.[24] If, as Polanyi argues, this made the English-speaking world a haven of democracy and order in the face of fascism and communism during the first half of the twentieth century, it may also have eased promulgation of the managerial ethics which so plague Britain in the latter part of the century. The other is to argue that all ethics ultimately have religious, or at least metaphysical underpinnings, and to try and talk about absolute educational values in an exclusively secular sense is to attempt the impossible. There have been, and clearly are, many deeply ethical people who would strongly deny any kind of religious or metaphysical basis for their beliefs, but as the postmodern denial of all values and truth might suggest, their position is arguably a residual and unstable one, rather than one with firm materialistic foundations.[25] My own inclination would be towards

[23] Paul Davies, *The Mind of God*, Simon & Schuster, 1992, p. 142.

[24] Michael Polanyi, 'The Eclipse of Thought,' reprinted in *Dumbing Down*, ed. Ivo Mosley, Thorverton: Imprint Academic, 2000, p. 231.

[25] This is a position implied, but not spelled out in Michael Polanyi's *Personal Knowledge*, Routledge, 1958, and discussed more explicitly in John Milbank, *Theology and Social Theory: Beyond Secular Reason*, Blackwell, 1991.

the latter view, but the fact is that we live in an inescapably pluralistic and polyphonic society, and discussions of public educational
policy must, therefore, be conducted, if at all, within the terms of secular discourse.

But if the values open to common secular discourse have (for good
reason) been those that have historically prevailed in British educational debates, it would be foolish to ignore altogether the metaphysical resonances beneath the surface. Agnostic parents have often
chosen to send their children to Church schools (of various hues) not
because they wanted them indoctrinated with particular beliefs, nor
out of religious nostalgia, but because they believed that teachers who
held quite different beliefs from themselves would show qualities of
commitment and dedication to their secular tasks that were not
always so evident in state schools. One of the greatest (and most often
overlooked) achievements of the British version of the modern, secular, pluralistic society is to have effectively tapped the very metaphysical roots that it has tacitly agreed not to discuss. Agreed silence,
however, is not the same as denial. Until the Thatcherite revolution,
British society had continued in what was essentially the Lockean tradition of pluralism by agreeing that no single person or group should
have the power to enforce agreement outside the specified area of secular discourse. As Desmond Ryan argues, post-Thatcherite government education policy (which manifestly includes that of New Labour)
has been to invade this hitherto protected 'space' by its emphasis on
testing and assessment. Nowhere does there appear to be more truth
than here to the charge that, by insisting on testing everything from curricula to training standards, the government has systematically
restricted knowledge to what is testable, turning education into training, and imposing its own ruthlessly narrow interpretation on what
had previously been left wisely undefined.

Among the unfortunate corollaries of the closure of this tacitly
protected metaphysical space is that secular advocates of liberal
education tend to rely on arguments for its economic utility that are
often slightly suspect. Quite simply, the vast majority of those who
believe in genuine education of the whole person do not do so for
economic reasons at all, but they believe (probably correctly) that
they will never be listened to by politicians and their bureaucratic ilk
unless they try to use the language of the market-place. But just as
bad money drives out good, so, in using this essentially false coin-
age, they have put themselves at a disadvantage, permitting their
own arguments to be subverted and corrupted into a debate about
economics rather than education. As Ryan has shown in the melan-

choly detail of recent history, the result has been to play into the hands of the most ruthless metaphor-mongers.

Thus I am convinced that Maskell and Robinson are entirely right to dismiss the economic arguments of the 1997 Dearing Report, showing that ever more students benefit the economy because in the past graduates have earned more than non-graduates (!), but their conclusion that university studies are, and should be, totally useless, is nevertheless a non-sequitur. I have no idea whether the target of their most withering scorn, the unfortunate Professor Norman Gemmell, of the Department of Economics at Nottingham University, is the most hard-headed New Labour apparatchik, a closet liberal, or even a secret Catholic Newmanite; subjected to literary analysis, however, his arguments bear all the characteristic hallmarks of someone trying to defend a deeply-held set of ideals that inform but do not quite coincide with his mode of 'proof'. What enrages Maskell and Robinson, of course, is the jargon and mystification of the language of managerial bureaucracy to which he has resorted to make his case — and it is indeed far from clear that genuinely educated graduates in Newman's sense would necessarily constitute a better workforce than one composed of (say) literate school-leavers. They would be more critical of time-wasting bureaucratic directives, more easily bored (I suspect) with silly and repetitive tasks, and would almost certainly show a degree of initiative and creativity that would be as wholly unwelcome in the ranks of current educational management as it would be in some commercial firms. All of which, however, in the greater scheme of things, provides a case for, rather than against Newman's view of the value of education. 'Transferable skills' may well be a nonsense — it certainly is an exaggeration — but an educated approach to life, in all its diversity, is in the long run likely to aid the economy — in so far as a really educated society sees the economy as an end, rather than a means to a whole lot of other ends.

Newman would also, I suspect, be delighted that his argument for the rationality of faith should also constitute a powerful argument not merely for the practical utility of an educated mind, but for the value of the study of a wide range of subjects. Like Robert Grant, he recognized the gulf between education and training; he also recognized that the difference was essentially one of how, rather than what subjects were studied. Though it is indeed hard to see how some of the subjects listed by Maskell and Robinson could easily lend themselves to university study (Embroidery... Global Futures... Pig Enterprise management... ?) and the present climate of university studies does not makes one inclined to give the benefit of any doubts, there are many practical studies that have a highly complex and theoretical component. As we have recently discovered, university centres for various regional studies, which combine history, law, culture, economics, politics and religion, such as Middle East studies (Bernard Lewis's Princeton base), Latin American studies, or South East Asia studies, have a vital political role in the conduct of contemporary foreign policy. Few would claim that such studies are not worthy of university attention — especially in view of the frequent manifested ignorance of these areas in the policy-making branches of government. We should also remember that law and medicine have always been part of the European university curriculum — and nothing Newman says suggests he would have wished them excluded. Similarly, the study of English (a key subject for Maskell and Robinson — as for myself) is a relative late-comer to the university scene. My own former Chair, the Regius Chair of English at Glasgow University, is one of the oldest (if not the oldest) in the world. It was founded in the 1850s at the same time as two others: the Chairs of New Testament Studies, and of Accountancy. Here was polyphony with a vengeance! The Cambridge English School, from which Ian Robinson (like myself) graduated, is the creation of the early twentieth century.

Nor should we regard modularization (another hate of Maskell and Robinson) as necessarily an intellectual and educational disaster — though, again, some cases of modularization have undoubtedly been both. Many of the interdisciplinary courses introduced by the new universities of the 1960s[26] were modular in design, but as well thought-out components of an overall course-scheme they proved as interesting for the faculty as they were for the students. I myself participated (with other faculty members of the appropriate discipline) in several at Sussex in the 1960s and '70s, including 'The English Romantics and their Society' (literature/history), 'Romanticism and Philosophy', and 'Landscape and Literature 1650-1850' (literature/art history). I count all of these, and others, as major milestones in my own intellectual development. From their comments, they were equally so for the students. I also recall Marjorie Reeves, the Oxford historian and Dante scholar, who was an external examiner for another Sussex course on Plato, Paul, Augustine, and Dante (Literature/Philosophy) which I had not taught, saying to me that, though she had had initial doubts about its intellectual validity,

---

[26]   The so-called 'Shakespearean Six': Essex, Kent, Lancaster, Sterling, Sussex, and Warwick.

when she came to look at the essays and exam papers she was totally won over by the quality of thought shown by the candidates.

In short, though Maskell and Robinson are rightly scornful of much of the jargon, the sloppy thinking, and self-seeking in government language and even the practice of some universities (their favourite target is Swansea), I cannot accept their conclusion that universities are only for the tiny minority who wish to learn to think along the lines of a (Leavisite) English Department. I believe, on the contrary, that universities are socially and even economically valuable to modern Britain, and that as many people (of all ages) who genuinely want to participate in what they have to offer should be enabled to do so. What is an unmitigated disaster is the combination of mindless egalitarianism and social instrumentalism that seem to be the main planks of present government policy. Though universities should offer equal opportunity, they are not about egalitarianism, but intellectual discrimination; though they have a vital social function, that function is not the Blunkett-Morris 'well-trained labour force'.

For a positive assessment of the modern university (not entirely incompatible with Newman's ideal) we could do worse than turn to the description of Frank H.T. Rhodes, President Emeritus of Cornell University:

> The university is the most significant creation of the second millennium... It manufactures no products, but it creates the science and technology on which those products depend. It produces no mass circulation newspapers, magazines, or television programs, but it trains their publishers, writers and producers. It informs public understanding, cultivates public taste, and contributes to the nation's well-being as it nurtures and trains each new generation of architects, artists, authors, business leaders, engineers, farmers, lawyers, physicians, poets, scientists, social workers, and teachers — as well as a steady succession of advocates, dreamers, doers, dropouts, parents, politicians, preachers, prophets, social reformers, visionaries and volunteers — who leaven, nudge, and shape the course of public life.[27]

If, as I suggested earlier, one vital aspect of a modern liberal education is its polyphony — not just in terms of the curriculum, but the relation between the parts of the curriculum — our universities are central to all our lives, public and private, not because they do one thing well or badly, but because they do so many — irreplaceably.

[27] Frank H.T. Rhodes, *The Creation of the Future: the Role of the American University*, Ithica: Cornell University Press, 2001, p. xi.

Desmond Ryan

Neo-Luddism

*How Thatcherism Destroyed
Britain's Potential to become
the Mindshop of the World*

Introduction
Great Transitions and the British Elite

Some ten millennia separated the agricultural revolution from the emergence of Britain as the 'first industrial nation'. A mere two centuries has seen the supersession of the first industrial revolution by the second. This has not yet acquired a definitive title. However, if we may denominate an era by its staple, we see the Age of Corn giving way to the Age of Machinery, and then the Age of Machinery being succeeded by the Age of Information. A new staple does not eliminate the old but, as more profitable, displaces it (even physically, to less mature economies in other countries). Just as industrial workers did not cease to eat while tending their machines or pondering their returns on investment, so the service workers of today still depend on the mechanical infrastructure which constructs their commodities and maintains their environment. But *value* in the economy is more and more derived from the quality and timeliness of information. Though food sustains it and iron and plastic construct it, information now drives the world economy. No one alive doubts that they are living through an information revolution.

This paper draws attention to an irony in the history of political economy: the British political elite making the same mistake twice in less than 150 years. The mistake in question is the misidentification of the long-term source of value in the British economy at the point of transition between staples. The first time, as every schoolchild once knew, the mistake was corrected by Sir Robert Peel when he sealed the end of the Age of Corn by repealing the Corn Laws. However, come the second point of transition, what do we see? Apparently mesmerised by the content of the historically dominant staple, the British governments of the 1980s ignored clear evidence that a new staple industry was emerging in the UK, one in which the country had both a clear superiority in the factors of production and a lead of a generation over most competitors in development and marketing. As I will show in this essay, Mrs Thatcher and her ministers persisted with a policy of promoting the interests of manufacturing industry long after it had become clear that Britain had no more lasting a comparative advantage in machinery than it had earlier had in corn.

This blind defence of the Iron Laws was at the expense of the dynamic but fragile 'information interest', emergent in the British economy since the eclipse of the imperial economic system in the late 1950s.[1] The emergence of this interest[2] derived from Britain's comparative advantages in scientific research, elite education, and quality cultural activities (design, media, art and music). All of these rising sectors depended for their vitality and competitiveness on the higher education system. Because British higher education then offered a comparatively unusual degree of formative contact with critical-creative minds at work, its most outstanding graduates, socialised to high expectations for fulfilling work, often competed to work in sectors allowing the most liberated exercise of the mind. Higher education thus became the live germ of a post-manufacturing production system with a competitive edge in imaginative ideas. To emphasise the parallel with the staple it displaced, we may select a term which resonates with 'manufacturing' and call higher education the 'mind-factory' of the 'mindfacturing' industries. It produced the producers of new, high-value, largely abstract goods and services, the 'new invisibles' of the post-imperial trading system.

The elite sectors of higher education (excluding certain lacklustre university departments but including certain colleges of art and design, of music and drama, and some polytechnic departments) had a number of distinctive characteristics: collegial self-management, the self-confidence in criticism of a competitively selected elite, respect for excellence in the specific skills of each aesthetic/intellectual practice, high social esteem for creativity/ innovators, and a positive attitude to risk taking. It is striking that, *as a*

---

[1]   P.J. Cain and A.G. Hopkins, *British Imperialism: Crisis and Deconstruction 1914-1900*, Harlow, 1993, pp. 275-91.

[2]   The fact that its emergence caused an earthquake in terms of the rights to social esteem and to symbolic territory claimed by different social classes was signalled by 'The Sixties', 'Swinging London', etc.

moral system, and despite the difference in the actual material being produced, these characteristics have so much in common with those associated with the transition from craft skills to industrial manufacture in the emergence of Britain as the first industrial nation. The reward for high achievers in this new productive system was, in international comparative terms, also distinctive: not high incomes and conspicuous consumption, but independent and interesting work. Having encountered intrinsic values in their education, they wished to continue to enjoy them in their work.

The interrelatedness of these characteristics suggests that this productive system was a niche-specific culture, flowering only under organizational conditions similar to those found in the higher education institutions where its workers had received their cultural formation. Herein lay the fragility. That higher education system, that formative cultural matrix, existed in an economic enclave protected by the state. This protection depended on a long-established but contingent view of its interests taken by the controllers of the state. By 1980 those controllers had changed, and with them changed the proclaimed view of the state's interests. In historical perspective, British higher education between 1945 and 1980 appears as the state-sponsored workshop of the discipline of originality for an elite destined for leadership roles across those parts of the culture which gave scope to people with critically trained minds and a disposition to creative originality. Today, however, as the source of a culture of intellectual adventurousness, of self-surpassing excellence in individual achievement, and of norm-questioning deep play, the British higher education system has been all but smashed — not by superior competition from the mindfacturing systems of other countries, but by its own former sponsor, the state. Of course there are still universities, indeed more than ever; they have not been closed down, their wealth confiscated, their occupants expelled, their work terminated, as with the state-suppressed monasteries of the 1530s. But it is only the name which remains; they are not the same institution, any more than Charterhouse is still a Carthusian monastery. In being organizationally reconfigured to take on a politically decreed role in the economy they have lost the right to collectively self-manage their own work, the vital ingredient in the discipline of originality. Losing that self-management has turned their occupants into employees, to be deployed (and 'let go') as utility dictates. Losing the discipline of creativity under criticism brought in consequence the loss of their cultural role in British society. From *producers of cultural norms* which animated a dynamic sector of society they have become the *consum-*

ers of procedural dogmas foisted on them by the new controllers of the state. Despite being dictated by government, these dogmas largely emanated from the moribund sector of society which had never had much regard for university products and which the universities were bidding to displace: manufacturing industry.

In squandering its emerging predominance in mindfacturing, Thatcherism has made Britain the butt of a Toynbeeian historical joke. Even while proclaiming themselves to be the party of the real world, the Thatcherites crippled the source-agency of the new economic system by imposing on it a fantasy-projection from the moribund system it was displacing. Rather than promoting investment in the fields which were attracting the energies of Britain's brightest entrepreneurs, the government reached nostalgically back to a model of production in which the UK had been a competitive failure for over a hundred years. The joke is that, rather than having flexibly intelligent companies run like universities, Britain now finds itself with stultifyingly mechanistic universities run like factories. And, domino-like, behind the political instrumentalisation of the universities has quickly followed the degradation of swathes of public service agencies in which collegial self-management was the basis of a low-key but efficient form of quality control. Managerialised to within an inch of their viability, the BBC and the NHS hang on to intrinsic values by the strength of the culture built up over generations; other agencies display the symptoms of terminal human disaffection (e.g. early retirements, retirements on the grounds of ill-health, recruitment difficulties, absenteeism). Neo-Luddism has imposed a culture more reminiscent of the eighteenth century than prophetic of the twenty-first. But these machines are abstractions, and cannot be smashed.

As a history undergraduate, I was fortunate enough to do the Age of Peel as my special subject under an inspiring teacher, the late Angus MacIntyre. The only way I could think of to share my understanding of the 1980s as the decade when a complex, organically evolving civilization was traumatically regressed by its 'no-alternative' therapist was to stand back and see it in historical perspective. Set against the 1840s, I see the 1980s as an instance of a ruling elite making a major historical mistake as a consequence of elevating dogma and will to power over the lessons of history. For in the Industrial Revolution our history already had a lesson on the importance of recognizing when quantitative economic advance became a qualitative historical transition. But the lesson never escaped from the history books into the dogma-riddled world of Margaret

Thatcher: despite Peel, the imposition of the 'philosophy of manufactures' on the 'mindfacturing interest' remained as explicitly the
policy of the Thatcher governments as the protection of the agricultural interest against the rising manufacturing interest had been the
policy of the crypto-Luddite governments of the 1820s and 1830s.

So, these clarifying preliminaries over, let us now step back to our
distance-giving vantage point, the moment of the assertion of manufacturing industry as a system, in conscious and rhetorical opposition to the landed interest. Its apologist — perhaps the last of that
great wave of luminaries collectively known as the Scottish Enlightenment, Fellow of the Royal Society, Professor of Natural Philosophy in the University of Glasgow before giving up his chair to
become a freelance chemist and the author of works both explaining
the workings and extolling the merits of the new industrial system
— Andrew Ure.

Andrew Ure and the Blessings of the Factory System

Few apologists for a new civilization have been less apologetic than
Andrew Ure.

> ...magnificent edifices, surpassing far in number, value, usefulness, and
> ingenuity of construction, the boasted monuments of Asiatic, Egyptian,
> and Roman despotism, have, within the short period of fifty years, risen
> up in this kingdom, to show to what extent capital, industry, and science
> may augment the resources of a state, while they meliorate the condition
> of its citizens. Such is the factory system, replete with prodigies in
> mechanics and political economy, which promises in its future growth
> to become the great minister of civilization to the terraqueous globe,
> enabling [Great Britain], as its heart, to diffuse along with its commerce
> the life-blood of science and religion to myriads of people still lying 'in
> the region and shadow of death'.[3]

As harbinger of the meliorations to be received from British commerce by the myriads then lying in the region and shadow of death
in distant parts of the terraqueous globe, Ure outlined those already
enjoyed in the region of Greater Manchester. In keeping with its
character as a political tract aimed at the governing classes, the bless-
ings listed were as much moral as economic. Indeed, what marks out
The Philosophy of Manufactures as an Enlightenment text is the subordination of the economic, the political and the military advantages to
be looked for from the factory system to the civil and the moral.

[3] Andrew Ure, *The Philosophy of Manufactures: or, an exposition of the scientific, moral
and commercial economy of the factory system of Great Britain*, Third edition,
London, 1861 [First edition 1835], pp. 18-19.

Accepted that there is such a thing as society, there are better and worse ways of ordering it. For Ure, the incomparable agency for ordering society was the factory system:

> At Quarry Bank, near Wilmslow, in Cheshire, is situated the oldest of the five establishments belonging to the great firm of Messrs. Greg and Sons, of Manchester, who work up the one-hundredth part of all the cotton consumed in Great Britain. It is driven by an elegant water-wheel, 32 feet in diameter, and 24 feet broad, equivalent in power to 120 horses....At a little distance from the factory, on a sunny slope, stands a handsome house, two stories high, built for the accommodation of the female apprentices. Here are well fed, clothed, educated and lodged, under kind superintendence, sixty young girls, who by their deportment at the mill, as well as in Wilmslow Church on Sunday, where I saw them assembled, evince a degree of comfort most creditable to the humane and intelligent proprietors. The Sunday scholars, equally numerous, belonging to the rural population, appeared to great disadvantage alongside of the factory children, the former being worse clad and worse looking than the latter, and worse behaved during divine service.[4]

After the elegance of the water-wheel, the sunniness of the slope, and the handsomeness of the house, the acid in the final brush strokes of this utopian panorama alerts us to Ure's rhetorical purpose. Though identified in the footnotes of *Capital* as an enemy of the proletariat, Ure had as the principal goal of his writings to undermine the ascendancy of the landed aristocracy. At almost every point of substantive comparison, agriculture and its people are disparaged. For example, immediately after we see the rural poor appearing to disadvantage alongside the factory children — worse clad, worse looking, and worse behaved in church — we learn that the girls have 'a man and a woman . . . also a schoolmaster and schoolmistress, and a medical practitioner' looking after them. Inevitably, their health is unequalled by any other class of work-people; their death rate is only one third of the Lancashire average; and in forty years no more than two have 'come on the parish', as a charge on the Poor Rate. A page later:

> Mr W.R. Greg says that the general state of education among their mill hands is remarkably superior to that of the agricultural people. He has attended sometimes a sort of little club established near one of their country mills, to which some of the farmers' people came, and he found an astonishing difference between their intelligence and that of the mill-workers.[5]

[4]   *Ibid.*, pp. 346-7. Cf. Michael Sanderson, 'Education and the factory in industrial Lancashire 1780-1840', *Economic History Review* Second Series, 20, 1967, p. 269.

[5]   Ure, *Philosophy of Manufactures*, p. 348.

As for education and intelligence, so for accommodation and material comfort, Ure vindicates the industrial system for its harvest of happiness. Yet the *point* of the following comparison is not material: rather, the curtain is drawn back on an animated moral icon, a human[6] scene both touching and uplifting, full of symbols of attachment to the religious and moral order, one well calculated to work on the hopes and fears of the rulers of pre-Victorian Britain.

> The houses occupied by [Mr T. Ashton's] work-people lie in streets, are built of stone, and are commodious; each consisting of at least four apartments in two stories, with a small back-yard and a mews lane....I looked into several of the houses, and found them more richly furnished than any common work-people's dwellings which I had ever seen before. In one I saw a couple of sofas, with good chairs, an eight-day clock in a handsome mahogany case, several pictures in oil on the walls, freshly painted for the family, a representation of one of the younger daughters like a smart peasant girl carrying a basket on her arm, one of the Virgin and Child at Bethlehem, and another of Christ crowned with thorns, all creditable to the travelling artist. In another house I observed a neat wheel barometer, with its attached thermometer, suspended against the snow-white wall. In a third there was a piano, with a little girl learning to play upon it.[7]

However vivid, tendentious description is not left to do duty for substantive argument. While 'philosophy' in his usage means more what we would now call 'technology', Ure's massive tract is philosophical in that it presents the factory system as a comprehensive advance in the application of reason to human affairs. It is because it is fundamentally more intelligent than agriculture that manufacturing will triumph, just as agriculture prevailed over societies based on hunting. Eulogising Arkwright as the man who first understood that the factory system both rose out of and required a new quality of *discipline*, Ure claims for him a place of honour in the history, not merely of Britain, but of civilization itself.

The main difficulty lay

> ...above all, in training human beings to renounce their desultory habits of work, and to identify themselves with the unvarying regularity of the complex automaton. To devise and administer a successful code of factory discipline, suited to the necessities of factory diligence, was....the noble achievement of Arkwright.... If...[the factory system] be not merely an inevitable step in the social progression of the world, but the

---

[6] 'The constant aim and effect of scientific improvement in manufactures are philanthropic....At every step of each manufacturing process described in this volume the humanity of science will be manifest.' Ure, *Philosophy of Manufactures*, p. 8.

[7] *Ibid.*, p. 349.

one which gives a commanding station and influence to the people who most resolutely take it, it does not become any man, far less a denizen of this favoured land, to vilify the author of a benefaction, which, wisely administered, may become the best temporal gift of Providence to the poor....Arkwright well deserves to live in honoured remembrance among those ancient master-spirits, who persuaded their roaming companions to exchange the precarious toils of the chase, for the settled comforts of agriculture.[8]

If the efficiencies of the factory were to be secured, discipline was indispensable: a subordination of every machine and worker to the source of power that gave life to each factory: its 'prime mover'.

> The term *Factory System*, in technology, designates the combined operation of many orders of work-people...in tending with assiduous skill a series of productive machines continuously impelled by a central power...[T]his title, in its strictest sense, involves the idea of a vast automaton, composed of various mechanical and intellectual organs, acting in uninterrupted concert for the production of a common object, all of them being subordinated to a self-regulating moving force.[9]

Twenty years before, the reverse of impressed with the human consequences of the 'intelligence' of the factory system, the Oxford divine Edward Copleston had accused it of reducing the living human being to the status of a component in a machine.[10] Ure glories in this reduction: as a triumph of contemporary practical science, and as the foundation of future progress.

> The principle of the factory system then is, to substitute mechanical science for hand skill, and the partition of a process into its essential constituents, for the division or graduation of labour...The grand object, therefore, of the modern manufacturer is, through the union of capital and science, to reduce the task of his work-people to the exercise of vigilance and dexterity...[11]

Through the operation of this reduction, Ure foresees the factory principle bearing many future benefits, for both the operatives and their masters.

[8]   *Ibid.,* pp. 15, 17.

[9]   *Ibid.,* p. 13.

[10] 'But while [the man] thus contributes more effectively to the accumulation of national wealth, he becomes himself more and more degraded as a rational being. In proportion as his sphere of action is narrowed, his mental power and habits become contracted; and he resembles a subordinate part of some powerful machinery, useful in its place, but insignificant and worthless out of it.' Edward Copleston, *A reply to the calumnies of the Edinburgh Review against Oxford,* Oxford, 1810, pp. 107-108.

[11] Ure, *Philosophy of Manufactures,* p. 20.

...on the equalization plan of self-acting machines, the operative needs to call his faculties only into agreeable exercise; he is seldom harassed with anxiety or fatigue, and may find many leisure moments for either amusement or meditation...How superior in vigour and intelligence are the factory mechanics in Lancashire....to the handicraft artisans of London!...The one set is familiar with almost every physico-chemical combination [of the various machines in the factory], while the other seldom knows anything beyond the pin-head sphere of his daily task.[12]

Impelled by the momentum of advocacy to overlook logical consistency, Ure adduces as the principal benefit to the master that he can dispense with the costly labour of these vigorously intelligent mechanics.

It is, in fact, the constant aim and tendency of every improvement in machinery to supersede human labour altogether, or to diminish its cost, by substituting the industry of women and children for that of men; or that of ordinary labourers for that of trained artisans.[13]

Then, in an attribution that has turned out to have epochal significance for the relationship between industry and science over the next one hundred and fifty years, Ure points up what larger lesson the manufacturers have learned.

This tendency to employ merely children with watchful eyes and nimble fingers, instead of journeymen of long experience, shows how the scholastic dogma of the division of labour into degrees of skill has been exploded by our enlightened manufacturers.

They are, in truth, much better acquainted with the general economy of the arts [of manufacture], and better qualified to analyse them into their real principles, than the recluse academician can possibly be, who from a few obsolete data, traces out imaginary results, or conjures up difficulties seldom encountered in practice....

The university man, preoccupied with theoretical *formulae*, of little practical bearing, is too apt to undervalue the science of the factory, though, with candour and patience, he would find it replete with useful applications of the most beautiful dynamical and statical [sic] problems. In physics, too, he would there see many theorems bearing golden fruit, which had been long barren in college ground. The phenomena [of physics] may all be better studied in a week's residence in Lancashire, than in a session of any university in Europe. And as to exact mechanical science, no school can compete with a modern cotton-mill.[14]

Though himself a former university professor and an able experimental scientist, Ure was impressed by the fact that the benefits of industry which he chronicled in such detail had been brought into

[12]   *Ibid.*, pp. 22-3.

[13]   *Ibid.*, p. 23.

[14]   *Ibid.*, pp. 23-5.

existence by men with minimal formal schooling. Their fortunes were self-made, but so also was their science. He clearly believed that a fertile union of making and knowing had been effected in the workshops of northern England, a union which had unprecedented powers of self-regeneration and innovation. He also believed that this new culture needed only to be generalised to all the other parts of the economy to guarantee Britain's continued economic supremacy.

> Great Britain may certainly continue to uphold her envied supremacy, sustained by her coal, iron, capital, and skill, if, acting on the Baconian axiom, 'Knowledge is Power,' she shall diligently promote moral and professional culture among all ranks of her productive population.[15]

So, not content with acknowledging that the Factory System brings the benefits of social progress for the world, of prosperity for the nation, of advances in moral and professional culture for the industrial districts, of comfort and security for the workers, and of education and health for their children; now Ure claims for it its own 'economy' of knowledge. We are at a fateful moment.

Why fateful? Because of what Ure, and others like him, understood powerful knowledge to be. What is really special about the British industrial (r)evolution[16] is how organic it was. Invention, innovation and development, capital, knowledge, training — the greatest part of these requirements were provided internally. The achievement had enormous short-run benefits for Britain but it also had a long-term cost which it is one objective of this paper to point out. While Ure is dotingly one-sided in what he claims for manufacturing, he is clearly an intelligent analyst of what he sees in manufacturing. What he sees is a productive system generating its own knowledge: knowledge for its own purpose, organic to its own institutions, structured in response to difficulties encountered in its own practice. Yes, knowledge was power; but Ure had no illusions that it was universities which would furnish the knowledge to empower the textile industry. It was the factory itself which was the growth point of the sciences. The Factory System was internally cognitively coherent, was rational: the largest and most complex rational system ever devised. Ure believed that anything from outside this system could only threaten it. Its self-sufficiency was taken to be the secret of its astonishing success. Thus in *The Philosophy of Manufactures* we see British industry insulating itself in its own culture. The fateful moment we are at is the laying-in of that peculiarly British contrary

[15] *Ibid.*, p. v.

[16] J. Mokyr, 'Was there a British Industrial Evolution?' *Research in Economic History*, Supplement 6, Greenwich, CN, 1991, pp. 253-286.

of reclusive academies, barren colleges, ivory towers: 'the real world'. Ure's views were soon triumphant, and have ever since provided much of the hidden bedrock of British industrial self-perception. In what follows I shall present some evidence that the privileging of 'the real world' of practical men who managed their firms with aggressive common-sense was still politically dominant 150 years later. I do this to suggest that the failure of the state to manage the evolution of the use of knowledge by manufacturing industry over that period led to a search for scapegoats for manufacturing industry's failure to overcome the competitive liabilities of this proto-industrial management style. I shall also suggest that it was the universities who were pushed into the role of scapegoat by Sir Keith Joseph,[17] the chief ideologue of the Thatcher government, ideologically as emphatically convinced about the connections between *manufacturing* industry and wealth-creation as Ure himself. In the final section I take my lead from an economic analysis of the competitive position of British universities to suggest that this 'real world' primitivism, having merely handicapped Britain for a century and a half as a manufacturing power, once imposed on the universities as a charter for relevance and wealth creation, may have maimed her completely for a leading role as an information power.

The Philosophy of Manufactures as a Political Rhetoric

Jumping a hundred and fifty years from Andrew Ure, we find still prevalent the assumption that industry means manufacturing. But its slopes are now less sunny, its icons less persuasive:

> Bright young people in Britain are 'actively encouraged to go into anything but industry', helping to erode the country's manufacturing industry base, said Mr Sam Toy, president of the Society of Motor Manufacturers and Traders, in a speech at Liverpool University.
>
> He said Britain was unique among industrial nations in the opprobrious way that it regarded industry in general, and engineering in particular.
>
> 'Careers such as medicine, the civil service, law and — God forbid — even the City are the so-called smart choices, whereas industry is something you do if you haven't got enough A levels to do anything else', he

[17] There are three important facts about Joseph which are relevant here: i) he actually represented a constituency in a long-declining industrial city, Leeds; ii) he had previously been the Secretary of State for Trade and Industry but was judged less than successful and was moved; iii) he was at the Department of Education and Science for a uniquely long time in recent historical terms. After his departure the terms 'industry' and 'manufacturing' could be found uncoupled, but by that time the power political pay-off of his attack was evident, more than compensating for its failure to have any economic effects.

said.

He said engineering, while an exciting and fulfilling career, was still woefully unrecognized and under-rewarded.

'On average an engineering director in Europe can expect to receive 63 per cent of the top person's income. But in Britain the figure is a miserable 48 per cent – the lowest ratio in Europe.'

Mr Toy gave his speech to commemorate the centenary of the establishment of the Harrison chair in engineering at Liverpool University.

He praised universities for doing more [*sc.* than they had been doing] to 'prepare undergraduates for the real world, rather than just concentrating on academic excellence for its own sake'.

But he said ministers and politicians should have a better relationship with industry and not, as in Britain, be 'made up almost exclusively of lawyers, ex-journalists and firsts in Oxbridge greats'.[18]

The President of the Society of Motor Manufacturers and Traders must be owned a linear descendant of Ure's philanthropic mill-owners. Here he regrets what Ure would most certainly have recognised as the survival of landed aristocratic values in the British political elite, echoing Ure's own strictures on –

> ...the gross ignorance evinced by our leading legislators and economists, – gentlemen well informed in other respects, – relative to the nature of those stupendous manufactures which have so long provided the rulers of the kingdom with the resources of war, and a great body[19] of the people with comfortable subsistence...'[20]

However he might have reacted to the persisting ignorance of the political elite, Ure would surely have been surprised to hear that British engineering industry was no longer profitable enough to pay salaries competitive with the professions, nor able to attract the high-fliers on their way to a political career. But he would have been amazed at *the reasons* given for the fate of the 'moral and professional culture' derived from 'those stupendous manufactures' in Lord Bowden's speech in the House of Lords debate on the universities in March 1976. Lord Bowden, formerly a professor of engineering at Manchester University, opened with this statement.

[18] 'Car magnate bemoans lack of interest in industry', *Times Higher Education Supplement*, 16.1.1987.

[19] Ure gives (pp.4-5) the figure employed in manufacturing in 1831 as 'upwards of one eighth of the population of this island....and probably not more than one sixteenth in agriculture'. This is within one per cent of the proportion of the population employed in industry in 1983; nearly four million jobs were lost in industry in the period 1961-83. J.R.Hough, *Education and the national economy*, London, 1987, pp. 4-5).

[20] Ure, *Philosophy of Manufactures*, p. 6.

...it is true to say that Englishmen no longer want to study those subjects which would fit them for a career in productive industry.

Mr. Mulley, speaking the other day in another place [i.e. the House of Commons], said that he had been talking to schoolmasters who said, 'Of course, our brighter boys don't want to go into industry.' A few months ago I myself lectured to 200 headmasters and asked them why they did not send their students to college or university, to study engineering. They all said the same thing. 'But of course if one of our brighter boys ends up at the age of 30 in a factory everyone — including himself, his family, his friends, and his schoolmates — will account him a failure who could do nothing better.' But it is upon the activities of these failures that we have to depend for the very food which we eat.'[21]

Later, he answers a question put to him by Lord Donaldson arising out of that early statement.

I ask myself why any responsible parent should allow his son to study engineering if the prospects thereafter are so poor....Why are prospects in industry so bad? The reason is that most industrial plants are so appallingly under-capitalised and that their equipment is poor and old. [A few months ago] I went round that enormous complex which used to be called Metropolitan Vickers and which has been at Trafford Park since the beginning of this century....and saw the enormous machining aisle in which some of the greatest artifacts ever made in this country were fabricated. The first 12 machine tools I passed were at least 15 or 20 years old....I also noted that every machine tool I passed was built by a local firm which has since gone bankrupt...Cravens of Stockport made very large lathes; they went out of business six years ago, and it is now impossible to get a big lathe made anywhere in England. No industrial country can hope to survive if it has no machine tool trade and the plant in its factories is wearing out....We now face a situation in which industry is under-capitalised and cannot attract engineers. Unless and until we are able to solve this problem, I do not see that there is any future for higher education, for hospitals, for the Health Service or for central or local government, because all those things depend on the product of the men making things in factories.'[22]

Mr Toy and Lord Bowden agree that the able young are neither being directed towards nor seeking out jobs in manufacturing industry — very much the reverse, in fact. Lord Bowden suggests that this is rational behaviour — that there is less and less industry to get jobs in — and adduces an economic reason — under-capitalisation while 'successive governments....have pillaged industry in order to support the recurrent costs of running the nation at the expense, in the end, of the whole of our economy and in the

[21] Official Report, Fifth Series, *Parliamentary Debates, House of Lords*, Vol.369, 31 March 1976, coll.1193-4.

[22] *Ibid.*, coll.1197-8.

long run of the universities as well'.[23] Mr Toy is less focused, hinting at some general cultural conspiracy causing his salary to be c.24 per cent under par, with government personnel not blameless. Of the resources Ure took for granted as available to Great Britain in 'the bloodless but still formidable strife of trade', both capital and skill have turned out to be problematic.

For the origin of the problems with capital, Lord Bowden is blunt: for '40 to 50 years....we have been suffering from an accounting process which has taken industry's capital away from it and has put it at the disposal of the Government to use as if it were current income'.[24]

Reluctant Partners:
British Industry and University Science

As to skill, a single moment can be fixed on with great precision: the traumatic experience of the 1867 Paris Exhibition. Between 1835 and 1867 a new word had come into existence: scientist. Self-originated technology ceilinged early; the self-sufficiency of British proto-industrial knowledge lasted only as long as mechanical improvements could be made by native wit and technical skill. From the moment that abstract scientific theory became the essential partner of industrial advance, the British Factory System went into secular comparative decline.

> At the Great Exhibition of 1851 in London, Great Britain was awarded the palm of excellence in nearly all of the one hundred or so departments. At the 1867 Exhibition in Paris she won in only ten of the ninety departments....'this defeat awakened England to the startling fact that the industrial sceptre was slipping from her grasp and she saw the result — her ships decaying in her harbours and the hammer falling from the hand of starving workmen'.[25]

Awakened is one thing, galvanised is another. The British government continued to place financial savings for the government above investment in scientific and technical education for the nation.

> Britain stood out during the nineteenth century for the contrast between its national wealth and its educational penury. Britain was the richest country in Europe until almost the end of the century, 'yet more parsimonious than any except perhaps France — even at a time of peace and great prosperity such as 1870 when revenue was buoyant, expenditure steady, income tax reduced...and budget surpluses almost embarrass-

[23] *Ibid.,* col.1217.

[24] *Ibid.,* coll.1198-9.

[25] Michael Sanderson, *The Universities and British Industry 1850-1970,* London, 1972, p. 9.

ing. In 1870 government expenditure was a much lower percentage of gross national product than in 1850; and in 1890 it was lower still.'[26]

Thus when the Thatcher government came to formulate its policy towards higher education, it inherited a debate which was over a century old. As the party proclaiming the need for fresh thinking and for risk-taking to overcome the sclerotic tendencies of an over-managing, 'nanny' state, it might have been expected to update the debate, to recast it in a more comprehensive economic framework, based on analysis of trends in comparative advantages in the international division of labour, current domestic trends in the factors of production, and signals from the key players in the various markets. To ask, in short, what was the real state of Britain, of its work and its institutions, and what that reality might mean for its place in the world. Instead, the government's policy was to ask, with such obdurate and pertinacious repetitiousness that it became clear that it did not expect an answer, the question Baroness Gaitskell had asked early in the debate in the House of Lord in 1976.

> My Lords, before the noble Lord [Lord Robbins, Chairman of the Committee on Higher Education 1961-63] sits down, can I ask him why in his fascinating speech he gave us no indication of the fact that the expansion was not followed by greater productivity in the country?[27]

Even by 1976, the question was old and obvious; but so old and so obvious that no one seems to have put it to themselves that, just *because* it was old and obvious, it had to be the wrong question. While for the first few years of the new government the consequences for the universities of not having the answer to it were merely financial — the public spending economies begun after the first oil price shock in 1974 were continued — before long there came with the cuts in resources a demoralising and politically disabling message which was to become a Tory refrain: higher education had only itself to blame for the cuts. Expenditure on higher education had all along been investment in industry — where were the dividends?

> Not ideology, not monetarism....lies behind the squeeze on higher education. The origin lies in the failure of the higher education sector over

[26] J. Wrigley, 'Technical Education and Industry in the Nineteenth Century' in B. Erlbaum and W. Lazonick (editors) *The Decline of the British Economy*, Oxford, 1986, p.164, quoting M. Gowing, 'Science, Technology and Education: England in 1870,' The Wilkins Lecture, *Notes and Records of The Royal Society of London*, 32, 1977, p. 82.

[27] *Parliamentary Debates, House of Lords*, 31 March 1976, col.1121.

the last thirteen years and more to demonstrate decisively [*nota bene*] its claim to a protected share of taxpayers' money.[28]

Such statements appeared at the time to be a politically deft blaming of the victim. But with hindsight they were more. They were an expression of the belligerent core of Thatcherism. Thatcherism was more than an ideology, more than a moral attitude; it was pure spirit, the will to power. One of Mrs Thatcher's most outstanding gifts was the ability to effect a brilliant interweaving of power and language into a form of communication with which no communication was possible. Even in 1982 Waldegrave, a skilfully plastic politician, was already deploying the paradox that was to underlie Tory higher education policy after their re-election in 1983. The universities were going to continue to be caught between the corporate state and the market — but the Tory government was going to be both. For it was another brilliant originality of Thatcherism to turn the market into an arm of centralization of power. It did this in two ways:

a) by using it as a rhetoric of legitimacy. In the general rhetoric of the market used by Thatcher governments to secure the moral high ground with the electorate, the incantation 'manufacturing industry' bore almost voodoo power. It was presented as the foundation stone of the architectonic of material prosperity and national self-reliance to be once more achieved through work, efficiency, and discipline.

b) by 'privatising' sectors whose ownership by the state had in the 1960s and 1970s become a liability for governments; which, in another idiom, had made this country appear 'ungovernable'.[29] Thatcherism set about ensuring that the days of multiple claimants impeding governments from governing were past. The state was going to be both less and more: leaner yet stronger.

One argument in the rhetoric with which higher education was to be reshaped took the following as its logical form:

> Future graduates will want jobs
> [A revitalised and successful manufacturing industry will provide jobs]
> [Successful industries are those which incorporate the most science and technology]
> Therefore students will want to study science and technology.

Thus the rhetoric of Mr Waldegrave in 1982:

[28] W. Waldegrave, *Speech at Westfield College, University of London, 17 November 1982, Discussion Paper 12*, University of Exeter Teaching Services, 1982, p. 2..

[29] M. Crozier, S.P. Huntington, and J. Watanuki, *The crisis of democracy: Report on the governability of democracies to the Trilateral Commission*, New York, 1975.

I do not need [*nota bene*] to tell you that a strong utilitarian wind is blow-ing through HE as students accurately [*nota bene*] assess the needs of a Britain which has a long slow job ahead of it building a better economic performance. This is a chill wind for some of the less well founded liberal arts and social studies departments, and for some of the less practical sci-ence courses too.[30]

Having warned his audience that the 'accurately assessing' stu-dent market going for *practical* science and technology would be fully supported by government, he then said the challenge facing institutions was:

to find ways of meeting quickly enough the legitimate [*nota bene*] claims and needs of students seeking new courses which genuinely [*nota bene*] relate to Britain's business needs. This will need flexibility and respon-siveness in meeting new demands, and learning from industry [*nota bene*] and commerce what is required in time to do something about it.[31]

The close reader of such texts might feel that in 1982 this rhetori-cian was a would-be truthful man in search of political preferment; ambitious enough of deceiving his neighbour, not yet politician enough to deceive himself. Note how the lack of 'flexibility and responsiveness in meeting new demands', identified for over a cen-tury as the principal weakness of British *industry*,[32] now appears in the debit column *of the university*! And yet how unerringly his but-tressing adjectives and adverbs lead us to what the junior minister with responsibility for higher education felt to be most vulnerable in his presentation: indeed, suggest to us that the factual truth is the very opposite of what he is politically required to say. For what evi-dence might Mr Waldegrave have had for his view that eighteen year old students could foresee — despite fifty years of pillage from governments — a return to prosperity of British industry? He had not yet the benefit of Mr Toy's view on the opprobrium attaching to industry in the mind of the public; but one pointer he would have known should have given him pause: Lord Bowden's speech.

[30]   Waldegrave, Speech at Westfield College, pp. 3-4.

[31]   *Ibid.*, p. 5.

[32]   Cf. 'British universities have served their country well in peace and war during the last half century. Alas, industry, or the financial houses, have failed or been unwilling to exploit the products of academia, whether people or ideas, and have permitted our rivals to do so. I find it especially galling when persons who should know better, but are evidently unaware of the facts, assert that universities are the haven of an 'anti-industrial culture'. My own experience is that for the last half century sectors of UK industry, through choice or ignorance, were anti-research and anti-graduate employees.'' Lord Dainton, *Times Higher Education Supplement*, 16.1.1987

I have to tell your Lordships that the expansion which was initiated with such enthusiasm and success 20 years ago came to a stop in 1970, and went abruptly into decline and reverse. Departments which were full of Englishmen in 1970 have hardly an Englishman left in them today...the department of chemistry, which had 140 student freshmen every year for years, now gets 60 students...Engineering departments are much worse...[In chemical engineering in Manchester] we used to admit year after year about 100 Englishmen and half-a-dozen foreigners as freshmen in the undergraduate course. This year we recruited 20 Englishmen and 24 foreigners....[When the entire Manchester machine tools trade collapsed] an industry in Manchester which had 15,000 men in it now has 500. Are noble Lords surprised that no one comes any more to study machine tools in Manchester? Last year we had 18 students, of whom four were British. For many years we have had what is probably the finest textile department in the whole world. It so happens that some of the big Lancashire mills are suffering very much from competition, particularly from Turkey. Are noble Lords surprised to hear that half of the students in the textile department are Turks, and that in some classes none are English?[33]

Replies to the Rhetoric

I have said that Thatcherism was distinctive for the originality and effectiveness of its manner of communicating: like an adept *schizogène*, it gave the impression of participating in a communicative exchange, when in reality the messages were all one-way. Electorally impregnable after 1983, the Tories withdrew from the traditional conservative engagement to keep the inherited institutional framework in working order, in favour of imposing a dogmatic vision. This was the vision of a reborn industrial Britain. But the rhetoric of competition was not supported by policies (e.g. on exchange rates) genuinely supportive of manufacturing industry; it served rather to cloak and justify attacks on established institutions seen by the Conservative leadership as 'overmighty subjects': the unions, the professions, local government.

The above speech by Mr Waldegrave is an excellent specimen of the discourses of Thatcherite politicians in these years. The staple ingredients are prominently visible:

—   the lofty and superior tone, as of a parent to a refractory child;

—   the ventriloquising of an exasperated public's recrimination for universities' failure to contribute to economic growth;

—   the threats of intervention, in the public interest, in universities' internal procedures;

[33]   *Parliamentary Debates, House of Lords*, 31 March 1976, coll. 1194-6.

- the self-absolution from responsibility for any such intervention, 'forced on the government' by the continued failure of HE to meet 'the legitimate needs and claims' of one or another market;

- the 'double-bind' of such interventions, requiring institutions to alter their ways of working to meet such new needs at the same time as 'protecting' those ways that have supported traditional excellences, of which the government declares itself proprietorially proud;

- the apparent reasonableness of asking the sector to justify 'to the public' why further cuts and interventions should not take place while themselves having no intention of hearing any such justification. Thus, for example, Mr Waldegrave's 'decisively' means the opposite of what it says: no demonstration *could* serve, as the decision (being part of the vision) was already taken;

- the straightforward ignoring of evidence that did not make for their case (e.g. of the fact that Britain *already had* a higher proportion of science and technology students than her industrial rivals),[34] or of appeals to reason from the most authoritative of sources, such as Lord Dainton.

No Newman, no Jaspers, no Ortega arose to reformulate the idea and mission of the university in reply to such speeches; no R.D. Laing or Gregory Bateson drew attention to the operation of pathological communication styles. Nonetheless, individual and collective voices were raised on behalf of the institution in public reply to government proposals. Authoritative voices raised in polite protest received a platform in the *Times Higher Education Supplement (THES)*, from where they passed into the scrap-books of the perplexed.

As was to be expected, representatives of industry and commerce also sought a hearing for their idea of the university. Unexpectedly — perhaps the *THES* was selective, or perhaps the scrap-book — these few representatives of Britain's leading firms seem to have been saying something that would have been as surprising to Andrew Ure as it should have been unwelcome to the government rhetoricians (though the second proved no more capable of hearing

[34] 'British research 'too segregated'' *Times Higher Education Supplement* 14.9.1984. The best reason for not acknowledging this fact was that often, as Lord Bowden had observed, a majority of such students were *from* her industrial rivals, learning the science of industries they had already captured on the basis of labour costs. Not the least of the advantages of late developing economies is not having to disentangle themselves from delusions about the superiority of knowledge generated in 'the real world'.

than the first) — they were satisfied with what they were getting. The importance of these statements is not proportional to their number; this is an autopsy, not a scientific survey. Our interest in such statements is as evidence of the degree to which the government, in such speeches as that by Mr Waldegrave above, genuinely spoke for industry itself. The answer appears to be partly yes, partly no.

The 'yes' part was that ministers did often speak for that part of industry which either could not afford or did not care to invest in training their own workforce. Although in an international perspective, British industry as a whole was admitted to be underinvesting in training,[35] within the national perspective, as the appropriate government minister publicly acknowledged, a distinction needed to be made between the market leaders, profitable enough to provide for their own needs, and the rest. Speaking for the more profitable, this time under the hat of Chairman and Managing Director of Ford UK, Mr Sam Toy, whom we have already heard lamenting the poor image of engineering in the public at large and expressing concern about the cultural origins of the political elite, made an important point about industry's training of graduates. In a metaphor that would have alarmed Edward Copleston, he said that 'graduates arrived at his company in the form of semi-finished components, because they had not received training in the specific fields in which they would be working'. The implication being that Ford UK expected graduates to have received from their higher education more important things than such training.

Reported on the same page of the *THES*, the chairman of Rank Xerox UK spelled out what that was:

> Mr Hornby agreed that industry needed some highly specialized graduates, for example electronics engineers. But he said that unless they had constant retraining their knowledge was obsolete within five years.... 'Careers for the future will demand a general appreciation of people, organizations, societies and how they work rather than detailed knowledge of one technical skill,' he said.[36]

[35] 'Criticism of UK management styles does not stop at research and development. Only the very major firms or those in high tech have ongoing training programmes for their staffs. In a recent *Times* article, Secretary of State for Employment Mr Tom King noted that 'British companies spent on average only 0.15 per cent of turnover on training last year — so little that it hardly shows up on the balance sheet. That is one-seventh of the American figure and one fourteenth of the best in West Germany.' ' Edward G Coll, 'A road map with no signposts to profit', *Times Higher Education Supplement*, 26.7.85.

[36] 'Warning on trained obsolescence', *Times Higher Education Supplement*, 27.9.1985.

Deficient training seemed more deeply rooted in the weaker, under-capitalised firms, whose more marginal performance gave them an interest in transferring their training costs on to the public purse by selecting recruits who had followed a more job-specific higher education. Some effects of this reluctance to invest in training came to light in a study of skill shortages in manufacturing industry in the economic upswing of the mid-1980s.

> Where there are shortages the [Institute of Manpower Studies] authors suggest they are self-inflicted. Companies insist on trying to solve them by recruiting fully-qualified staff, instead of retraining existing staff or recruiting at a lower level and [then] training.
> This trend is disturbing, says the institute, suggesting that it is caused by a lack of in-house training or by fear of competitors poaching trained staff.'[37]

The 'short-termism' of such companies was also identified in a surprising place, a report from the Institute of Personnel Management on personnel managers' attitude to company training. While ninety per cent of those questioned claimed to have absolute or considerable discretion in the sphere of training:

> 'Far from defending training vigorously against the scepticism of managerial colleagues, the personnel manager increasingly espouses the same set of values as his colleagues. Thus training, with its longer-term pay-off may fall out of favour within the personnel function'.... personnel executives are tending to fall in line when their colleagues argue that unless there is a short-term advantage training should be cut off or put off.[38]

The recruitment behaviour of British companies in the 1980s seemed to be continuing the innovatory approach so sensitively picked up by Ure in the 1830s, of allowing advances in technology to downgrade the skills required of the workforce. However, the loss of their powers of recapitalisation in times of recession had by the mid-1980s left such firms without the resources to re-equip with the increasingly expensive high technology required for this strategy to be effective, leaving them with such options as poaching trained

---

[37] At 'a gathering of academics, university officers and industrialists, attended by Sir Keith Joseph' at Mr Toy's old college, Fitzwilliam College, Cambridge, 'there were murmurs of cynicism both from academia and industry, with representatives from both sides complaining that the Government was not providing incentives for them to forge stronger links'. 'Joseph pleads for 'healthy enterprise'', *Times Higher Education Supplement*, 27.9.1985.

[38] '"Tough guys" stamp on company training', *Times Higher Education Supplement*, 21.11.1986.

staff off competitors, relocating to cheap-labour areas off-shore, etc..
Or to go to the wall, as so many did.

In research, too, the government's ventriloquism of industry's
needs as being for research that was *relevant* and *applicable* was more
likely to be contradicted by those British firms powerful enough to
be still playing in the world league. For example:

> Universities must be allowed to retain the capability to do fundamental
> research without having to consider commercial applications, a leading
> industrialist said this week.
>
> At an open meeting of the Royal Society of Chemistry Mr Robert
> Malpas, a managing director of British Petroleum, pointed out that the
> fundamental knowledge is needed for applied research in industry. He
> warned that, 'without first class basic research, industry's applied
> research would quickly decline in quality'. British industry would be the
> loser, he added.
>
> Universities and industry needed to work closely together, he said,
> and 'we must ensure that universities can turn out top class scientists
> who do fundamental research'. He said it was necessary that their prime
> purpose should be 'to push back the frontiers of knowledge and under-
> standing with no specific commercial application in mind'.[39]

Sir Bruce Williams, the Australian director of the Technical
Change Centre, set up in 1981 with substantial joint funding by the
(then) Social Science Research Council and the Leverhulme Foundation, was also of the view that the universities ought to continue
doing what they did well.

> There was a real danger that higher education institutions would be
> financially pressured into activity in which they would not be very pro-
> ductive....Speaking on technology transfer, Sir Bruce said that he did not
> think the British research councils were equipped to pick out applied
> research in universities and polytechnics which was likely to produce
> results of great industrial relevance....The problem of developing
> research findings commercially was a problem for British industry, not
> for higher education. 'In the field of industry the possibilities for the uni-
> versities and polytechnics to get involved more in applied research and
> innovation is extremely limited', he said.[40]

And in research, too, there were those who saw the inherent tendency of industry as to go for the short-term interest, to protect what
was already here rather than to develop what would do well in the
future. Lord Butterworth (Vice-Chancellor of Warwick University
1962-1985) claimed in a speech in the House of Lords that it was nec-

[39] 'Get back to basics says MD', *Times Higher Education Supplement*, 17.10.1986.

[40] 'British research 'too segregated'', *Times Higher Education Supplement*, 14.9.1984.

essary for research to be conducted outside the industry concerned because if:

> the research is wholly within the industry, there is a danger it will be confined too much to the existing products and in defence of existing capital investment.[41]

The *Times Higher Education Supplement* published a contribution from an American university president, on a study visit to form a view of the pluses and minuses of industry–university links in Britain.

> As a university president who works extremely hard to strengthen and expand corporate ties with his institution, I wondered how other educational systems in highly industrialized countries interacted with business and industry....In eight weeks I have become somewhat conversant with UK universities and their considerable array of talent. I am impressed, to say the least. In eight weeks I have also gained a better understanding of UK business and management styles and observed some of the philosophies at work in British industry and commerce. In this regard, I am somewhat less impressed and even a little dismayed.
>
> My interviews with academics, business executives and industry consultants revealed some recurring criticisms of British business attitudes:
> — too much concern with immediate profit and little vision for the future;
> — little priority for research and development budgets within the corporate structure;
> — lack of an appreciation for an academic degree by senior executives who themselves are not university graduates;
> — the absence of continuing education for staff within the UK corporate community;
> — the significant lack of personal involvement by business executives in the education system which is providing their future employees.

Then, with the clarity of the outsider, the President of Alfred University, Alfred, New York, made some concluding observations and asked a most pertinent question:

> The Green Paper affords a golden opportunity for British education to step boldly forward and show its capabilities. But the policy makers must remember that it always takes two to tango. What happens, as an example, if the UK campus structure is moulded to accommodate the nation's industrial needs in an era where its industrial leaders focus heavily on today's profits while ignoring tomorrow's opportunities? It would be the ultimate irony if the Green Paper created a vast reservoir of teaching and research talent that serviced primarily the commercial needs of the UK's international competitors who were smarter and quicker to take advantage of such a national treasure. At best, it would create a new dimension for the term 'brain drain'.

[41] 'Avoid stripey toothpaste philosophy', *Times Higher Education Supplement*, 28.11.1986.

> The Green Paper is....a good concept, but ignores the second half of the
> equation: UK business and industry....Who now devises the Green
> Paper for the profit sector?[42]

Not only was there not to be a Green Paper for 'the profit sector',
but rather it was the 'business and management styles....and some of
the philosophies at work in British business and industry and commerce' which were to be imposed on the 'impressive' UK universities. This self-spaying of the universities was effected by means of a
report from the Jarratt Committee, established (after 'proposals' by
the Department of Education and Science) by the Committee of
Vice-Chancellors and Principals in March 1984, with the remit to
carry out 'efficiency studies' comparable to those earlier conducted
into Civil Service departments by Sir Derek Rayner. One hundred
and fifty years after its publication, the *Philosophy of Manufactures*
was to be extended to the professorial classes; the reclusive academies were to be rescued from their idle formulatings.

In a discreetly packaged way, the demands that emanated from
the Jarratt Committee were that university internal governance
should change to reflect the best in the management of British industry and commerce, from which came a good third of the Committee's
membership.[43] But the discreet packaging can no longer disguise the
fact that the recommendations of the committee fell into the prevalent Tory style of pathological communication. Distinguished in
their other lives though the members were, the committee was not
an open-minded search for ways of making something good better,
it was a means of imposing constitutional change. Above all it was
not a debate. If there had indeed been a real debate, common-sense
criticisms of some of the key premises of government policy should
have been welcomed as a means of avoiding costly or damaging error

[42] Edward G. Coll, 'A road map with no signposts to profit', *Times Higher Education
      Supplement*, 26.7.1985.

[43] However, the fact that exactly similar demands were being imposed on the
      Health Service at the same time in consequence of the first report of Sir Roy
      Griffiths (Department of Health and Social Security, *NHS Management Inquiry*,
      London, 1983) makes it difficult to suppose the Jarratt conclusions were reached
      without government prompting. Cf.: '[In Cox's case study] it was very evident
      that the difference between administration and management was a key issue
      amongst those implementing Griffiths....Whereas administration was seen as
      servicing the needs of the professionals... general management was a matter of
      taking overall responsibility for the delivery of a service...[and] involved
      planning, setting targets, managing implementation and monitoring
      performance against pre-set criteria.' D. Cox, 'Health service management – a
      sociological view: Griffiths and the non-negotiated order of the hospital', in J.
      Gabe, M. Calnan, and M. Bury, (editors) *The sociology of the health service*,
      London, 1991, p. 94.

— the usual justification for taking wide soundings before implementing a radical change of policy. With regard to the internal governance of universities, the retrospective evidence suggests that the government had a vision of the internal management system it wanted to see in place and no counter-arguments made any difference.

Substantive Critiques

However, some practising academics behaved as if the debate was open. Many of the counter-arguments were specific, targeted at one or another proposal by a critic deemed significant enough to quote in the press. Hence the more fundamental critiques tended to lose their impact by being lost in a fragmented chorus of protest and rage. However, to give an idea that they could indeed make fundamental points, here are quotations from two authored pieces. The first, by the registrar of Leeds University, appeared as an article.

> It was a delusion to expect that the worst industrial management and the best university system could exist in the same environment....The Jarratt report contrives to be both a strategic and a tactical blunder on the part of the leaders of the university system....Simply because everyone has now realized that our wealth depends on industry does not....entitle the representatives of the dismal performers in that field to lecture the excellent performers in another. The tone of the report suggests that at the deepest levels the search for scapegoats for our national failings is never ending....The main fault [with universities] as expressed by Jarratt is that universities are not like businesses and they don't plan like businesses. They have too many committees and nobody is the boss. Much of this is true and much of it is also irrelevant. We aren't businesses; we aren't armies, and we aren't parliaments either....In a document dedicated to efficiency the failure to quantify savings is surprising. It betrays perhaps the basic fallacy of the premise itself, the fallacy of the sub-optimal use of resources ('if you have a lavatory, why are you not sitting on it?'). [The failure] will be rectified elsewhere. The government also is interested in efficiency, and its performance indicators are brutally simple: pound notes.[44]

[44]   James Walsh, Registrar, University of Leeds, 'Brains above all', *Times Higher Education Supplement,* (date mislaid). Cf. Lady Warnock at the 1985 Conference of the Confederation of British Industries: 'Lady Warnock said it was astonishing that education was being urged nowadays to become more like business when everybody knew that British industry was in a parlous state. Our universities were recognised, however, as extremely efficient compared with others in the rest of Europe.' 'Grudging praise from Sir Keith on efficiency', *Times Higher Education Supplement,* 22.11.1985.

Pausing only to point up Walsh's emphasis on the *tone* of the report, I pass on to the second example of reasoned criticism, this time from a professor of industrial sociology, i.e. from an expert in the organization business. After reading it, any thoughtful person would have been left wondering. As possibly the most pointed document of the (non-)debate, I reproduce it in full.

> Sir, — In your editorial [o]n the Jarratt revolution (*THES* April 5) you express two doubts about the strategy recommended: first, because changes in management structure will not change the 'ambiguous environment' in which universities operate, and secondly because increasing the power of 'managerially minded' but still disciplinary orientated senior academics may threaten the 'indispensable pluralism' of universities. Such doubts are justified. But there are more fundamental doubts about the Jarratt approach to university management.
>
> First, the transfer of one private industry model to universities is inappropriate. There is no one appropriate model for universities, any more than there is for private industry. Management structures should be adapted to the objectives of the organization, the resources required and available, the production methods used, and the environment in which the organization operates. Objectives, resources, methods and environments differ between universities, and between universities and private industry. As teaching institutions the objective of universities is to 'produce' well-educated, adaptable, and if possible creative graduates; as research institutions to create new knowledge. The resources include, most importantly, highly trained manpower. The methods used vary widely, and depend partly upon discipline. The environment, both on the 'supply' side and on the 'demand' side is highly variable.
>
> Management structures should take account of variable contingent factors, and not be based upon a mechanical comparison with models used elsewhere. To use traditional management science terms, organic models are more likely to be appropriate to universities than mechanistic models, but not always.
>
> Secondly, private industry in countries which have achieved much greater economic success than the UK does not operate according to the Jarratt model — notably Japan, but also elsewhere. Decision-making in Japanese industry is often slow, and involves wide consultation — it is not a matter of making 'hard' decisions at the top and enforcing them upon subordinates. More important for organizational success is employee commitment to the goals of the organization.
>
> The major management task for British universities is not transforming the management structure, or developing clear performance indicators (which leads to 'chase the indicator' instead of doing the job as well as possible), but maintaining commitment in the face of diminishing resources and demoralizing insistent criticism. Will following the Jarratt model increase that commitment? I doubt it.[45]

[45]   Roderick Martin, Professor of Industrial Sociology, Imperial College, London, *Times Higher Education Supplement*, 19.4.1985.

Although as a letter telling and succinct, as a substantive communication it does not go beyond the knowledge and principles to be encountered in a first year management science course. The dawning realization that epochal transformations in the constitutional fabric were being made by people who were assertively ignorant of the absolute basics of what they were dealing with was, to this writer, cause for great perplexity. There had to be something larger going on.

Symptomatic of the lack of engagement in any form of reasoning which would have made for a real debate was this report of Jarratt's own response to criticisms of his committee, perhaps to this very letter. Speaking to a conference on University Purchasing (*sc.* purchasing *by* universities, not *of* universities):

> The committee had also been accused of proposing the imposition of industrial management on the universities. 'Frankly, this is rubbish. Any organization which involves bringing together people, buildings and services should be concerned about how it uses these resources to achieve its purposes. There are not different systems of management for different types of organization.'
>
> Participation and consensus were essential in the build-up to a decision, said Sir Alex, but in any successful decision-making structure, the ultimate responsibility must lie with one person or body.'[46]

It is difficult to see in this statement more than dogmatic re-assertion. Not only are Martin's arguments not addressed, for somebody who had spent a year chairing discussions with the likes of Sir Robin Ibbs and Geoffrey Lockwood, Sir Alex reveals a large ignorance of the scientific basics of his problem. Such a statement could not have been made by anybody who had had brought to his attention the central works on university governance (as, for example, compellingly synthesized by Burton Clark),[47] or even the work in one of the most significant traditions in studies of management in industry itself, that emanating from Burns and Stalker, who state

[46] *Times Higher Education Supplement*, 20.9.1985. Our first-year management science student would identify these as the views of the Scientific Management theorists, some of whose prescriptions were current long enough ago to have convinced Lenin. Cf. A. Bryman, *Leadership and organizations* London, 1986, p. 169. Cf. also: 'In management we are learning that the type of organization, and the sort of people we employ in particular parts of it, have to be contingent upon — depend on — the task to be accomplished. This in turn means a willingness to allow, and indeed encourage, variety.' Thomas Kempner, Principal of Henley, The Management College, 'Playing the university game', *Times Higher Education Supplement*, 4.5.1984.

[47] B. R. Clark, *The higher education system: academic organization in cross-national perspective*, London, 1983.

categorically: 'The beginning of administrative wisdom is the awareness that there is no one optimum type of management system.'[48] Is it unfair to see 'the great and the good', when wheeled on by ministers to impose major changes on fields they know nothing about, as direct descendants of Ure's class of 'enlightened manufacturers', 'exploding scholastic dogmas' merely because they had not been verified in their own experience? Is it wrong to see the inability of this crypto-government committee to take heed of the findings of research on the problem it was supposedly addressing as of a piece with the secular inability of the leaders of British industry to appropriate scientific research and expert training for the greater competitiveness of their enterprises? Was not *this* the moment when the potential cure of ailing Britain was given the disease?

Perhaps feeling themselves compromised by their sponsorship of the Jarratt Committee, perhaps mesmerized by their close proximity to the big stick, individual university leaders may have hazarded that it was better not to speak out too assertively, lest it should be sooner rather than later that the soft grunting should give way to the wielding. Only one statement from a vice-chancellor found its way into the scrapbook, coincidentally a statement made on foreign soil. At a conference organized by the International Association of Consultants in Higher Education Institutions in Ennis, Ireland, Sir Peter Froggatt, Vice-Chancellor of Queen's University, Belfast, is reported thus:

> It is probably impossible to make universities like businesses without damaging their core constitution and it would be wrong even to try...There was a simplistic notion that if universities were made like businesses then something magical [*nota bene*] would happen in society, he told a conference in Ennis, Co. Clare...
>
> The British government wanted to break staff security of tenure, make the vice-chancellor chief executive, introduce performance indicators, managers, budgetary units, and corporate plans. It wanted a university council which would act like a board of directors. It also wanted to see universities raise private capital if necessary through capital markets and it openly favoured a general dogma of privatization.
>
> Sir Peter told the conference....that the diffusion of central power in the university hierarchy was not understood by businessmen because it was anathema to their own model.
>
> But the whole university machinery was ideally suited to allow staff to teach, to research, to debate, and to publish — in fact to conduct their contractual activities — without let or hindrance except the laws of the land, and with at best minimal direction from their employer....[49]

[48] T. Burns and G.M. Stalker, *The management of innovation*, London, 1961, p. 125.

[49] *Times Higher Education Supplement*, 20.9.1985

The individual and collective voices raised on behalf of the university in public reply to government rhetoric had no apparent effect. By this time it was clear that the Thatcherite counter-revolution was driven by a belief that the government should be sovereign, not needing 'to consult or negotiate with any one else'.[50] The rhetoric of the market legitimated interventions, whose ultimate purpose was given out to the public as to secure the benefits of competition — 'the pre-eminent advantages [which] arise from the principle of allowing capital to run in an open and unrestrained channel'[51] — but whose proximate effect was to create a unitary higher education system without legal privileges, easily steerable in any desired direction. Behind the rhetoric there lay a political strategy: to break the constitutional independence of the university, to subjugate universities to the rules of 'the real world', to end their centuries-long run as an estate within the state: cherished by the Treasury, buffered by the UGC, an anomaly from pre-industrial times. The government would see that they received the best of management practice in British industry and commerce, to support their drive for greater efficiency in 'meeting national needs'.

As with any good double-bind, behind the market rhetoric lay the political pay-off: the reality of centralization, compulsion, and control. Within five years an apparently untouchable estate, formerly the source of ever-rising demands on the public purse, was reduced to a subordinate client system, easily manipulable as an electoral lever over the marginal middle classes, as John Major was to show. The short-term interests of ministers in reducing public spending coalesced with the long-term interests of civil servants in 'tidying up' a rag-bag of conflicting jurisdictions, incommensurable indicators, multiple funding formulas.[52] Ure would have been impressed to see the emerging outline of

> a vast automaton, composed of various [administrative] and intellectual organs, acting in uninterrupted concert for the production of a common object, all of them being subordinated to a [politically]-regulated moving force....[necessarily] training human beings to renounce their desultory habits of work, and to identify themselves with the unvarying regularity of the complex automaton.[53]

[50] Aubrey Jones, *Britain's economy: the roots of stagnation*, Cambridge, 1985, p. 140.

[51] Ure, *Philosophy of Manufactures*, p. 107.

[52] William Taylor, 'Rationalization, whatever its merits, is hardly facilitated by having in separate hands decisions about resources, need, and academic quality.' *Times Higher Education Supplement*, 20.3.1981.

[53] Ure, *Philosophy of Manufactures*, p. 13.

The *Philosophy of Manufactures* and
Post-industrial Industry

While most of the replies to the Thatcher governments' critique of higher education remained within the organizational terms of debate established by that critique — costs, rationalization of structures, improvement of efficiency, emphasis on the management function, etc. — there was one notable exception. This contribution (widely publicised: given as a Suntory-Toyota public lecture at the London School of Economics and published in at least three publications) was Professor Robin Marris's essay on the Great British University Miracle.[54] As if acting to the letter on Edward Coll's advice for British higher education to profit from the opportunity of the Green Paper to step forward and show its capabilities, Marris argued that, strictly as commercial enterprises, British universities were ace: effective, efficient, the leader in the world market.

Marris's argument was simple, scientifically coherent (no criticism of it appeared in any publication), well supported with appropriate evidence, and was actually submitted as commissioned advice to the Department of Education and Science. Nevertheless, it sank without trace.[55] Though technically an exercise in economics, it is as a contribution to historical thinking that Marris's work is most significant to our purpose. Essentially it was making the same case as Ure's *The Philosophy of Manufactures*: that a new productive system had arisen in Great Britain; that in this system of production Britain had great comparative advantages; that these comparative advantages were such that it had already 'augmented the resources of the state, and meliorated the condition of its citizens', while it 'promises in its future growth to become the great minister of civilisation to the terraqueous globe, enabling this country, as its heart, to diffuse along with its commerce the life-blood of science and [e.g. liberal knowledge, humane values] to myriads of people...'.[56]

> It is doubtful if there is any other sector of public activity, and probably not too many in the private sector, which can show a riskless real return of [8 per cent]. If universities were actually in business, and could recapture the full economic value of the benefits they create, investors would be flocking to buy their shares![57]

[54] Robin Marris, 'The Great British University Miracle', *Times Higher Education Supplement*, 6 April 1984; 'Higher education and the mixed economy: the concept of competition', *Studies in Higher Education*, 11, 2, 1986, pp. 131-54.

[55] Marris, personal communication, 1993.

[56] Ure, *Philosophy of Manufactures*, 18-9

[57] Marris, 'British University Miracle'.

As apologists for rising productive systems, Ure and Marris each found that the representatives of the failing productive systems — systems with a falling share of overall employment, unable to attract the best-qualified young people, unable to give remuneration perceived as adequate to those obliged to labour there, unable to sustain the nation in the 'bloodless but still formidable strife of trade'[58] — had used their control of the legislative and executive organs of the state to disadvantage the rising industry.

> The Government via the University Grants Committee....has produced a set of cooked demographic projections designed to show that 'demand' for student places in the long run is going to fall...[and has] briefed its unfortunate spokesman in the House of Lords to give information on the economic return to higher education which also appears to be cooked.[59]

It seems now to be largely forgotten that the 1980s remodeling of higher education was for a very specific purpose: to make higher education more adapted to the interests of manufacturing industry. Whatever we may now know about the Conservative governments' differential responses to the needs of manufacturing and the City, the legitimation then offered to justify the destruction of higher education as an independent estate was to make it of greater service to the manufacturing economy. The 'protectionism' embodied in the 'Iron Laws' may have appeared in the 1980s to be political common sense, as the extension into a new economic conjuncture of the competitive politics of material interests. But whose material interests? The government's reply, as we have seen, tended to be: manufacturing industry's. But did manufacturing industry actually regard this policy as representing their interests? We have seen signs that such British manufacturing industry as was doing well in global competition did not. Their philosophy had moved on from Andrew Ure. What they wanted from university education was the most developed human beings; what they wanted from university research was the most fundamental, strategic knowledge. As to training of personnel and as to pragmatic applications of research, they could

[58] 'The present is distinguished from every preceding age by an universal ardour in arts and manufactures. Nations, convinced at length that war is always a losing game, have converted their swords and muskets into factory implements, and now contend with each other in the bloodless but still formidable strife of trade. They no longer send troops to fight on distant fields, but fabrics to drive before them those of their old adversaries in arms, and to take possession of a foreign mart. To impair the resources of a rival at home, by underselling his wares abroad, is the new belligerent system...' Ure, *Philosophy of Manufactures*, p. v).

[59] Marris, 'British University Miracle'. Cf. Ure, *Philosophy of Manufactures*, pp. 5-6.

look after themselves. Just as, a decade after the publication of *The Philosophy of Manufactures*, Sir Robert Peel told the House of Commons that properly capitalised 'high farming' had little to fear from the abolition of protection,[60] so the representatives of 'high' industry in the 1980s had no interest in programmed robot-graduates who would be obsolete after five years. What the progressive sector of manufacturing wanted to buy was not shallowly 'relevant' knowledge, or time-limited competences, but mind: the deep intellectual resources, scientific and human, capable of contributing creatively to managing new challenges under unforeseeable circumstances in the mid- to distant future.

A more reasonable conclusion, therefore, is that the interest most served by this policy was the government's own. The 'universities-as-factories' fantasy was politically functional. One value of revisiting the records of those days is that we see the political resolve progressively stiffening, the scale of the change growing. But we also see the ambiguity, the duplicity of the policy: the *motive* also changes. The rhetoric of national needs and societal impatience so exemplarily deployed by Mr Waldegrave turned out to be covering an aggressive political strategy derived from the Thatcherite analysis of the obstacles to governability. Mrs Thatcher's government sought to destroy the 'privileges' of established institutions so as to enlarge the relative weight of the governing party. Ignoring the existence of the Great British University Miracle meant that the government could shackle these recalcitrantly expensive institutions with ways of working which would both drive up the indicators of university 'productivity' and also symbolically reinforce the work ethic of the Factory System. This in turn would reinforce their claim to be the guardians of what they had declared to be the true economic interest of the nation — the culture of enterprise — and thus secure their re-election as the only party fit to be entrusted with its government. Driven by the power they had, drawn on by the power they wanted, the Thatcher governments were building a state that only they could govern.

I make no claim to be able to answer the questions raised by this claim: When did the power motive become the driver? Were they sincere about manufacturing at the beginning? Were only some sincere? Did anyone appreciate how much collateral damage was being inflicted on the delicate eco-system of political 'arrangements' (à la

[60]   D. Read, *Peel and the Victorians*, Oxford, 1987, p. 169.

Oakeshott)[61] inherited from previous generations? Nor is there the space. I shall close by re-emphasising how ironic it is, considering the Thatcher governments' espoused belief in 'wealth creation', that the dissolution of the universities under the banner of protecting the interests of 'the workshop of the world' may prove to have been terminally destructive of Britain's capacity to acquire a significant 'station and influence' in the post-manufacturing era.

Luddites passed into history as anachronistic antagonists; for nearly two centuries they have been construed as breakers of machines, benightedly *holding out against* a mass industrial future which our Whig textbooks told us was inevitable. But they may well have seen themselves more as conservatives, *holding on to* a desirable present: a communitarian vision of work, of craft, skill and family integrated around a living wage, human rhythms, and household interdependence. They saw themselves in danger of losing the world in which that vision had meaning and in which they themselves had acquired their identity. In breaking machines they struck out against the only object they could see to blame. Thatcherism was in like case, and from its beginnings proclaimed itself as the party of restoration: again, as protecting an acquired identity by restoring a vision of work, a 'Victorian' vision, productive and hard-working craftsmen producing quality technological manufactures in the workshop of the world, disciplined by a sharpened 'Two Nations' divide between the living standards of the employed and of the parasitic unemployed, the scrounging folk-devils of the Thatcherite nightmares.

But, just as the original Luddites did not see that the new mechanical *forms* were in fact expressions of a new socio-technological *system*, so also the Thatcher governments mistook a species for a genus. They hypostatised as 'industry' the manufacturing industry that makes things in factories for foreigners to buy, in return for which we buy their food: Lord Bowden's 1976 industry. In this perspective, indeed, 'industry' was still Andrew Ure's 1835 industry: that factory system which had been in its time a massive 'step in the social progression of the world', one which had given Britain 'a commanding station and influence' for a century and more.

But Ure himself would have been the first to see that the motive for preserving the identification of 'industry' with manufacturing lay in envy of the political emergence of a new order of the commonwealth. Ironically, considering the conservative governments'

[61]   M. Oakeshott, 'Political Education' *The Voice of Liberal Learning*, New Haven: Yale University Press (1989).

espousal of the idea of 'wealth creation', attacking the culture and traditions of the universities to protect the interests of 'the workshop of the world' may prove to have been terminally destructive of Britain's capacity to acquire a significant 'station and influence' in the post-manufacturing era. The machines the Luddites smashed were merely the material manifestation of a new productive system; destroying its culture was beyond their grasp. The spirit of the Factory System, the philosophy of manufactures, this only the landed aristocracy in Parliament could have destroyed. But the neo-Luddites of the 1980s *were* in Parliament: they *did* have control of the legislative machinery, of the Privy Council, of the UGC, CNAA, and NAB; they could set up Jarratts and Crohams to apply mechanical management to these antiquatedly organic institutions. They had the authority to infect the life-germ of the emerging wealth-creating system with an alien culture. Which they did.

The imposition of 'modern management' on the universities shows to what extent the philosophy of manufactures had floated free from its historical base in factories and workshops. Ure's utopian vision of factories as the great minister of civilization to the terraqueous globe became the ideology of a party of radical reactionaries who thought that, following economic dogma, they could compel history to repeat itself. A century and a half after emerging as the theory of an integrated sociotechnical system, the philosophy of manufactures became the instrumental rhetoric of cargo-cult politicians promising a grieving people a return to a past of power and plenty by means of an education-led reindustrialization. The historically ironic character of the imposition of managerialism on the universities in the 1980s thus requires us to see 'Luddite' as a *structural* role. In every age Luddites defend established socio-economic systems by attacking the institutional manifestations of new socio-economic systems. Luddites resist new cultures; they have only incidentally been associated with breaking machines.

Furthermore, after the 1980s we know that they have only incidentally been associated with losing.

Of course, things in these islands do not seem very different. We are still part of the global economy, the site of production and consumption, of mortgages being paid, of children going to school, of operations being performed. But we are no longer a great minister of civilization. For we are no longer Britain.

Part II

Testing to Destruction:
The New School Environment

Diana Mabbutt

From Board School to Boardroom

*Changes and Consequences of Educational
Policy in Primary Schools*

Nearly forty years ago, when I first taught in inner-city London primary schools, my ideas came under the influence of colleagues who
had trained just after the war. It was an exciting and innovative time
to be young and starting out on what was then thought to be a life-
time career. These people, by then in positions of authority, were
men and women of vision, willing to discuss ideas, to experiment
and to effect fundamental changes on an educational system still
more geared to the ethos of the Victorian Board School than to the
spirit of the post-war world. Not all the experiments worked as we'd
hoped, of course, but the discussions and ideas inspired a high
morale among young teachers. There was a feeling that the job was
important and worth doing, that long hours and hard work were
going to make a real difference and that what we were doing *mattered*, and would have a significant influence on a new generation.
That enthusiasm was passed on to the children. Equality of opportunity came a step closer as pupils who hitherto had received a
restricted curriculum now had access to art, dance, music and literature. Those for whom it would once have been impossible now
began to plan their further education. It is true that a few pioneers
were already working along these lines, but by the early Sixties there
had been a huge expansion in teacher training, and young teachers
were streaming out of college in droves, full of enthusiasm and new
ideas. It is sad to reflect that, today, at the end of my teaching career, I
see little of that enthusiasm either in the teachers or in their pupils. So
much of what has been derisively termed 'progressive' has been rub-
bished by those who didn't understand or were afraid. True, some
teachers have brought this upon themselves by failing to understand

the intellectual rigour and organisational skills required by truly progressive education. There have admittedly been some disasters, but to rubbish a whole movement begun in such glory because of a few failures is, in itself, a catastrophe. An enormous wealth of sound educational thought and inspirational teaching has been buried.

In the last fifteen years or so there have been fundamental changes in the whole field of education, brought about by successive governments determined to exert greater central control. Schools have entered the world of business: everything and everyone is accountable. Teachers begin their careers armed with a 'career plan', updated every year in their annual appraisal. No longer is their primary aim to improve their teaching skills for the benefit of the children in their care. Now they must improve their results and their school's position in the league tables if they want to be promoted. Quantifiable results have replaced ideas in importance. One might suppose that to improve teaching skills would be to improve results: unfortunately, it is not so easy. The government decides first on the results, and then on the method of achieving them. This may work in business where there is a direct correlation between input and output, but the field of education is rather more subtle — or so we once thought.

Education has moved from the child-centred philosophy of Piaget to an attainment-centred system where the child is merely a mechanical hurdle-jumper. The teaching skills required to expose young people to a whole range of cultural and artistic experiences and skills which they can absorb, develop and express as their understanding grows, have been replaced by the teaching skills of instruction — the ability to impart knowledge which will, in turn, be regurgitated in a series of tests at ages decided by an adult. As a result, the curriculum has been narrowed. While some of our young people are rejecting the rat race, our very youngest are actually being trained for it. With the introduction of the National Curriculum we have replaced education with knowledge.

I do not believe this was the intended result. There was a genuine desire to raise standards, and indeed in some areas there was a real need for improvement. True educationalists, however, people with an understanding of how children think and develop, have been silenced by the scaremongers, and the cause has been taken up by those who see a political advantage in pandering to such people. These 'reformers' have focused on the end product and have often wrongly diagnosed the causes of failure. Quite arbitrary rules are laid down in order to achieve the goals, regardless of individual growth and developmental patterns.

This results-culture now influences every aspect of primary education. Playgroups, as the name suggests, were designed for children to interact socially with each other. They have now largely been replaced by nursery schools or provision in mainstream schools. Of course, these establishments still concentrate on social development, the vitally important skills of learning to share, to play and to communicate, but this is no longer their only concern. Parents are informed that this pre-school period is the Foundation Stage. There are 'early learning goals' which set out what most children are expected to achieve by the end of the Foundation Stage — pointers to help people (often not trained teachers) who work with three to five year-olds to focus on what they need to learn to achieve those goals. Consequently, very young children are being taught to read, write and count in spite of research showing that most children's fine motor skills are not sufficiently developed at this age and that the majority are not able to tackle phonics until the age of six. Nursery schools are accountable; they must produce results. Compare this with the United States and the continent where, although there is good nursery provision, formal education does not begin until children are at least six years old.

A disturbingly small proportion of today's youngsters enjoys the rich variety of nursery rhymes, finger games, action songs or playground games which my generation did. Working parents have little time to play with their children, and nurseries, although they attempt to do the things once done largely by mothers and grandmothers, also have to make sure they are meeting targets and completing paperwork in order to meet the requirements of Ofsted inspections. Our anxiety-ridden culture, where parents worry about the achievements of pre-school children, has discarded childhood. These early experiences have a knock-on effect. 'The two groups of children who cause most concern to teachers in ordinary schools are those that don't learn and those that don't behave.'[1]

Any teacher will tell you that children are more badly behaved than they used to be. I suspect that all generations say this, but teachers in primary schools are certainly dealing with more behavioural and learning problems than ever before. There are a number of contributory causes, but recent government legislation and pronouncements must take some of the responsibility. After all, teachers have always battled with the social problems of deprivation, poverty and

---

[1]   From *Special Biographies* by Tony Booth, produced by the Open University Educational studies, Open University Press, Walton Hall, Milton Keynes, MK76AA.

poor parenting. One of the major differences now is the low morale of the teaching profession. For the past ten years at least, the government has relentlessly attacked teachers. Anyone who trained when I did learnt that the only way to get good results is to be positive and build confidence. 'Start from what the child knows, not from what he doesn't know.' 'Give praise, not criticism.' Thousands of teachers live by this creed when dealing with children, but they themselves have been told repeatedly that they are failing. Their 'failures' have been broadcast on radio, television and in banner headlines in the press. There are 'failing schools', schools which have to be 'turned around', 'super heads', and teams sent into schools, SAS fashion, to kick the staff into submission. The brief of the Ofsted inspection is to find out what is wrong, not what is right. The Ofsted inspector is not viewed as an ally working with his colleagues in the classroom, but more like something out of the Spanish Inquisition. I have seen sound, caring, hardworking and experienced teachers reduced to tears because their paperwork wasn't up to scratch.

As a result parents have become alarmed. They are being forced to take responsibility for something they used to believe could be done by specialists trained for the job. Nobody wants his or her children to be trapped in failing schools, taught by inadequate teachers. Parents are loth to see their offspring 'wasting' time painting, dancing or singing when there are important tests looming — from early years' assessment at five to the major Statutory Attainment Tests [SATs] at seven, eleven and fourteen. They are caught up in panic and fear fanned by media reports of failures and government pledges to put them right. They are worried by conversations with other parents and urge their children to win the reading race against their friends. Look in any bookshop and you will see a whole range of books coaching for SATs, comprehension tests, spelling lists and grammatical exercises. Whatever happened to reading for pleasure?

Many parents no longer trust teachers, and indeed many teachers have begun to doubt their own abilities. Those brave enough to point out that not all children learn at the same pace and that it is not necessary for every child to read fluently at six are accused of making excuses for their own poor performance. This is a dreadful downward spiral. Unintentionally perhaps, teachers have become the scapegoats for everything that has gone wrong; from poor test results to bad behaviour. Parents who were once confident about their children's progress have become unnecessarily alarmed and have jumped on the band wagon, blaming teachers. Children hear their teachers criticised at home, and know their 'rights'. Some hear their parents shout at and about the people who, at early primary level, are a vitally important part of their lives.

In order to meet the ever-increasing demands of parents, attainment targets, test results and league tables, teachers are expecting little children to spend more and more of their time sitting still and listening, concentrating on such things as formal reading exercises and handwriting skills. A sizeable minority of five and six year olds can cope with this. There are many who cannot. We are putting our primary age children, many of whom lack the social and play skills that were once common, under pressure from home and from school and making them face what are sometimes unreasonably high expectations. Is it any wonder that so many are resorting to unacceptable behaviour? In addition, with the closure of so many special schools and units, more pupils with behavioural problems are in mainstream schools, often with no additional support. Many teachers are coping only at a crisis management level.

When the National Curriculum was introduced it was a bold scheme to exert centralised control over what was taught in primary schools throughout the country. Interestingly, however, it was not considered necessary to make it statutory for independent schools. In deciding that there were to be core subjects of English, maths and science, with specified amounts of time allocated for each, this measure immediately, if unintentionally, marginalised the non-core subjects and changed the whole teaching approach for primary pupils to one geared much more to specific subjects. In order to justify such a radical change, results must be seen to improve, and tests were introduced in a simplistic attempt to ascertain how well the new curriculum was being taught.

In learning as in business, forecasts and targets have become essential. Teachers are required to predict how many children will be able to reach each National Curriculum level by the end of each Key Stage. This means making predictions about a five year old child's performance possibly two years ahead. I myself have actually witnessed situations in which teachers, against their better judgment, tried to do this honestly and professionally. When too many 'low' results were predicted, the authority asked them to re-assess and raise their expectations. Reluctantly, they raised the levels, and when those targets were not met, the teachers were told that their teaching was not good enough. This is a statistical exercise; it has little to do with children's learning and is an insult to teachers' professional judgment. Immediately, a blame culture is established. 'Good' teachers will make sure that their children all reach at least level two at the end of Key Stage one and the appropriate level for their age thereafter. 'Bad' teachers presumably will not. For some teachers old enough to remember the eleven plus exams, there are disturbing similarities. Teachers have been assured that the intention of these tests is merely diagnostic. Perhaps so — but parents don't see them as diagnostic and neither do many schools, since they have to publish results and positions in league tables. Moreover, most state primary schools have unstreamed classes composed, in many rural areas, of two different year/age groups. Primary school teachers have for decades been taught how to teach young children of mixed abilities in large groups. It was never assumed, however, that all children would absorb information at the same rate. In the modified National Curriculum 2000 this problem is addressed. It states

> The National Curriculum programmes of study set out what most pupils should be taught at each key stage — but teachers should teach the knowledge, skills and understanding in ways that suit their pupils' abilities. This may mean choosing knowledge, skills and understanding from earlier or later key stages so that individual pupils can make progress and show what they can achieve.[2]

The clear intention of the policy, as expressed in this document, is that all pupils should achieve success and that the programme of work must, in some cases, be modified. In spite of this, both the National Curriculum and (for example) the Literacy Hour programme carry specified teaching schedules for each year and, in some cases, for every term. The tests remain for each key stage. For teachers of mixed ability, mixed age-group classes with little additional support, the task is impossible.

For children with special needs the implications are obvious — such children will lower the school's results. Some schools, especially popular institutions in urban areas, can carry out a surreptitious programme of selection. Some church-aided schools, for example, have decided that only children of communicant parents can be accepted. Other schools, such as those with falling rolls in rural areas, or which have received a bad press, cannot afford to be so choosy. The inevitable result is that they produce poorer results. They are classified as 'failing', find it difficult to recruit new staff and quite often have less supportive and less wealthy parents.

Provision for children with special educational needs [SEN] is an important issue. The 1980 Government White Paper stated that:

---

[2]   All quotes from the *National Curriculum*, DFEE., Sanctuary Buildings, Great Smith Street, London SW1P3BT.

'Whenever it is educationally and economically viable, children with special needs should be educated in ordinary schools alongside children without such needs.' The Warnock Report, supporting that view, stated that planning should be based on the assumption 'that about one in six children at any time and up to one in five at some time during their school career will require some form of special educational provision .' Implicit in the 1981 Education Act was the promise of money, resources, more teachers and more training. For the children, this should indeed have been an improvement. Every child with an identified need would have an individual education plan, reviewed regularly with the child, the parents, the teacher and any other professional involved. Parents were to be encouraged to be partners in their children's learning. In practice, many special schools and units have been closed or made unavailable to primary aged children other than in very exceptional circumstances. The special needs budget has become part of the whole school budget and certainly does not provide the kind of professional support previously available in special schools.

Teaching assistants with minimal training have been provided to support children with behavioural and learning difficulties. Thus class teachers, already struggling with the problems of meeting National Curriculum targets with unstreamed classes, also have to provide individual programmes of work for these assistants and perhaps four or five special needs pupils. There is a serious lack of educational psychologists and the amount of their time allocated to schools has, over the years, been reduced, with additional time, if available, paid for out of the school's budget. Children with special needs inevitably take up a disproportionate amount of a class teacher's time, particularly where there are a lot of children with behavioural problems. Despite the very best intentions, many of these children are not getting the attention they need, because they are in a class of children who have targets to achieve and tests to pass. Similarly, many teachers, struggling to provide adequate SEN provision, feel that they are failing the other children in the class. In the revised National Curriculum 2000 it states that teachers should respond to pupils' diverse learning needs:

> When planning, teachers should set high expectations and provide opportunities for all pupils to achieve, including boys and girls, pupils with special educational needs, pupils with disabilities, pupils from all social and cultural backgrounds, pupils of different ethnic groups including travellers, refugees and asylum seekers, and those from diverse linguistic backgrounds. Teachers should plan their approaches

to teaching and learning so that all pupils can take part in lessons fully and effectively.

Who could disagree with such laudable intentions? For them to be fulfilled, however, schools will require money and expertise. While attainment is to be tested, results published and schools rewarded or blamed, the full range of all pupils' needs can be met only by increasing the ratio of qualified teaching staff and by the recognition that not all pupils can achieve the academic targets set by central government.

The declared aim of increasing parental choice is another good idea that has failed to materialise. In many areas, parents have no choice at all. The effect of the league tables has been to create inequality and competition between schools rather than collaboration. Similarly, with parent participation. Quite rightly, parents have been encouraged to take an interest and indeed to participate in their children's education, particularly where the latter have special educational needs. It has now been decided that all children from year one should have some form of homework. Many parents welcomed, and indeed requested this, but in the case of the youngest children, such homework may require a lot of parental attention in the form of conversation, reading, trips to the library and little tasks to be done at home. Often there is neither the time nor the inclination for this, and parents may also lack the confidence or ability to help. Children from these homes are immediately disadvantaged. Some parents, fuelled by fears of teacher incompetence, see the invitation to parental partnership as an opportunity to exercise their 'rights'. They consider it their 'right' to tell teachers how to do their job, to influence the curriculum, to demand that a reading book is changed, to decide which class their child should be in. At worst, parents become abusive and even violent. A parent knowing his 'rights' and determined to cause trouble knows that he has only to accuse a teacher of inappropriately touching a child for that teacher to be suspended. A teacher is usually alone and vulnerable, with no such rights.

This situation has arisen because parents have been encouraged to come into school, ostensibly to share in their child's learning, but in reality because schools are short of both staff and money. Schools have been grateful for help from parents: parents who raise money for books and equipment, parents who decorate classrooms and tend gardens, parents who help in the classroom. It is good that parents are no longer afraid of teachers, but an important dividing line has been crossed. In many cases, respect has been replaced by an inappropriate familiarity. Parents are not the professionals: they know their children better and in a different way from teachers, and their role is entirely different. Even parents who are trained teachers are not the professionals in this instance and, while teachers may welcome parental co-operation, there must be a point at which the professional is allowed to be just that. Unintentionally, the teacher has become de-valued.

So why, when the present government set out with such a high profile agenda for education, are so many teachers demoralised, off sick and taking early retirement? Why is it so difficult to recruit new staff, and why, when we are told that exam results are getting better each year, are schools still apparently 'failing', so that disaffected youngsters leave poorly equipped for adult life?

Bureaucracy has become the scourge of all teachers. It is significant that the majority of primary school teachers are women. Traditionally they have been bright, hard-working girls from the middle classes, essentially practical people, good organisers and good communicators. Their expertise is in dealing with the complex needs and demands of young children. They care, and they are not accustomed to failing. These people have taken everything that successive governments have thrown at them. They have changed, adapted, tirelessly attended training courses and have tried to come to terms with ever increasing paperwork, explaining and justifying their every move. Teachers have always had to plan. Now they have to predict, target, justify, evaluate and record.

Much of this paperwork is repetitive and unnecessary. After 35 years' experience, I was producing more paper work to prove what I was doing in the classroom than had been required when I was a student on teaching practice. No doubt the government will consider this to be progress. I consider it to be insulting. Any inspector with primary school experience should be able to see almost immediately on entering the classroom whether the teaching is well planned and organised. There should be no need for pages of written intentions and evaluations. Now pupils have to be told what they are going to learn, how they are going to learn it and, at the end of each session, what they have learnt. The structure has become what is important, not the spontaneity. Teachers are weighed down with paperwork; they are too tired to be spontaneous — and in any case they must not deviate from the lesson plan. Primary school teachers generally, and particularly in small schools, are not paid for non-contact time. By the end of the day they are exhausted — and they still have hours of planning and evaluating to do. Young and old are leaving. The traditional trust between parents and teachers, particularly important at primary level, has, in many cases, broken down, and teachers have been left feeling vulnerable, undervalued and defensive. The results-oriented blame culture has in no small measure contributed to their distress. Financial incentives might be the answer to recruitment, but most teachers I know are more concerned about their conditions of work and their feelings of inadequacy than their salaries. Money becomes an issue only in the absence of job satisfaction.

We are told that test results improve every year. Maybe they do — but at a cost: the drastic narrowing of the school curriculum. After the prescribed number of hours are taken out of a primary school day for numeracy and literacy, not to mention registration and assembly, there are approximately ten hours a week left for everything else. Creative and physical education have been sidelined. Whatever the test results show, some children are not going to achieve the standards required by the government, and will continue to be low achievers. What happens to them? In spite of the stated inclusion policy of the National Curriculum, there is no real place for such youngsters in the brave new world of structured learning, target setting and results-orientated education.

It is difficult to see where we go from here. High standards are important, but high test scores should never be the only goal. The current pressure to perform has made it more difficult than ever to convince some parents that there is more to life than passing tests. Many are already unhappy with the system. It is ironic that only independent schools are currently able to provide the broad curriculum once available in most state schools. Teachers need to feel confident about their ability to do their job and parents need to have confidence in the teachers. Such confidence can only be created by longterm support and encouragement from the government. 'Naming and shaming' is a puritanical concept which produces more negative results than positive, and the profession is still further demoralised by the introduction of endless new initiatives surrounded by more and more bureaucracy . Only when teachers are treated as respected professionals, provided with the necessary resources in terms of equipment and manpower, and allowed some independence in interpreting and broadening the National Curriculum will their confidence be restored and perhaps the pleasure put back into teaching. When that happens, children, parents and teachers alike will be getting a better deal.

Margaret Sutcliffe

Bureaucracy and the Growth of Anxiety in a Small Independent School

Having recently retired from the post of head teacher at an independent preparatory school, I can look back at my career with a certain degree of detachment. It is an interesting, if somewhat depressing, exercise to assess the effect of the changes imposed by government on this important sector of the British educational system.

Our school opened its doors in 1977 with a minimum of red tape and seventy-four pupils. We registered with the Department for Education but, apart from sending an inspector to check that our premises were suitable and safe and that the children were learning effectively from a broad and balanced curriculum, very few directives were imposed on us.

The first prospectus proclaimed, with complete honesty, that we taught English, maths, science, geography, history, French, religious education, art, craft, music, cookery and physical education. The school day started at 9am and finished at 3.30pm. Homework was an integral part of the experience, teaching the children to work with a degree of self-discipline and independence. Within this curriculum structure, designed to prepare pupils for entrance examinations to secondary schools at the age of eleven, the children flourished. Even those who were not required to take entrance exams transferred to secondary schools well-schooled in basic numeracy and literacy with a marked degree of confidence, which was a reward in itself. I state this, not as any form of self- congratulation, but simply to illustrate that the formula fitted the bill, the children were happy and the parents were obviously delighted. Our numbers doubled within five years and at the time I retired our school role had reached its maximum capacity of 180.

In those early years there seemed to be sufficient time in the day to offer a balanced educational diet *and* achieve good results — without teachers spending hours outside the school day on anything other than commonsense preparation and record keeping.

The foundation of the school was the nursery class, where children were initially allowed to come for as little as three mornings a week. We subsequently changed attendance to a compulsory five mornings in the interests of continuity: half days were the norm and full days the exception rather than the rule. Admittance was in the September after the child's third birthday in order to place him or her in the correct academic year. Staffing was arranged on a commonsense basis and three staff, including one fully qualified teacher, met the needs of twenty two nursery children aged between three and four years.

Shortly after the school opened we were required to complete an annual return for the Department for Education. This covered pupil numbers and dates of birth and asked for details of changes to staff and buildings. Although it was a time-consuming exercise, it was assumed that this data would be valuable for the compilation of useful statistics, and it was willingly provided.

It goes without saying that the school was totally self funding, and special needs teaching was incorporated as part of the school's permanent provision. Parents were asked to pay extra for uniforms, lunches, educational visits and individual lessons in music or speech and drama.

We did believe in testing the children on a low-key regular basis. These tests took the form of word and number recognition in the younger classes followed by weekly spelling and multiplication-table tests. When children joined the upper school aged eight and upwards, they were given tests once or twice a year to train them in exam techniques. This also served to provide evidence of their strengths and weaknesses, and reports to parents or secondary schools were based on the results of these tests. The achievement of good test results was certainly never the sole, or even the main, goal of the teaching staff. Good standardised tests were available from The National Foundation for Educational Research (NFER), though class teachers frequently devised their own class exams based on the work the children had covered during the term. These tests proved to be more than adequate yardsticks. The majority of children approached them with healthy respect and a degree of enjoyment. Parents, in fact, were often unaware that the tests were taking place at all, and pre-test hype was therefore mercifully avoided. At this stage the all-pervasive and prescriptive SATs had not appeared on the scene.

By the time the National Curriculum was introduced, the school had been running for a good ten years. As an independent school we regarded it with only mild interest at the beginning. I agreed with other heads that one of the joys of being independent was that we had time to consider the implications of new government initiatives before adopting them ourselves. Our optimism was short-lived. It was not long before we too received draft proposals for the implementation of the National Curriculum. A set of expensively produced booklets with an extremely complex format quickly had the staff room ringing with frustration and anxiety. No sooner had we come to terms with what was being asked of the country's teachers than another batch of National Curriculum booklets arrived, even more expensively produced and just as complex as the first. These contained the same directives, now modified in response to nationwide reaction and feedback from hundreds of teachers. More booklets, more clutter, more anguish. Teacher morale wavered badly.

One of the most contentious aspects of the new directives was the introduction of a record-keeping system which required each class teacher to tick boxes in order to assess whether little Harry had completed certain attainment tasks. It was soon realised that if every teacher of every large primary class complied with this there would be no time at all to prepare, teach and mark the children's work in the normal course of a school day. I sent for some prototypes of books which an enterprising educational publisher had produced to meet this demand, but very soon decided against adopting them for class use. I seriously wonder how many teachers really complied with this onerous form of record keeping, and for how long.

We also had to rename or renumber all our classes. The new National Curriculum was written for what came to be known as the *Key Stages*. KS1 was for children aged five to seven years and KS2 was for those aged seven to eleven. The classes in our school were Nursery, Transition (often known as Reception), 3, 4, 5, 6, 7 and 8. It quickly became apparent that we were going to run into difficulties if we stuck to this form of numbering and a decision was made to change the designation of the various classes to Y1 – Y6. Although this did turn out, in fact, to be more logical – particularly since secondary schools had decided to call their intake class Y7 – it caused quite an upheaval.[1] So far, so good... if we exclude the added stress

[1]   It also avoided confusion and helped with the transfer of children from other independent schools as there was often no uniformity in class names in the

caused by demands for unreasonably detailed record-keeping mentioned earlier.

The first of the really worrying developments followed soon after: a blind insistence that all primary schools teach design technology. This subject took us into territory totally unfamiliar at the time and clearly requiring special training for as many staff as possible. Until that point the children had all enjoyed the subject known as 'craft': during these classes they worked with a wide range of different mediums and ended up with simple end-products of which they were justifiably proud. They learned to sew, knit, embroider, beat copper, produce clay models and wicker-edged trays, to name but a few. Now the skills themselves became more high profile and models with working, moving parts became the order of the day.

The government was also strongly pushing information technology at primary schools such as ours, actually offering grants for the purchase of computers. Once again teachers were going to have to re-train in totally new skills so as to keep abreast of unforeseen developments: the level of anxiety amongst staff began its inexorable rise.

The worst aspect of these changes was the time factor.

If these new subjects were to be introduced into an already full timetable, something else would have to go. The first to be hit was a cookery and drama class held each Friday afternoon: the children in this class had derived great enjoyment from it and were sorely disappointed when it was cancelled. After a fairly complex timetable change they found themselves tackling the rudiments of design technology for the first time. (I should add that, with a little encouragement, our noble staff managed to squeeze some cookery — or *food technology*, as we were now advised to call it — into geography or DT classes). Instead of the smell of fresh baking on Friday afternoons, we now saw a great deal of lip biting and worry. The children struggled to measure accurately and cut safely as they designed and constructed artefacts which had to work, drive and stick together effectively. Disappointment was rife as children found through their mistakes what did and did not work. One of our brightest pupils ever could not come to terms with the fact that it takes more than some smooth wood and a lot of determination to construct a grand piano, even a miniature one!

Religious Education was given a low profile and, although we were over-controlled in many areas, very little help was given to

independent sector. To be told that a child was in Lower 111 was not always helpful.

independent schools as to how this subject should be approached or what should be taught. Surprisingly, given the very precise instructions that accompanied the national guidelines for other subjects, R.E. did not actually feature in the National Curriculum. Eventually a framework emerged for general guidance at county level. It was 'suggested' that fifty percent of all religious teaching should be Christian and the other fifty percent should encompass at least two other world religions. Although this was interesting to teach, I was quite determined that all children should still have a good general knowledge of the Old Testament stories — though we learnt how to celebrate Divali (even at nursery level), heard how our Jewish families remembered Hannukah, and had several visits to mosques and other religious buildings.

The government's next intervention was to push us into introducing a programme of Outdoor Pursuits. My PE staff were unenthusiastic, as the children were already playing netball, soccer, rounders and short tennis — as well as swimming, gymnastics and modern educational dance. Where were they to find time to bring in another activity? Eventually a compromise was agreed. The top class would attend a residential activity centre in their final term and the rest of the school would take part in a whole school walk alongside all the usual activities organised as part of their PE programme.

So before we realised it we were paying more than lip service to a national demand for uniformity in schools, not because our syllabus was ineffective — but because another word had infiltrated the staff room and school office ... OFSTED

Until this point our school inspections had consisted of visits by a single friendly inspector. This person's job was to visit and monitor each independent school on a roughly four or five year cycle. If the school was doing a good job it had only a verbal report, occasionally supplemented by a request for extra information. But *inspection* had become a buzzword and no school was immune. Independent schools, like state schools, were now to expect regular OFSTED inspections (and boarding schools came under even greater scrutiny with the introduction of the Children Act). Policy documents were requested on absolutely *everything,* from mathematics to equal opportunities. It was important to get it right, and countless courses on Preparing for Inspection were held up and down the country. These were attended by Heads who arguably should have been running their schools, rather than taking notes on how many pieces of paper they would have to produce for a main OFSTED inspection.

Accountability was to be the order of the day in primary schools, just as in Bruce Charlton's universities.[2] Regardless of a school's track record at providing a successful education for the children in its care, written planning of every lesson was to be set down in detail, each lesson evaluated and every child's performance discussed by all the staff involved. This gave rise, predictably, to supplemental costs which put a severe strain on the independent schools' budgets. The practicalities of complying with these demands were earth-shattering.

I was hardly surprised, therefore, when two very experienced and effective class teachers decided to retire from class teaching; two years later one of my best teachers came to me and announced that she had decided on a career move. Another extremely conscientious teacher, a true perfectionist, was obviously on the verge of a classic nervous breakdown. Within a term, another member of staff found that she could no longer cope with the load of paperwork and decided to alter course. Although we were all aware of the government's national expectations, I had been careful to avoid pressurising my already very hardworking teaching team, knowing that we were likely to have reasonable warning of a main inspection. I could in any case see that they were all stretched to the limit.

At this point, national tests known as SATs were introduced to measure the performance of pupils and teachers. These were to take place at the end of the two Key Stages in the primary school. Was fun going to disappear out of the seven year old's classroom experience completely? The SATs extended the range of anxiety out of the school to include parents: our teachers were repeatedly asked whether little Harry was going to make the grade and worry about the children's school performance spread to their home environment.

Six or seven year-olds can still vary enormously as to their level of maturity and the SATs tests often provided no indication at all of the standard we could expect from the same children at eleven. The tests were also very time-consuming administratively and I found it necessary to allow our special needs teacher and other support teachers to help the Y2 class teacher. The maths tasks (part of the testing procedure at KS1) had to be given on a one-to-one basis, which meant that another member of staff had to teach the body of the class while the class teacher worked with individual pupils. Many young children were slow to understand that in this instance the teacher was not allowed to help with the answers!

[2]   See 'Audit, accountability, quality and all that'(this volume).

The Y6 children took their SATs in May. This did not present such a problem, as they were quicker and easier to administrate. Most of our children were well practised in sitting tests by then, and it gave those children who had not sat an entrance exam before something to work towards. The Assembly Hall became 'the exam room' and the majority of the children took the experience in their stride. The papers were sent away to be marked externally and we received the results in time to incorporate them into the end of term reports.

While all this was going on in independent schools another government initiative was being launched; that of free education for four year olds.

It soon became apparent that all nurseries worth their salt were expected to give parents the chance to claim vouchers entitling their child to twelve and a half hours of free nursery education per week. There were real teething troubles in the school or nursery offices up and down the country as extra paper work piled. Nurseries or nursery classes which cooperated in the voucher scheme had agreed in essence to become government funded, and therefore had to prepare to be inspected. Predictably, an enormous amount of paperwork was required before, during and after the subsequent inspection.

With so much formality creeping into nursery provision and the media fanning the flames of parental concern, it soon became obvious that children were 'wasting their time' if the nursery was spotted as teaching-through-play. Having worked with this age group for many years and in fact lectured on the importance of play as a learning medium, I was most certainly *not* going to change course. However, our nursery department was not immune to the pressures of OFSTED and each child had already generated a fat profile of paperwork by the end of its first year. The nursery staff found their workload virtually trebled.

Incredibly, the government then decided to extend the offer of free nursery places to three year olds. More chaos in countless school offices — and ours was no exception. As we now even had a pre-nursery class for two year olds, life became complex indeed. The voucher scheme was scrapped and another method of payment introduced — which mercifully worked better. What a pity the powers that be had not worked that out in the first place!

There can be no doubt that countless well-run small private nurseries up and down the country drowned under the pressures of paperwork and administrative complexity and reluctantly closed their doors.

The constantly changing scene and moving of the goal posts continued. Shortage of time remained the biggest problem for even the
most robust and resourceful teachers in our school. We constantly
found ourselves having to water down or trim the syllabus which
had worked well for so many years in order to do any sort of justice
to the new programmes of study. Geography and history were rele-
gated to half a term each at certain stages. The study of the Middle
Ages was taken out of the primary school history syllabus altogether, a move I was most reluctant to endorse, since it had fired the
imagination of every seven to eleven year old I had ever taught.

The National Curriculum was desperately over-prescriptive. As
every primary teacher worth his or her salt will say, some of the most
valuable teaching is done on the spur of the moment. A child stag-
gers in with a jar full of frog spawn or a picture of a famous astronaut
cut from a magazine. A good teacher does not waste the opportunity
but springs into action to give an instant lesson on metamorphosis or
current space travel instead of the planned lesson. Such spontaneity
was not on the curriculum and was therefore no longer permissible.

It is generally accepted that independent schools are expected to
provide a 'value added' element. Parents are paying twice over for
their child's education and therefore can be forgiven for hoping that
their child will receive that extra something from an independent
school. I was more than happy to provide those extras, and it was
without doubt a major selling point. It was also part of my philosophy that children should have an opportunity to discover all the joys
of creativity by making music, painting, acting or singing. Sport was
not only an essential part of the prep school curriculum but a wonderful safety valve for potential classroom 'stirrers'. The energy and
healthy aggression released during a football session, for instance,
was invaluable. However — and here's the rub, were we still going
to be able to offer all the added value? It would have to be provided
during lunch hours and after school, organised and supervised of
course by the already overworked staff. Fortunately we were able to
call on some wonderfully dedicated peripatetic music specialists
who visited us on a regular basis; I continued to be amazed by the
stamina shown by so many of the class teachers, who took on extra
responsibilities for the good of the children.

In referring to parents' expectations in the previous paragraph I
am reminded of the vexed question of discipline. Government directives, books on child psychology and overblown media coverage
have made many modern parents positively terrified of saying *'no'*
to a child... and meaning it. There is some idea that the child's devel-

opment will somehow be stunted if it is thwarted. Things have come to a pretty pass when a child, whether in maintained or independent school, knows unacceptable behaviour is highly unlikely to be punished effectively. As Diana Mabbutt has said,[3] the role of the teacher has been greatly devalued over the past two decades, and parents are far more inclined to question the school's handling of a point of discipline. Twenty years ago teachers were considered the professional experts and were left to get on with their important job. Today's parents never see their child's behaviour in class, and frequently have a distorted idea of how he or she interacts with teachers and other children. Although they desperately want their child to succeed, such parents cannot accept that children need to learn how to work hard *and* behave well in order to achieve.

Another change has been the new reluctance of teachers to have physical contact of any sort with a child. Members of the teaching profession are constantly reminded of the risks they run, with abuse cases trumpeted far and wide. It is sad indeed that we are afraid to take a child on our knee to comfort it, clean it up after an unfortunate 'accident', or help to speed up the drying process after swimming lessons when the bus is waiting to leave.

We found ourselves holding parent/teacher evenings more and more frequently. Some of these were to report on pupils' progress, others were information evenings that explained to the parents what work the children could expect to cover and how various aspects of school policy could affect *their* child. Greater familiarity between teachers and parents sometimes resulted in parents demanding that a reading book be changed; or they might be unhappy about their child's neighbour in class; or complain about the role their child had been given in a school play. When these comments and complaints came my way I became adept at saying no and smiling at the same time! The more frequent contact with parents also had some useful consequences. Teachers acquired greater understanding of the child's home environment, and parents learned about their children's programmes of study. It also gave parents a chance to meet the individual subject teachers. These were all plus points. Every parents' evening, however, was yet another demand on the poor class teachers' ever diminishing free time.

At the beginning of every OFSTED inspection the parents are called to a meeting and asked how they view the school. Are they made welcome? Are the channels of communication effective? In almost all cases the answers are non-contentious but a parent can

[3]   Diana Mabbutt: 'From Board School to Boardroom' (this volume).

make waves with the greatest of ease. Nowadays parent power is a force to be reckoned with!

In reviewing the changes that have taken place in independent education over the past twenty years I have to acknowledge that some great strides have been made but we must not lose sight of the fact that some of the experimental teaching methods have failed. Whatever happened to whole class lessons based on 'talk and chalk'? I find it hard to believe that I successfully taught forty-three lower juniors by this method in a maintained school in the sixties and I can remember groups of excited seven to eight year olds in an independent school who learnt world geography by travelling the world on a 'Magic Carpet', a whole class at a time.

Even a small independent school like ours is reeling from the amount of legislation that has been foisted on us. There are more staff meetings. Planning meetings, Key Stage meetings, whole staff meetings, and parents' meetings pepper every staff room calendar. There is ongoing preparation for inspections, a rolling programme of In-Service Training (INSET), all eating into the limited time which the teacher actually spends on teaching. The paperwork is frequently totally unnecessary, particularly in the case of the tried and tested, experienced teacher. My successor has already had to extend the school day by starting earlier in the morning, with a later lunch break, in order to deliver the syllabus. What effect does this then have on teachers' time management and morale?

The biggest change must surely be the teaching of information technology. Handwriting is in danger of becoming a dying art, and the long-term effect on eyesight and computer-bound bodies is still unknown. Children may enjoy the technological challenges they meet on a daily basis, but the enjoyment of books is in decline. Three cheers for Harry Potter whose adventures have brought many a primary school child back from the brink!

It is no wonder that a recent teachers' conference has seen the teaching unions being promised more non-contact time by the Secretary of State for Education. Whether this promise will be fulfilled is anybody's guess. Teacher shortages are now so acute that giant steps will have to be taken to recruit new teachers and it is no longer any use for exhausted staff from maintained schools to turn to the independent sector for respite. We are all in it together.

Against the Grain

It would be good, one day, to see some genuinely independent research into why parents go private. It would probably work best if a truth drug were involved, because it is a subject involving a great deal of embarrassed spin-doctoring. Apart from a very few unrepentant snobs ('Can't send them to the Council School!') and flashy nooves ('Only the best for Daddy's little princess'), most parents are deeply equivocal about buying private education. Either they have a bad conscience about conspicuous consumption and the fabled ill-effects on the state system, or else they just feel like mugs with more money than sense. There is plainly no inherent pleasure in handing over large sums, out of taxed income, for something which you are already supposed to have paid for through the said taxes.

Even in contemporary fiction, most novelists shy away from this particular social and family dilemma — the exception being brave Joanna Trollope in *The Rector's Wife*, Mrs Vicar defiantly takes a job as a shelf-stacker so that her daughter can be rescued from the rough comprehensive and sent to some nice nuns. The author hedges her bets by carefully stressing that the siblings had done perfectly well at the comp, and that this is merely a matter of personality and vulnerability in one child. Even so, I remember reading more than one venomous press comment about the essential ghastliness of a heroine who only breaks convention in order to send her child to a private school, yah boo.

Plenty of private-school parents suffer, usually in glum silence, under the lash of such smug contempt from *confrères* who got into the best state schools by deliberately buying into the inner catchment area or executing ruthless middle-class backflips with the appeals system.

Again, we may exclude the resolute and carefree rich from this, but in the income bracket which can just about manage private school fees, there is a strong current of opinion which says that having a kid at state school is virtuous, responsible and *communitaire*: having a kid at private school is selfish, snobbish and elitist. Call it the 'McCartney effect' — I have rarely read an article about Paul and the late Linda which did not admiringly point to the fact that their children went to the local school despite their great wealth.

We should meet this unease head-on, examine it, and tease out the real reasons why parents go independent even when ideology, social comfort and financial prudence militate against it. Is it entirely academic? Is it driven by league tables, and the prevailing middle-class terror that inadequate qualifications at eighteen will wreck a whole life and propel your child into a dead-end or workless underclass? Or are there more subtle ambitions in play here: inchoate yearnings for an education beyond what an increasingly stern and centralized Whitehall rule decrees?

I do not speak only for myself here, but may as well lay the cards on the table for the sake of frankness. We live in a rural area, where for geographical reasons parental choice of secondary school barely exists. We had a most excellent state primary school: a model of flexibility, humanity, good-humour and intellectual adventurousness, which sadly only ran up to the age of nine before colliding with one of the country's few surviving middle-school systems, which we did not favour. This, and the general ill-tempered chaos and uncertainty of educational reorganization in the early 1990s, led us into private secondary education. The first private schools were not right for either of the particular children; both ended up, at twelve and thirteen respectively, at yet another fee-paying school. We were lucky in that we found one which takes most of its pupils on massively supported fees provided by the Greenwich Hospital charity for the children and grandchildren of seafarers, so that while there are some outsiders on normal fees (like us), the social and intellectual mix is far less claustrophobically exclusive than at most private schools.

But we went through all the decisions, all the doubts, all the desires, of any parent in those circumstances. We had a mixed background: mine in a series of schools abroad, and then boarding in a British convent, and my husband in a Sheffield grammar school. Both of us, I suppose, were searching to reproduce the best bits of our own education. In his case that meant order, rigour, good behaviour, clarity of purpose and proper teaching of science. My inchoate desire was for inspiration, love of learning for its own sake, cultural breadth, music and theatre, pastoral kindness, an ethos where good values could be imbibed without noticing, and tolerance of a certain quirky individuality, even eccentricity. The state primary school, I should say, had had all of these.

It went down to the smallest things. One of the deciding factors about one of the schools we chose for the buffer period was the fact that a teacher brought a ridiculous dog in with him daily, which lay growling quietly through his Maths lessons and romped through the playground all day to the evident irritation of more staid staff members. I was still dazzled by the receptiveness and creativity young children show, and remember saying grandly 'Sod the qualifications, but I will not have them frightened and I will not have them *bored'*.

Talking to other secondary school parents over the last eight years, I have found much common ground. Those who got lucky in the awful lottery of British state education often praise exactly the same things — in their state schools — that some of us pay money for. The comp we liked best, but were unlikely to have got a place in, had much of the old-style independent about it — a Latin club at lunchtime run by the headmaster for fun, plenty of music, odd sports like judo, a decorous atmosphere and code of behaviour, and a staff which had managed to avoid going on strike during the awful mid-1980s, because they couldn't bear to. You walked in, looked at the artwork on the walls and saw the easy relationship of teachers with pupils, and felt the buzz. You felt safe and stimulated . On the other hand, class sizes were big, and rising and, even then, the staff privately expressed a sense of panic, and pressure, and resentment at the mounting load of paperwork which took them from their teaching.

Conversely, there were independents whose apparent virtues — high league table places, discipline, tradition, small classes — had somehow turned into vices. There is a horrid, unkind, competitive rigidity about some well-regarded schools, an ethos which freezes the blood. One acquaintance had a daughter at a very well-reviewed establishment some fifty miles away, and I congratulated her when she told me. She snapped 'Wrong. Great results in the exams, but they've never had a school play or a school trip in three years, and the headmaster is a cold-fish careerist. I'm moving her. She's only young once, poor little toad'.

So what do parents look for, when they happen to have enough money to buy a genuine choice and not a hard-fought *faute de mieux?* I would suggest that from years of anguished conversations and personal experience, the list goes something like this.

Small classes definitely count. For all the weasely governmental statements of recent years, for all the barmy comparisons with Japan, Korea etc, parents continue to want their children taught in reasonably small groups. This is particularly important in primary school, but continues to matter to secondary parents. Instinct and commonsense tell us that in a smaller group, a child has more chance of having its questions answered, its views heard where appropriate, and its private bafflements noted and overcome. One of the most alarming remarks of recent times was made by the education minister Malcolm Wicks in a letter to *The Times*, regarding larger sixth form sets caused by the AS level reform. 'There is no reason' he said, 'why sixth forms cannot manage a few extra students, since discipline is not as big an issue at that age'. It was not so much the immediate sentiment that was alarming, but that an education minister should be under the impression that the ONLY reason for small group teaching is to prevent the students throwing things and spitting.

But then, discipline also counts. There are, everybody knows, parents who send their children to private schools for unforgivably snobbish reasons: so that they get 'naice' accents, so that they meet affluent fiiends, and don't have to mix with any riff-raff. That is regrettable, if typically British. Far easier to excuse and sympathize with is the genuine dread of throwing your gentle, thoughtfully reared, nonviolent, bookish child into a maelstrom of rude, rowdy, disruptive, aggressive and troubled peers who will actively impede his or her learning and make the playground a daily hell. I would not pretend that bullying is universal in state schools and unknown in private schools — crikey, the reverse applied with us, as the first time one of ours was mugged for a break-time snack was the first week we paid fees. Nonetheless, the breakdown of discipline, decorum and routine courtesy in some state schools is something which a parent has an absolute right to flee from. A child only has one chance to be young and love learning; even one year's disruption and fear takes that away forever.

If schools have disruptive pupils, through no fault of their own, they have to be resourced in a way that enables the horrors to be weeded out and reformed without grinding the whole class to a halt day after day. The mildest parents feel that in an independent school they have a right to demand that this happens: to complain vociferously about disruption and bullying and to assert their rights as paying clients. In a state school — though they are also paying clients — this feeling is much diluted. 'They're doing their best, but with the Scumville Estate just round the corner, what do you expect?', goes the tired refrain. 'The kids have to learn to take people as they come.' But sometimes the kid can't take it, and it is not snobbery but compassion that decides to reach in, at any cost, and fish him out to swim in a smaller, quieter pool.

Results count, too, but less than you would think. The old chestnuts of A-C grades at GCSE, A level scores and university places are raw data which any parent would be crazy to disregard. Yet parents are gradually growing more leery of these raw figures, learning for example to take into consideration the degree of selection at entry and the question of whether the school 'culls' unpromising candidates out of key subjects. Under the tutelage of honest independent heads, ever more parents come to understand the unfairnesses in the tables. For instance, when only 16+ results in GCSE are counted, where is the justice? I have a daughter who got a hatful of A grades at fifteen, and did her school league table place no favours at all. Other schools — specializing in less mainstream pupils — produce numbers of creditable seventeen plus GCSEs, which don't count either.

Culture counts, immensely. Remember, most parents are making their choice for a child of eleven, and when your child is eleven it is actually quite difficult to focus on the distant goals of public examinations. What counts more at that still magical, still uncynical age is the wider vision of the school. You want your child to have contact with music and a chance to make it. In many maintained schools music is squeezed right out, or limited to a very few pupils and very few hours. A parent is pleased to think that a child would stretch his or her lungs and sing every day, as a matter of course, even if it is just an assembly hymn. You are more likely to get that by paying fees these days, just as you are more likely to get membership of a choir or an orchestra, even if your child is not especially talented. Drama is another draw: it is not just the ritzily equipped school theatre that lures punters in to St Plutocrats, but the presence of creative, relaxed, enthusiastic staff who want to put on plays and revues just for the hell of it, without justifying them in narrow curriculum terms.

The same goes for games. If you happen to have a boy who adores his football, longs for the rugby pitch, or has a real talent for athletics, but who needs persuading of the value of school lessons, you are likely to want a school where games are part of life, part of the system, and where there is somewhere to play them daily, to run free and breathe. Moreover, if his maths teacher is also the rugby coach, he will be that bit more co-operative in maths; and if your unacademic daughter's beloved dance and drama clsses are timetabled into her working day, she will be less inclined to write off the whole of school as 'boring'.

Of course, the best state schools offer the same kind of whole-child integration of activities . But independents — because they are that bit freer, that bit more oriented to what real people want rather than what government departments order — certainly find it easier. Especially, no doubt, because having shorter terms they may work their staff harder and expect extra-curricular dedication as a matter of course.

Teachers count. It is a truism of business that people who feel valued will perform better; and it is equally a truism in the arts professions that if you want creativity, you have to give your people space and tolerate some veering-away from rigid templates of behaviour. This grows harder and harder for teachers in the maintained schools, and parents notice this weariness and crushedness and resignation, and do not like it. Again, it is not universal: the best state schools are as full of bouncy individualists as anything you could pay for. But not all state schools are the best and no parents voluntarily sends a nervous, wondering eleven-year-old into a world that seems defined by hunched shoulders and a resentful atmosphere.

Communication counts. An overworked, under-appreciated teacher, with an overload of genuine problem children and a constant need to cover for colleagues who have collapsed with stress illnesses, will find it hard to be responsive to queries and worries and to set up a partnership with each anxious parent. A cheerful, valued, reasonably loaded member of a contented staffroom is, quite simply, easier to deal with. If a twelve-year-old is panicking each night about a subject, or overloaded with badly co-ordinated homework, you want to sort it out quickly on the phone or in person. And you want to talk to the subject-teacher, not to some specially appointed liaison person or professional parent-fobber-offer or distant Year Head who has to pull out a manila file to remember which your child is. This individual, focused responsiveness — not just on twice-yearly parents' nights — is one of the luxuries that you get with a good private school (you don't with a bad one, believe me). It is, many parents will say, worth paying for.

In fact, it's all worth paying for. Culture, music, exercise, space, peace, safety, eccentric individuality, teaching so enthusiastic it soars way beyond the curriculum. It is not snobbery, or a desire to steal a march on others, which makes parents want these things for their children. In these post-Gordon Brown days of imminent positive discrimination, it is certainly not a conviction that it will get them into 'Oxbridge'. No, the desires of parents who buy private education in Britain are perfectly healthy ones, and we do no good at all by denying it.

The fact is that all children deserve an education as good, as relaxed, as culturally wide and unfearful as the best of the independents can provide. The other fact is that it costs money to provide such an education. Even more money in areas where parents' associations can't contribute much, and where many of the children import vast intractable problems from their home life. But rather than rail at the unfairness of independent education, the goal of everybody concerned with school planning at every stage should be to ensure that none of us is driven to it.

Rowan Williams
Statements, Acts and Values

Spriritual and Material in the
School Environment

'Spirituality is a powerful force that determines what we are, our self-understanding, our outlook on life, others and the world, and consequently shapes our behaviour'.[1] The general approach represented by such statements is a great and solemn orthodoxy, and it is only with some trepidation that I dare enter a protest or two or three, as I find myself puzzled and frustrated by its implicit assumptions. I hope the overall discussion of the 'spiritual' element in the process of education may actually benefit from a bit of emperor's-new-clothes questioning; and that is what I propose to try in what follows.

Adrian Thatcher, in a perceptive article on the notion of 'values' in the curriculum,[2] has recently pointed to the strangely unhistorical character of talking about values that might be identified as common in a society. When people ascribe value to a pattern of behaviour, when they recognize it as worthwhile, worthy of imitation or whatever, they are acting out of a process of prior *learning*. They have come to recognise this or that way of behaving as desirable, normally because of other beliefs about what human beings are like or what the universe is like, or even what God is like. A 'value' — and it helps to remember that speaking of *a* value in this way is a very recent habit — isn't a self-evident policy that can be communicated independently of questions about the sort of creatures human beings are or are about what it is that human beings want or ought to

[1]   *Education for Adult Life: The Spiritual and Moral Development of Young People*, SCAA Discussion Papers no. 6, July 1996, p. 6. The paper is the report of a conference held in January 1996 in the wake of consultations on the National Curriculum and the new model syllabuses for Religious Education.
[2]   Adrian Thatcher, 'Values — Secular or Christian?: a Response to Mary Grey' in A. Thatcher (ed.) *Spirituality and the Curriculum*, London, Cassell, 1999, pp. 33-54, esp. pp. 37-42.

want. Nor is it, as Thatcher rightly insists, a sort of optional gloss on the world of facts. The so-called fact–value distinction is deeply built into a particular kind of modern moral philosophy that has some-times served to reinforce belief in the absolute givenness of certain processes and states of affairs, and muffled criticism.

This does not mean, of course, that there can be no agreement about what is desirable, because every moral agent's desires are con-fined by one tribal myth or another. It does, though, pose the prob-lem of how desire itself is educated, and how we are to avoid in this area a dangerous level of abstractness about how judgements of worthwhileness are to be made. Certainly the 1993/95 SCAA[3] paper on 'Spiritual and Moral Development' recommended 'learning experiences' that would enable students to ' understand why people reach certain decisions on spiritual and moral issues', as well as developing 'a sense of belonging to a community'. But there is not a great deal on *which* experiences in learning actually shape such deci-sions. Judgements of value arise from situations in which you come to *see* in particular ways. It's not that there are neutral bundles of things and events which you later elaborate by adding value to them: the way you are led to see and speak about things and events already carries evaluation, subtly teaches you what is worthy or desirable.

If this is correct, in any discussion of spiritual values in education Christians should focus on what kinds of learning experience will at the very least keep open the door to understanding — and thus, potentially, to sharing — the Christian commitment, the Christian account of what human beings are. It will be no use trying to com-municate Christian teaching or Christian moral perspectives, even in a Church school, in an environment that refuses the experiences that will make sense of them. I'm not referring to what the textbooks might call 'religious experiences', not even to experiences of awe and wonder and so on, but to the fundamental experiences of being a human person in the learning environment. Of course, to have any clarity about this requires a level of clarity about the Christian vision itself; so, in order to reflect on what environment might assist in nur-turing the sense of this vision as a lively possibility for a growing individual, I want briefly to look at some of its main characteristics.

The basic question for the Christian educator thus becomes how to create an environment that allows for the emergence of a sense of the possibility of living human life in this way. It is, I want to suggest, a

---

[3]   School Curriculum and Assessment Authority, a predecessor of today's QCA, or Qualifications and Curriculum Authority.

prior question to the content of religious education. If the messages being given by the whole way in which educational institutions and practices work are hostile to this possibility, no amount of substantive doctrinal or moral instruction will make any difference. To borrow a very suggestive phrase from the American philosopher Jacob Needleman, we shall be addressing a person who isn't there. The images and ideas of our religious discourse relate to a purely abstract human subject, whose sense of what is humanly possible is shaped by experiences in which there is no room for the possibilities opened up by the gospel. And I suspect that a fair amount of confusion and even damage results from not attending to this prior issue when we are talking about religious education, as if the content of instruction could be separated from the environment in which it is delivered. If that environment tells you that the humanity presupposed in Christian language is not to be taken seriously, Christian education simply doesn't happen.

These conditions for making sense of Christian possibilities can at least be discussed and examined without immediately appealing to revelation. They make Christian understanding possible, but they also make other things possible, including other kinds of both religious and imaginative perspectives. The Christian educator, that is to say, can argue for these prior conditions in the educational environment as something more than just a confessional convenience. This ought not to create too many theoretical problems if we are, as believers, confident that the gospel releases what is most significantly human in us. The task of the explicitly Christian school then becomes — and I think this a challenge of real importance — to *show* the connections between the general human environment of an institution and the gifts and demands of the gospel.

So what are these 'conditions'? They relate to three areas at least in the life of an educational community: the use of *time*; the understanding of the *body*; and the use of *language*.

Let us look first at time, so conspicuously a problem in the contemporary educational process. All educators are bitterly aware of the pressure on schedules, and the prevailing atmosphere in most schools is of relentless 'busy-ness'. Thus time becomes a scarce commodity that needs always to show a rapid return on investment. This is evident in several different ways: in the continuing erosion of dinner hours and the anxiety about cutting down 'dead' time at the beginning of the day; in the current passion for testing, which so clearly declares that the expenditure of time has to be justified; and in the vulnerability of fringe activities in an overloaded day, leading

to the marginalising of sport, music, or drama in a school determined to improve its 'performance'. Wry smiles of recognition will
always greet comments on the time pressures of the modern school.
But this is more than a matter of practical stress and overactivity; our
use of time already carries messages about our human priorities. An
anxious and overloaded timetable tells students that the fundamental requirement upon them is to *justify* their interests, projects and
pursuits because of the scarcity and preciousness of time. The effect
is to foreshorten perspectives and foreclose expectations. If you have
to have a rapid result from the investment of time, you need to know
with some precision what result you're expecting: you cannot afford
to wait and see. It then becomes even harder to defend more impon-
derable and longer-term expectations, although they may prove in
fact to be more appropriate. It is an image of the constantly shrinking
short-term perspectives of our economic life, reflected, too, in the
patterns of educational funding — but that is another story.

This, in essence, is my worry about the use of time: if reactions and
results are short-term predictable, what is lost is the time or room to
digest experience. And this is a problem that affects other areas as
well as English teaching. More pertinent, perhaps, to the theological
context sketched earlier, a prevailing atmosphere of anxiety (not to
say exhaustion and stress in educators) is a major obstacle to the
Christian vision. As Christians, we should certainly fear God, and
this extends to taking responsibility for our use of time. The worst
possible way to honour this, however, is to seek exhaustive utilitarian justification of every moment in the hope of being acceptable to
God or to others. And the believer's vision ought to be such as to be
hospitable to the idea that effects are, in a grace-haunted world,
unpredictable and disproportionate to effort. A school or other institution perpetually panicking about its timetable is communicating
very effectively a model of human living inimical to religious faith in
general and to Christian belief in particular.

To address the question of attitudes to the *body* is a bit more complex. For one thing, although we still use that remarkable phrase
'physical education', our basic models of education have to do with
what we fondly imagine to be disembodied subjects. For a long time,
few people thought systematically about the impact of the material
environment on the educational process. Even when this began to be
a serious consideration in the design of new buildings for educational purposes — usually primary schools — alternating and conflicting dogmas made it difficult to arrive at a reasoned view. The
issue is not so much about details of design, or even philosophy of

design, as about what makes an environment look nurtured or loved, what humanises it in ways that contribute to the humanity of students. In order to understand the 'spirituality' of an institution, it may be more useful to look at the displays which greet visitors in the main entrance; whether there *is* a main entrance; what sort of simple physical space there is overall for functions other than core curriculum activities (how large is the library and does it invite you to spend any time there? What is the space provision for music practice?); and many other questions like these. I would add as well that I am not talking simply about what is provided for pupils: a cramped and overcrowded staff room contributes to the 'message' that bodies do not matter, quite apart from its effect on stress levels among teachers. And, although the subject is usually just a matter for comic clichés, the diet of a school will also carry its own messages about the body and its significance.

To ask for more resources will sound like crying for the moon in our present climate. I want to say very emphatically that, from the point of view of any serious reflection on 'spiritual values' in education, these are not luxuries, but absolute necessities. Material environment sends out messages as clear as does the use of time in the institution. Children begin to appropriate — or fail to appropriate — a sense of their own real and potential worth by the care given to material surroundings, and where the material surroundings of their domestic lives are likely to be chaotic or ugly, there is more, not less, need for the school to pay attention to this. My own experience of visiting schools in 'deprived' areas often leaves me amazed and moved at precisely the degree of care shown in the creation of a physical environment, an uplifting celebration of colour and wit and confidence, often in disgracefully inadequate premises from an architectural point of view. But if a school is going to do all this, often by literally displaying the achievements of its students, architectural detail does matter. One of the depressing effects of many visits is the realisation that so often very little thought has been given to what physically greets student or visitor on entering a school. Our current anxieties about security have of course led to some obvious qualifications about offering free access to all. The issue remains, however, and needs some sustained attention from those who are thinking about 'values' in the curriculum. Let me repeat the point again: moral or spiritual instruction in the curriculum will be largely empty if the overall environment, the use of time and the valuation of the body, send clear messages that are at odds with the content of any such teaching. And if the Christian gospel looks to a state of affairs in which material life is weighted with the meanings of God, if the body really is a shrine for God's Spirit, these are not at all secondary matters, not at all the concerns of dilettante idealists. Schools that include in their codes issues about care for the school environment (even if it is only the standard prohibition against running in corridors!) have seen the point; but it is that much harder to reinforce in forbidding physical surroundings.

There are other dimensions to the body that cannot be examined closely here because of limitations of space. Sport must be mentioned, however briefly, not just because it teaches pupils about competition with others, but because it brings home some sense of what care for and enjoyment of the body might involve. And there is one last important question which I would like to address in connection with the body. Contact between the healthy majority and those other pupils who have special physical needs can be of enormous significance, not only in nurturing compassion or 'charity', but in relation to just this matter of the body's life and needs. It provides a sharp and necessary reminder of the vulnerability of bodies, even their mortality — always a difficult and abstract notion for the healthy young. There is a crucial lesson here: dignity, integrity, even a strange kind of personal independence are quite compatible with bodily limitation and chronic dependence on others. This, in fact, offers a more deeply spiritual insight than many of the abstract notions which are debated as part of the curriculum. It seems to me that when there is imaginatively fostered contact in schools between those with special needs and others, a dimension of experience is again *made possible.* This is too often sidelined in the current climate of anxiety and functional austerity, with their foreshortened perspectives.

I have mentioned the importance of contact between pupils of different abilities and physical needs, and this carries implications regarding the importance of *language,* in the broadest sense. Our 1993/95 SCAA document stressed the value, in 'spiritual and moral development', of experiences that would allow the growth of relations 'with adults and peers'. The level of conversation between different generations is often a good mark of the maturity of an institution. When focusing on the use of language in this context, I don't mean the literary or rhetorical quality of what is said in the classroom or the prevalence of swearing in the yard, but the ease of communication in informal settings between students and others (including maintenance and kitchen staff) around the institution. Pressure on time is one of the main things that erodes this, of course, and that is yet another of the hidden costs of overloading the curriculum. Much can be garnered about an institution's health from casual exchanges at the staff-room door or conversations at the day's end between staff and pupils.

Of course I do also have an interest in the quality of language used in other settings, in the extent to which there is a conscious effort to warn students about the dangers of dead speech. The deadness may be of various sorts — the deadness of bureaucratic jargon, the deadness of uplifting waffle, the deadness of acronyms and target setting. In any particular area of study, it matters that the language used does not flatten out the depth, and a concern for the spiritual once again should include concern for this. We are not talking simply about exposing students to good aesthetic experience, or to the rather overworked sense of awe and wonder which we hear a lot about; it is a lot less marginal than that. The linguistic world we inhabit is the most immediately available index of our *human* world. The fact that adolescents are almost inevitably inarticulate must not deter us from asking how we convey to them that language is a medium of risk and adventure and excitement. It is too important to be left to English departments, crucial though they are. I wonder how many schools invite students to read a bit of Darwin at first hand, or start a year's work in science with a passage of Loren Eisely or Oliver Sacks or Fritjof Capra. I well remember the impact, in my A-level History course, of being encouraged to look at some pages of Carlyle's *French Revolution*. Once upon a time children were taught rhetoric as a matter of course, so that they should be able to recognise the sorts of things that others might say as a form of persuasion: language was something that was exhilarating but far from innocent. This is not about teaching arid ideological suspicion, but about sensitivity to the dangerous and miraculous possibilities of speech in all areas of our life and study.

Education socialises; but unless it teaches us how to distinguish between empty talk and authentic talk, between manipulative talk and talk that invites conversation and mutual understanding, we shall be left not socialised but homogenised, bound into conformism and unquestioning acceptance. David Holbrook makes a distinction between becoming civilised and becoming socialised, and points to the 'darkness of the intuitive faculty' and the 'inaccessible area of our make-up, beyond . . . consciousness and will'.[4] This, surely, has to be near the heart of any possible concern over the 'spiritual'. Here too the discourse of Christianity cannot begin to make sense unless

[4]   David Holbrook, *The Secret Places*, Methuen, London (1964), p. 270.

the darkness of the spirit is faced in some way — the darkness of
sheer obscurity, but also the darkness of evil. The bland language of
mutual tolerance as a spiritual value and priority misses something;
the room is too small. The difficulty we have in teaching some of the
classics, like the difficulty of worshipping with the Book of Common
Prayer, is not first and foremost a problem with lexical meanings,
but a problem with the register of the language. We don't have these
days much of a resource for the extremities of experience, obsessive
passion or jealousy, adoration, despair; and the missing 'keys' in our
music make it hard to become attuned to language that is at home
with words for extremity. There is no quick answer to this [certainly
not in the simple imposition of premodern forms in worship or
schooling], but there is a major issue here about how far our educational processes collude with a general deadening of public utter-
ance.

How do you talk to someone who is not there? As I have indicated,
this is to my mind the underlying and inadequately addressed question that needs to be asked prior to specific considerations of how
doctrine or ethics may be communicated. What I have been discussing is in no way an alternative to such communication. There is a
serious problem if the self that seems to be taken for granted in most
institutions is a self quite unconnected with the self that is capable of
growing as spirit in Christian terms. Spirit — or soul (with due
respect to long traditions of theology, this is not the place to argue
that distinction) grows where the self is set free from narrow func-
tionalism, connected afresh to the experience of the body, including
the painful or limiting aspects of bodily living, and encouraged to
articulate this in language that is free from embarrassment about the
unusual or extreme. This is not an agenda restricted to the 'soft' subjects in a curriculum — nor indeed restricted to the curriculum at all:
scientific education is capable of doing all these things. And, let me
stress again, this is not a prescription for producing Christians
through education. The worth of these considerations may be as
apparent to an agnostic as to a believer, as obvious to a thoughtful
religious practitioner of another tradition as to a Christian. My concern has rather been to sketch what I think to be generally necessary,
though not sufficient, conditions for Christian language, if it is to
make any experiential sense. If we are to continue talking about
spirit as *the self* in drastically transformed relations, existing as a
body bestowing its material resource for other material persons,
freed from anxiety over achievement and celebrating its new world
in new and and surprising speech, we have to look as critically as

possible at these perhaps prosaic issues in connection with schools and comparable institutions. I might add, a bit depressingly, that most of the considerations I have raised apply with painful force to the environment and ethos of much Christian worship. Many Christian buildings fail to give the immediate impression of being designed to help one believe in the resurrection of the body, just as quite a lot of Christian language will not suggest that the gospel is about liberation from fear, nor indeed, about extremes of darkness and celebration.

St. Francis de Sales is supposed to have said, in reply to an aristocratic lady who wanted him as her confessor, that he would begin the job when she had learned to talk more slowly, walk more slowly and eat more slowly. A recommendation to take things more slowly is likely to be met with ironic applause in the contemporary educational scene, but our assumption that time is scarce and that its 'waste' is the sin against the Holy Spirit does not seem to be producing maturity, reflectiveness, critical openness or even plain old happiness in our culture. My vote is for St. Francis de Sales.

I hope that church schools at least may feel that they should bestow a little of the credit upon Francis for the way they manage things. How often have you heard it said that parents opt for church schools because of their ethos rather than their actual teaching? Frequently that means that parents sense that certain sorts of space are being made. The church school cannot of itself alter the statutory constraints under which it operates; what it can do — and remarkably often does, in my experience — is to work at an environment where there is room for the spirit. Those who have some wider responsibility in policy making should be supporting these gentle subversions and arguing for their central character in the humanising process of education at large. There is no need to apologise for the fact that such things are recommended because, among other considerations, they form part of a *praeparatio evangelica*. If they are to be desired, then it must also be because they are recognisably humanising — which should not be too great a surprise if we really believe that faith in Christ is what human beings are made for.

To put the whole argument in rather different terms, much of our problem in being clear about 'spiritual education' comes from approaching the issue rationally and contractually. The SCAA document that I quoted earlier speaks of the need for a school's 'values' to be agreed and made available in a plain statement. 'Parents and children', we read, 'need to agree that, having selected the school in the full knowledge of those values, they are prepared to abide by them.

It is important to remember that children, especially older pupils, are more likely to feel a commitment to abiding by the values of the school if those values are openly and explicitly discussed with them'.[5] Admirable: but here the basic model is that of a contract concerning the nature of the product on sale. There is not much sense of the fact that both parents and children are more likely to feel committed if they see an institution actively devoted to making possible the sort of humanity they think desirable, and this may not be easily summed up in an all too often bland and uninformative statement of values. In fairness the same document goes on to make some more far-reaching points about teachers as 'moral agents' whose values are proclaimed by 'the way they address pupils and each other, the way they dress, the language they use and the effort they put into their work'.[6] To speak of teachers in this way is actually a powerful reminder that the process of education is an interaction between embodied beings, who observe dress, language and so on, picking up and transmitting signals in a whole host of different ways.

This may be an appropriate point to note how few of the real problems of educating are to be solved by the fashionable messianism around information technology. I have no quarrel with the idea that more computing resources will probably benefit most institutions. As I have argued elsewhere, however, computers are binary systems, unsympathetic to issues that cannot be dealt with by reduction to a choice between two alternatives. They are an excellent and economical way of conveying settled and uncontroversial information, and an appalling and unthinkable substitute for personal interaction [the word 'interactive' as used in this context of IT is very strictly metaphorical]. What IT cannot do is shape a moral environment. Any lessons conveyed by it about the use of time, the body or language, tend to reinforce the least constructive elements in our educational culture. If IT is to be a good servant and not a really corrupting master, it must be used in an environment already clear about its human objectives.

I hope, then, to see a little less attention being paid to *statements* of values, a little more attention to the material conditions of *acts* of valuing [that is, acts of recognising what is desirable and admirable]. Talk of values is bound to be empty and boring if we do not actually know what a moral agent looks like and have not established what room is needed, materially as well as intellectually, for such an agent

---

[5]   *Spiritual and Moral Development*, SCAA Discussion Papers no. 3, as previously, p. 8.

[6]   SCAA Discussion Papers no. 3, p. 9.

to be nurtured. Commitment to the matters I have been outlining does not involve accepting the Christian revelation as true. It might, though, involve the [perhaps telling] acknowledgement that the conditions for achieving moral maturity and for opening up the intelligibility of the Christian gospel are remarkably convergent — if indeed it is agreed that education in moral discernment absolutely requires certain elements in a material environment. Is that agreed, I wonder, in discussions of this whole area? People will regularly appeal to the undoubtedly true fact that some students develop moral sensibility or even spiritual understanding in materially deprived settings. But I suspect here a rather narrow definition of 'material privation'. It is quite difficult to imagine the development of any kind of moral sensibility which does not also engage with the material surroundings, such as conversation, time and attention given, and even the sheer enjoyment of the learning process. At the very least, suggesting that we might without cost get used to the absence of any or all of these, as if that would have no effect on the moral and imaginative horizons of young people, presages a future in which some kinds of *depth* become inaccessible to us.

I do not think there is anything very revolutionary in suggesting that the 'learning experiences' which contribute to spiritual development include the whole environment of a school, and not only those exercises specifically designed to help us feel aware or whatever. We are in constant danger of imagining that this whole area is susceptible to organisation as a curricular affair and of losing sight of what I want to call the *integrity of learning experience*. Our treatment of these issues needs continued attention within the actual and material circumstances of educating. It is no use speaking of 'values' if building and timetables don't convey a *valuation* of humanity in which there is room for the spirit. And that is where questions about spiritual development in education become, rather urgently, questions about the resourcing of education overall; questions about how the work of the individual teacher is valued in relation to the gifts of communicative patience that will educate students in un-anxious habits; questions about the proper place of technology; questions about our widespread expectations that schools will produce what families and society often do not want to think about, the need for sustainable common visions of what is humanly good. This is an enormous political and social agenda, but it should not be evaded. Once we start talking about religious education seriously, we are bound to arrive at the question of what it is to educate religiously, to educate the spirit. In arriving at any interpretation of what *spirit* means in our theological sources, we inevitably become involved in a debate about what is humanly desirable. We should be grateful that the educational agenda still presses these matters on us as a society, and it is all the more important that we as Christians be ready to respond.

Part III

Managerial Ethics and the
Corruption of the Future

Stephen Prickett

Conclusion

Metaphors, Managerial Ethics, and Unintended Consequences

This is a book about public commitment to education, and the disastrous unintended consequences of the monocultural climate of current policies. The policies have been disastrous because they have assumed the world is simple, when in fact it is not. The real world is mixed, confused, untidy and the product of many competing forces. Education in the real world cannot therefore be about serving one particular policy, one particular definition, one particular set of objectives. To insist, for example, that a 'university' is solely a place where one learns to think clearly is as unrealistic in the pluralistic society that is modern Britain, as it is to insist that it exists solely to produce flexible units for the labour force of the 'knowledge society'.

Reminders of the polyphonic roots of our own cultural heritage are important when we come to consider the metaphors of education used today — especially in the form of problems posed by the nexus of emotively resonant but weakly-conceived concepts which I have here termed 'managerial ethics'. The phenomenon I am describing is, strictly speaking, neither managerial nor ethical, but a hybrid (and sterile) vampire that draws what strength it has from that most dangerous of combinations, two concealed metaphors — both in themselves relatively harmless — but which together form a deadly compound whose corollaries include not just the crude idea that education should serve the needs of the labour market, but also underlie the whole *moral* rationale behind the push for accountability and testing.

Managerial ethics is not so much a theory as a set of sloppy and unquestioned assumptions. Few who deploy its jargon are likely to use words as precise as 'managerial ethics', or rigorously examine the content of their rhetoric. They are too busy — not of course with teaching, nor even with organizing teaching, but with 'management'.[1] Managerial ethics does not debate first principles, indeed *any* principles. It offers, rather, to find ways of making the status quo not so much acceptable, as seemingly inevitable.

Yet the notion of management as essential to educational organization is, at first sight, apparently uncontroversial. It rests on a clear implied syllogism. (1) Education is very complex and expensive (the second largest drain on the public purse, even before we get to the private sector).[2] (2) Complex and expensive enterprises require management. (3) *Ergo*, education requires management — with the obvious rider that this means 'professional management', since headteachers and professors are themselves simply jumped-up teachers, and, unless given a proper sense of the seriousness of their calling, are liable to go on teaching if they can, to the obvious detriment of their managerial roles.

But *is* the idea of 'management' as a commercial and people-handling skill, as applicable to the needs of education as current dogma seems to suggest ?

Since any kind of school or university requires some structure and organization the case might seem straightforward enough. From the mediaeval *trivium* and *quadrivium*, to the comprehensive school timetable, classes must divide knowledge into suitably graded pieces, and occur at clearly-announced times that do not conflict with other classes that may be attended by the same students. But this is 'organization' — the concept of 'management' as it has now been introduced into education is a metaphor from the commercial world, that implies not merely organizational effectiveness, but skills in control and motivation of people, a knowledge of the principles of economics, accountancy and bookkeeping.

We should be clear at the outset that there is nothing sinister or inherently malign about management *per se*. At its best it involves tact, sensitivity to individual needs and problems, and the ability to spot, bring on, nurture and motivate talents that even the possessor

[1]   Frank Furedi, of the University of Kent, has drawn attention to the way in which the new generation of educational managers tend to treat dissidents as not as people to be reasoned with, and met with arguments, but as people with personal problems in need of therapy. 'Management' is, after all, an 'ethical' activity. 'I hear what you are saying: perhaps if we could arrange some course on computer programming, spread-sheet analysis, modern management theory, personal counselling, you might understand that education has to change, to meet the needs of its 'customers', its paymasters, the country at large...'

[2]   Health, at £46bn., is the largest, followed by education, at £38bn., and defence, £24bn. Cited by Duke Maskell & Ian Robinson, in *The New Idea of a University*, Thorverton, Imprint Academic, 2002, p. 15.

may not have recognized. It frequently involves responsibility, vision, innovation and skills of implementation. Successful managers in the commercial world show such qualities in abundance, and are correspondingly well-rewarded. The problem is that though the term 'management' is now a hurrah-word in circles of educational administration, very few of the conditions that pertain to the business world apply in the same way to that of education.

What has actually happened over the past fifteen years is that one form of totally inappropriate control has been imposed upon education using the terminology of another, quite different but equally inappropriate form. Though the metaphors of the new educational management are those of industry and commerce, the structure of control is essentially bureaucratic — drawn not from the world of business, but from the civil service. This symptomatic confusion was made curiously, if, one imagines, unconsciously, explicit in the University of Glasgow in the early 1990s, when the management consultants, Coopers and Lybrand, were called in by the new Principal (a former civil servant) to survey the entire operations of the University and to recommend 'efficiency' changes. Needless to say, given such a brief (with corresponding fees), no firm of management consultants has ever failed to find the need for radical re-structuring of the hiring institution. What was significant, however, about this restructuring was the honesty of the report and its diagrams of the management process. Almost no mention was made of education, or the processes by which it might be facilitated, but Heads of Department were helpfully labelled (in brackets) 'line managers'.

Yet they were *not*, of course, line managers in any normal or recognizable sense. Heads of Departments need many skills — those of the psychiatrist, the priest, the con-man and the escape artist all come in handy — but they have limited powers of hiring, almost no powers of firing, and at the end of the day, no easily definable 'product' by which their success or failure could be measured.[3] In the new structure they were being absorbed into what was essentially a quite different kind of role — that of a middle-ranking bureaucrat. Unlike businesses, cases of universities actually going bankrupt are about as rare as countries doing so (i.e. almost never) and, beyond recording income and expenditure, their activity cannot be stated in

[3] Again compare with the American model which British universities are supposed to be imitating: 'The American university remains an organizational enigma, whose loosely coupled structure and collegially based organization defy the established canons of management.' Frank H.T. Rhodes, *The Creation of the Future: The Role of the American University*, Ithica: Cornell University Press, 2001, p. 14.

directly fiscal terms. There are no rewards for making a profit (i.e. spending less than they receive) or indeed for selling more. Universities do not make a widget to be marketed, and (at Glasgow at least) with ten applicants for every place, they have no need to seek popular approval. What these 'line managers' are supposed to 'manage' is a group of between five and thirty assorted cantankerous and semi-autonomous individuals (whose individuality is one of the reasons they were chosen for the job) and whose agreement must be sought for all but the most trivial changes. Incompetent or, more often, lazy, teachers exist, and can be admonished, and fail to gain promotion — but, at Glasgow, at any rate — promotions were not in the hands of the Head of Department, but involved recommendations to a Board of Review, whose decisions depended more on internal politics and the availability of money than on the deserving nature of the cases sent up to it.[4]

This is, as we have observed, a familiar administrative style; not that of industry or commerce, but of a Civil Service bureaucracy. Yet the language in which university teachers are exhorted to pursue their calling is borrowed from manufacturing industry with shameless opportunism. 'An education sector produces human capital for use in the production sector' write Sausman and Steel in the Dearing Report (1997).[5] It is not difficult to see from where Blunkett is getting his terminology. Metaphors like 'input' and 'output', 'quality control', and 'throughput' are used to shore up the increasingly tortured analogy. Applied to the rote learning of multiplication tables, 'quality control' might have some residual meaning, but by the time one gets to the history syllabus, it begins to suffer badly from metaphor-fatigue.[6]

[4]   The sheer arbitrariness of such proceedings is well illustrated by one case I personally witnessed where a distinguished scholar whose work did not strike any chords with most members of the Review Committee was simultaneously turned down for promotion to a Senior Lectureship, and then appointed by a (much more competent) search committee to a vacant Chair in the same department.

[5]   Maskell & Robinson, *The New Idea of a University*, p. 17.

[6]   Another, marginally more honest, example of this tortuous attempt to use industrial metaphors comes from Norman Gemmell's section of the Dearing Report: 'To capture the production externalities of higher education it is clearly necessary to have an accurate measure of the extent to which HE augments the quality of labour input. However, measuring the output of education in general, and HE in particular, is notoriously difficult. As a result input measures tend to be used... It is very difficult to know how close these proxies are to their conceptual equivalents.' [3.7]. *Ibid.* p. 11.

Yet as the above account should make abundantly clear, *neither* the blatantly flourished metaphors of commerce, *nor* the (thinly disguised) procedures of the civil service are appropriate for what an educational institution actually does. The real world that the university confronts cannot be reduced to the monolingual simplicities of their bottom lines. If teaching at its best involves imparting some skills, as other contributors to this volume have stressed, what they actually seek to produce is more like a quality of mind, or even of life. Moreover, this is done within a particular context which is neither commercial nor bureaucratic, but *collegial*. Members of a school staff or a university department are *colleagues*. They are collectively responsible for the development of their pupils, and for the advancement of their discipline.[7]

Nor is collegiality simply a matter of a community of teachers. It includes all pupils whose work makes them a part of the community of scholars. So far from simply imparting knowledge, the good teacher makes his or her pupils part of the enterprise. Educationally, what matters in the last resort is how individual teachers encourage or promote the growth and development of their students — and I include under that heading not merely conventional teaching, but even a great deal of writing and research. This will certainly involve the acquiring of specific skills, but that is never more than part of the picture. A recent series of advertisements in the *New York Times*, urging qualified graduates to return to teaching asked some pertinent questions to make precisely that point: 'When did you last hear of a teacher leaving to take up something "more important"'? 'When did you last hear of an ex-employee seeking out a middle manager ten years after leaving to thank him for how he had helped him?'

There is, in effect, within any educational institution a tacit 'hierarchy of respect' that has little or no counterpart in either the commercial world or that of public administration. In any effective commercial or administrative management, the hierarchy of respect must conform closely, if not exactly, to the official hierarchy of command, because that is the purpose of the system. In teaching, however, the headteacher, professor or dean, may be the most highly-paid member of the team (and no doubt rightly so) but every-

---

[7]   This simple fact has a profound, but often ignored, effect on the human relationships within the institution. Heads of Department, like Headteachers, remain in an important sense no more than *primus inter pares*; they have to live, often at close quarters, with their colleagues. In many cases in universities they will have to continue to work with these same colleagues after they have ceased to be Heads of Department. They are not like the captains of naval vessels who must take their meals alone.

one may also be aware that the best teacher, the best researcher, the best scholar — the person who is turned to for advice by students in trouble, or colleagues seeking arcane information, may well be someone relatively unrewarded by the official power-structure. This is not the same as the 'good old boy' in the firm who has been there for forty years and 'knows the ropes'. These, especially in universities, may be the best scholars in the department. Nor is it, I believe, an incidental and contingent phenomenon of educational institutions, but actually an important quality intrinsic to them — and those without such a parallel hierarchy of respect are already institutions in serious trouble.

It is, therefore, worth asking ourselves how what is arguably the most important single activity of government (and one that was hailed as such by Mr Blair) — the education and training of the next generation of citizens, has now been doubly wrapped in not one, but *two* sets of ill-fitting borrowed clothes. Some of this has been achieved by means of what one might call 'metaphorical transformation'.[8] The metaphor of 'management', however, has a glamour not shared by that of 'bureaucracy' and it is not difficult to see why civil servants might feel better, not only if they redescribed their own jobs in such terms, but also if they extended the redescription to those responsible for the 'output' of the universities, the schools and the health service — especially if it suggested the appropriateness of managerial salaries. Despite the fact that Britain has long been a by-word for poor management,[9] 'management' has now succeeded in establishing its metaphorical outreach into almost every activity that depends even peripherally on organization — and few human activities involving more than one person do not. But if it has conquered the health services, The Royal Opera House, the football club, and the amateur dramatic society, nowhere has it infiltrated more effectively than in education — and metaphors are rarely innocent infiltrators.

[8] We can see a similar process at work in the metaphorical extension of another loosely-defined word, 'politics'. From being the work of government, the word has been inserted into other spheres of activity to stress possible analogies: thus we get 'academic politics', 'sexual politics', and even 'group' and 'personal politics' — and certainly 'managerial politics'. Though they occasionally require similar skills (which is the point of the metaphor) none of these are of course 'politics' in the original, core, sense.

[9] See the quixotic defence from Peter Drucker 'What's right with British management?' in his *Drucker on Management*, Management Publications Ltd., 1971.

The whole purpose of a metaphor is to show something, by comparison, in a different, or new light, and so to change our perception of it. A metaphor that corresponded exactly with the thing described would no longer be metaphoric. Indeed, often the *less* resemblance between metaphor and object ('tenor' and 'vehicle') the *more* powerful and effective the metaphor. When Burns compared his love to 'a red, red rose', it is not clear if he was describing the lady in question, or what was happening inside himself — or both.[10] Indeed, the ambiguity is part of the impact of the line. What nobody imagines is a one-for-one correspondence between roses and the girl in question. Yet when the Department of Education and Science describes the role of a headteacher or of a university dean as that of a 'manager', the implicit corollary is to question why the other skills associated with commercial management are not also being exercised. Teachers with excellent qualifications in French or biology, who have always got on amicably with their fellows in the staff-room, and who have shown sufficient leadership qualities to become headteachers, are being asked why their accountancy skills are not up to scratch, or why they have not read the latest book on 'negotiating deals'? Budgets that used to be regulated by people with expert training in finance in the Town Hall, are 'devolved' to them, money may be 'vired' from one fund to another, and words like 'internal market' are bandied about. Whereas formerly every responsible person in public services *did* some managing, now, if you are responsible, you *are* a manager. In effect, the metaphor originally describing a part is now, by extension, dictating the whole.

Which brings us back to David Blunkett's conviction that 'the Department for Education and Employment's role stems from its responsibility for ensuring that the UK has a well-functioning labour market.' Not merely is this crudely 'mono-tonous' in both literal and root senses, it is tone-deaf to the kind of caveats suggested alike by Libby Purves and Rowan Williams. Blunkett was avowedly less interested in what children might know for its own sake, than in what training they needed to perform particular tasks. Since it is clear that many of the actual skills needed for the early twenty-first century will be rapidly outdated, he also believed in transferrable learning skills, enabling 'educated' people rapidly to up-grade their knowledge as appropriate to meet new situations. Given his general

[10] The floral industry, however, has reaped a vast commercial harvest from that one metaphor — to the point that anyone trying to buy a flower in the USA anywhere near February 14th which is *not* a red, red rose has considerable problems.

position, it was logical to assume that *everything* could be treated in the same way. If we need better citizens, then we need classes in citizenship; if we need clearer values, then we need classes in values. If a thing was of value to society, then it could be taught. And if a thing can be taught, then the effectiveness of that teaching could, presumably, also be measured.

Neither, of course, did this view of education suggest much appreciation of the distinction between education and training that was, ironically, to be the cause of his eventual conflict with Chris Woodhead. Up to November 2000 Woodhead had seemed to many to be the living embodiment of the new instrumentalist ethic. Though he had been hired by the last Conservative administration in 1994, Woodhead had slipped effortlessly into serving the new regime with the same abrasive zeal that he had served his former masters. His continued presence had flagged the fact that New Labour's much-advertised desire to make education its prime social objective was not a change of direction, but simply in an intensification of earlier policies. Yet in 2001, even its chief instrument recoiled in horror from the consequences.

Though this may sound like Thomas Cromwell complaining that Henry VIII had severely weakened monastic life in England, his criticisms are worth hearing. Woodhead, unlike Blunkett and the present Morris regime, is not an out-and-out instrumentalist, since he did not and does not see children primarily as potential units in the UK labour force. However misguided one may believe his methods to have been, he at least claimed to believe that education is intrinsically valuable to the individual, and could not merely be measured by its economic contribution to society. He is however a 'transmissionist'. He believes that the chief role of education is to transmit the best that has been thought and said in the past to each new generation. His most withering contempt is reserved for those who see education primarily in terms of self-expression, or even in terms of 'learning how to learn', since in his view there are *no* transmissible learning skills separate from the actual acquisition of knowledge. Blunkett's idea of classes in values was always, it now seems, a nonsense for Woodhead, who never believed that 'wisdom' could be taught at all. It is the fruit of intelligence, thought, and what he calls 'character' over time.[11]

[11]   Woodhead, of course, having resigned from OFSTED, has now gone public on his educational views. They make instructive reading (Chris Woodhead, *Class War: The State of British Education*, Little Brown, 2002.). He is rightly contemptuous of the flaccid platitudes emanating from both government ministers and university departments of education, but his contempt is

Though neither Blunkett's or Woodhead's position is particularly new, and both have been well-represented in past educational debates, there is here a deep theoretical division — accentuated, no doubt, by Woodhead's apparent damascene conversion to freedom from central control, though it is still unclear how this is to be squared with his passion for testing, which appears undiminished. Perhaps the only surprise is that they have taken so long to fall out — and no doubt their recriminations will continue to reverberate through the pages of *The Daily Telegraph*. What has not been commented on, however, is that however deep the theoretical gulf between them, the practical gulf is much smaller — a mere ditch, in fact. The historically unusual feature of this particular partnership is that both sides took it for granted that their goals could readily be achieved through overtly 'managerial' practices. If schools (or even 'educational workshops') are properly organised, if teachers are closely enough monitored, if the products are sufficiently tested, rigorously and often, then the desired outcome can be achieved. Though a certain rhetorical gloss of personal values and human relationships is deployed, such ethical values are essentially 'managerial ethics'.

generously extended to almost everyone who disagrees with his own, fairly narrow, view of what education should consist of. Not merely is there knee-jerk opposition to anything even vaguely 'progressive' in content, ['my biggest single doubt about OFSTED stems from the fact that some inspectors are unwilling or unable to jettison their progressive educational views.' p. 110.] he is convinced that teachers have 'nothing to learn' from their pupils. [p. 77] Having myself taught in primary and secondary schools, as well as in a number of universities, world-wide, I find this does not conform remotely to my own experience. Teaching would be unbearably boring if that were really true. University teaching, if the teacher listens, is full of interesting surprises, both in terms of facts and ideas. One is less likely to learn new *facts* in secondary or primary school teaching, but there are certainly plenty of new ideas to be heard in most classrooms. For Woodhead, one suspects, 'facts' are what make up education, and his declared inability to hear anything else tends to confirm what many have long suspected: that he is a *very* poor listener.

Yet even Woodhead's use of facts is curious. He dismisses evidence that the standards of public exams are rising by citing a wealth of plausible and worrying evidence for grade-inflation. But having cast (equally plausible) doubts on the effectiveness of much of OFSTED's work, he then proceeds to use success in both public exam results and OFSTED reports as 'hard evidence' for improvement in the standard of failing schools, and, indeed, for the success of OFSTED's work in general. Similarly precise figures surface elsewhere in his argument: in 1999-2000 those same 'soft' sources reveal that ten percent of headteachers were ineffective, or failures. [p. 4] The second time such figures are aired [p.103] they have moved from 'estimates' to hard figures. He can, it seems, have it both ways — in a manner that one of his (ideal) teachers would not allow a properly-inspected pupil. But then, logic does not figure on the Woodhead curriculum. There are, remember, no transferable skills.

Here is the real cost of replacing polyphony with monotony: the instrumental replaces the intrinsic, the manager replaces the leader, and the hierarchical displaces the collegiate. Here too we find continuity between Mrs Thatcher's oft-repeated belief in 'TINA' — that 'there is no alternative' — and the Blunkett-Woodhead managerialization of the school system and Dearing's vision of the university as a productive sector. Why have alternatives, if you already know that the *only* way to go is the way that increases 'output'?

Yet the justification for the time and money devoted to the new managerial ethic is peculiarly hard to resist, since it comes in a wrapping certifying not merely its efficiency but its self-evident *morality*. On the one hand, comparisons of annual tests allow politicians and ministry officials (Woodhead, Blunkett, Morris — it matters not) to claim 'hard evidence' of rising standards; on the other, the aim, that of providing more and better opportunities for all our young people has an ethical appeal few are prepared to challenge. The problem must, therefore, be nailed right at its source.

As Grant trenchantly argues, right at the heart of this whole massive edifice is an enormous nonsense. Training and education are fundamentally different things. You cannot use the methods of the former and hope to get the latter. Similarly, sometimes good ethics can be good management — and vice versa. But this is usually coincident. 'Management', freed of the disciplines of the market-place, and structured as a covert bureaucracy, is always as much about power, control and prestige, as it is about getting things done. Ethics, on the other hand, though their effect is universal, begin by looking inward. How we treat others grows from the way we see ourselves.

The point is not just that managerial 'ethics' are usually bad ethics (which they are), it is also that they are almost invariably bad management. The reason is inherent in the rhetoric. Applying the metaphors of commerce and the administrative methods of the civil service to an organization that by its nature depends on independence and collegiality is no way to produce clarity of perception — or anything else.[12]

The inclusion of the word 'ethics' licenses moral indignation, so that disagreement about methods becomes (in extreme instances) a moral crusade. If we assume, for instance, that Gordon Brown's out-

[12]   Indeed, as Ryan points out, it is ironic that the principal of the civil service's own training institution, Henley Management College, Thomas Kempner, was in 1985 calling for management to learn from the model of universities, perhaps echoing the professor from the London Business School who said 'Universities are the prototypes of the organisations of tomorrow' (Charles Handy, *Gods of Management: How they work and why they will fail*, Souvenir Press 1978, p. 188).

burst about Laura Spence's rejection by Oxford was not (as some curmudgeonly commentators persist in believing) simply a piece of cynical political posturing, we are left with the view that he must somehow believe that his moral commitment to equality of opportunity licences his certainty that he *must* know better than Anthony Smith and the black arts of the Magdalene College admissions tutors about which candidates to admit.

It is alarming to observe how the rhetoric of managerial ethics pervades the modern British educational system. Charlton's discussion of 'accountability' shows how a term from accountancy was deliberately flavoured with an ethical gloss. We live, we discover, in a nakedly — even flamboyantly — ethical society. Not merely does government self-evidently always have our best interests at heart, but contemporary commerce — 'customer relationship advisors' — aglow with mission statements, seem only to exist for the public good. When banks close branches in the pursuit of profit, or Railtrack (as it used to) declares profits for shareholders, public opinion was vaguely affronted, as if something politically incorrect had been momentarily glimpsed beneath the hemline. At the same time, as common shareholders ourselves in the Great Business of State, we demand not merely selfless integrity from those who run our country, but the highest managerial skills. The responsible society, we tell ourselves, is a well-run society. Good management is good ethics. Thus testing is simply the expression of the concern and efficiency of a caring state. It is the way we ensure and maintain quality.

The Emperor was always clothed in clichés. 'Quality', declared a Teaching and Learning executive at a recent motivation session, evidently quoting somebody to be quoted, 'is not an added extra; it is built in from the start.' The maxim sounded good: if only for an instant. But then the questions begin to surface.[13] What *is* 'quality' in education? The question is actually a very difficult one. Is it a form of attainment that can be measured or tested, is it something to do with inner-directedness, an ability to find things out and think for oneself, is it in Newman's terms, to give 'real' rather than 'notional' assent to the values one lives by? If, as I suspect in our polyphonic society, it is

---

[13] What, for instance, is this a metaphor *from*? Building? Engineering? In what context might that word 'quality' have a meaning — any meaning at all? Does it mean, for instance, that all the components of a car should be made of better steel/plastic/fibreglass? Not if modern production-engineering theory is to be believed: components should be strong enough to do their specific job. More is waste. Not, perhaps, such a good slogan in education.

all of these, then the slogan is more foolish, the Emperor's loins chillier, than ever.

But behind the notion of managerial ethics lies the idea that society can be changed from the top by policy — and the fact that some things clearly can has historically muddied the waters. In the later 1960s, Oliver MacDonagh attributed the phrase 'Revolution in Government'[14] to the nineteenth century in what he described as 'the pattern of Government growth', observing that when a particular abuse was finally deemed to be 'intolerable' (for example, dangers inherent in working down the mines), a set pattern could be discerned, of public enquiry, report, parliamentary debate and legislation, frequently revisited, to counter the perceived evil, the establishment of a public body (an early quango) with a chairman and board/commission members and a cadre of inspectors to ensure that the legislation was being observed. Examples of the pattern were legion from the 1830s onwards, in (to name but a few) the fields of public health, teacher training, safety in coal mines and on ships, alkali manufacture, lunatic asylums and many other spheres.

A similar pattern can be observed from the 1980s in that it came to be thought 'intolerable' that that standards of performance and accountability throughout public service were self-evidently woeful and that considerable amounts of public money were being wasted. 'Sleaze' in political life constantly hit the headlines as did the apparent failure of publicly funded activities to deliver the quality and service which taxes funded. Consequently a whole new regime of governance, audit and accountability came into existence and grew exponentially. All the different bodies shared characteristics in origins and of purpose. They also shared effects.

At the centre of this so-called managerial revolution is what a recent BBC documentary saw as the deliberate political destruction of the old professionally independent middle-class. Earlier in the twentieth century two kinds of middle-class activities could be clearly distinguished: the managerial, and the professional. The former was essentially administrative. Whether in factories and business, the civil service or local government, it was the job of such figures to interpret and implement policies laid down from above. Their effectiveness as managers was assessed by their success or failure in carrying out the specific tasks allotted to them. Their wages

<hr>

[14] The phrase was first used by Geoffrey Elton for his studies of the growth of central control in the Tudor period. For this, and much of the historical analysis that follows, I am indebted to an unpublished article by Anand Chitnis of the Higher Education Foundation.

were determined by their success, and those who worked their way to the top of their hierarchies (especially in manufacturing and commerce and banking) could expect to become rich. In contrast, doctors, lawyers, school and university teachers — with a few exceptions — were never likely to become as rich; as Grant argues, however, they as professionals were used to a high degree of independence and, often, prestige within their fields. They usually enjoyed greater job-security; their judgements were listened to with respect; provided they were perceived by their peers to be effective in what they did, how they did it mattered less.[15]

One feature of the revolution in managerial ethics emphasised by Onora O'Neill in her 2002 Reith Lectures has been the systematic destruction of this tradition of professional independence through the institutionalization of suspicion and distrust. Each new medical scandal, each crooked lawyer, each paedophile teacher or priest exposed justifies further regimentation, inspection, and control of the entire system, so that the middle-ranking professional in almost every field is no longer a specialist consultant giving professional leadership, but an interchangeable bureaucrat dignified with the name line manager.

Nor has this process been accidental or unconscious. At a weekend meeting of academics and senior civil servants in the early 1980s (under Chatham House rules) after a few drinks one of the leading members of the Department of Education was quite explicit about the need to bring academics under greater central control. 'You guys have had it far too easy for far too long', he commented. 'I have the same class of degree as you have. Why should you enjoy longer holidays and greater freedom than me ?' The rhetoric of managerial ethics of the last twenty years has in reality masked the greatest centralization of bureaucratic government control of the professions in British history — with a correspondingly great re-allocation of resources from actually 'delivering' education (health-care etc) to the 'management' and control of those professions. It is, perhaps, small wonder if teachers who find themselves mendaciously described as line-managers opt for the better pay, conditions and

[15] Hence that tradition of great eccentric specialists, who in fact and fiction alike did things 'their way': Sir Launcelot Spratt in *Doctor in the House*, Rumpole of the Bailey, unorthodox professors like Wittgenstein, or Donald Mackinnon, who enjoyed baffling and perplexing their students by unexpected teaching methods — even to the extent of one Oxford tutor *reputed* (probably with undergraduate exaggeration) to give tutorials to students of both sexes while lying in the bath.

freedom of action given to *real* line managers in the commercial and industrial world.

In a parallel development to the regulation of education, from the autumn of 2000 NHS organizations have expressed increasing concern over the resources to be devoted to the range of inspection, quality assurance and accreditation programmes in the NHS, where inspectors can be anyone from the medical Royal Colleges to Investors in People — a title given to any company which pays its fee, passes some notional and undemanding 'tests', and fills out the requisite forms.

What such a history also reveals is a steady progression from areas where legislation and inspection are appropriate and effective into areas where it is less and less so. It is the political equivalent of the creation of 'myth' in science. A detailed and limited study of a topic reveals that certain things behave in particular ways under specific conditions. This result is then generalized into a universal 'law' which in science (unlike the law) means it is applicable under all conditions and cannot be altered. The idea of 'entropy', lifted from the sealed thermal system in which it began, and grandly applied to the universe as 'proof' that all energy will eventually run down, is in this category. But in politics, even more than in physics, measurement means power. Thus we are tacitly encouraged to believe that values can be defined by acts of parliament; that reliance on trust and integrity can effectively be replaced by systems of measurement and compliance; that professionalism can survive a system that cannot allow its practitioners to take risks or to show initiative or creativity; that a culture of blame and litigiousness is somehow the price of living in a 'modern' world.

The Corruption of Education and the Creation of the Future

What then is to be done? One thing is clear: we cannot do nothing. As thousands of parents, if not Estelle Morris, know very well, the system is already in crisis. The desperate remedies listed in the Introduction tell the story more clearly than any government rhetoric. Indeed, the mere fact that the government is now trying to *re-assure* us ('standards are rising', etc) reveals how *bad* they have become. If we continue, our schools will reflect Disraeli's two nations: one, a private system for the seriously rich, another, increasingly inferior, for those who cannot afford the cost of private education. The latter will teach fewer foreign languages, less history and geography (increasingly now they are 'alternatives'), mathematics only where they can find qualified maths teachers, much less classical music, drama, and even sport.

As with schools, so with universities — which are only as good as the quality of their entrants. A.N. Whitehead once wrote that 'The task of the university is the creation of the future, so far as rational thought, and civilized modes of appreciation can affect the issue.'[16] Though that idea of the creation of the future may still have a meaning in British political rhetoric, it has largely lost its meaning in the educational scene. If education is not about a well-trained labour force, it seems to be about mechanical transmission. The current contrast in mood between British and American universities can be judged by the two new books about the state of the respective national systems, already cited above, which appeared in 2001. The American one, which takes for its title, Whitehead's phrase, *The Creation of the Future*, though rightly critical of much that is happening there, is confident and forward-looking, not least because what is happening is under the control of the academics. The tone is the more poignant for a British reader in that it is written by an Englishman, Frank Rhodes, whose description of a university I quoted earlier. He taught at Durham University and held an administrative post at Swansea (one presumes in the time of Ian Robinson!) before moving to the USA and eventually going on to become President of Cornell University. The British counterpart, *The New Idea of a University*, is, as we have seen, a justifiably angry and embittered book, which was written in the belief that in the UK universities, no longer under their own control, have reached the end of the line, and that most are scarcely worthy of the name.

If present trends continue, for British universities the future is in fact fairly clear. Britain already has on paper the highest HE participation rate in the world, with 35.1% of twenty-four year olds with a first degree.[17] Mr Blair's declared aim is to push this up to 50%, but (apparently) with no corresponding increase in finance. This, if achieved, will only confirm what various writers have already pointed out: that the great university 'expansion' was, of course, a barely-concealed *contraction*. Some ten to fifteen institutions will remain internationally competitive, the rest will be largely

---

[16]   Alfred North Whitehead, *Modes of Thought*, NY: Free Press, 1968, p. 171.

[17]   Comparable figures for the US are 32.1%; Japan 28%,; Norway, 25.8%; Germany 24.3% (China, 1.4%). (U.S. National Science Board, *Science and Engineering Indicators – 2000*, Arlington VA, vol. 1, appendix table 4-18, 2000, (Rhodes, *Creation of the Future*, p. 17)).

non-research institutions, with few, if any, post-graduates, and heavy teaching timetables for their overworked faculty. These 'universities' will, of course, decline in quality as their faculty realise what is happening, and either leave teaching altogether, or take better conditions and pay overseas. As potential postgraduates come to perceive the growing gulf between the inner ring and the rest, serious post-graduate teaching will die out among the latter. Of the places available in the major research universities, more and more will go to overseas students (Oxford already has more foreign postgraduate students than it has native; other top universities are not far behind). Laura Spence's own moves were revealing: having failed to get into Oxford she took a scholarship to Harvard rather than go to her local university, Newcastle. She will be typical of a new generation of students who know their own value, and the weakness of the British second-tier system — and, outside the world of political posturing, who can blame them?

Only the most blindly chauvinist of little Englanders would take this growing internationalism as a weakness in itself. A first-rate *university* should be open to all comers. A student body or faculty that does not draw on world talent is not, by definition, world-class. Just as Laura Spence was free to gain admission (and a scholarship) to a university of her choice in the US, so US or EU students should be free to come to the UK — paying fees, or competing for scholarships with the locals. Informed student choice is one of the best registers we have of international standing. The problem is that world talent will be less and less eager to come and work in a manifestly second-class system. Nevertheless, international comparison may yet be a source of relief to our beleaguered universities. The son of a British professor with a first-class degree from a provincial institution recently applied to do a Ph.D. in one of the sciences in Oxford. He was greeted courteously by the Head of Department, who asked with some curiosity why he wanted to come to Oxford. The young man replied that he wanted to be at the cutting edge of his chosen field. 'OK', came the reply. 'You don't want Oxford. I've got a friend at MIT,[18] I'll give him a ring and we'll see if we can get you in there.' Repeated pleas by the British scientific community for better funding may find shame a more effective weapon than either pride or logic.

On a world-view we could end up with something like the mediaeval trans-national fluidity, where those graduating from cer-

[18]   The Massachusetts Institute of Technology in Cambridge, Boston, USA. One of the finest science research institutes in the world.

tain institutions owe more allegiance to their class and education than to their country of origin. On the one hand the present expansion, if it is pushed through at present or comparable levels of funding, will produce a low-level vernacular system for the masses; on the other, a small number of elite and largely fee-paying institutions (unlike the mediaeval world, they mostly teach in English rather than Latin) will draw their students from around the world, and send their graduates into a disproportionate number of top jobs in banking, government, medicine and highly-paid research.[19] A case might be made for such a brave new world, but it is far from clear that this is what the British public actually wants, or the government is trying to achieve. Moreover, for the British, such a future is a corrupt one, in which the means persistently distort the ends.

One problem, of course, is money. In Britain we spend something like £38 billion a year on public education, with some £6 billion of that going to Higher Education alone. As Evan Harris shows, there is still much to be done to broaden the intake (not for the sake of politically correct 'social inclusiveness' but because good potential students are still being excluded by poverty). More money *is* urgently needed to fill empty posts, to provide better facilities — even, in one government initiative, to make a larger section of the sixteen year-old cohort stay on at school. But the real problem may not even be the total amount spent, but where it is *coming* from. In the USA attitudes towards public and private expenditure differ sharply. To the average citizen who has had no direct contact with universities, the news that a professor in a state-financed university may teach formal classes for perhaps five hours a week spread over two days often seems like an outrage: a blatant rip-off of public money. The news that a professor in a major *private* university in the USA may work similar hours, or fewer, and be paid perhaps 30-50% *more* than his colleague in the state system commonly provokes not anger, but awe: 'Wow! They really must be experts if they can command salaries and conditions like that !' The fact that in the US the rich will pay up to six times the fees charged by the state universities to send their children to the great private institutions clearly indicates to them that the private universities *must* be better — and, indeed, on the whole they are right. Certainly a minority of able students from poorer backgrounds agree with this assessment to the point of being

[19] See Rhodes on the degree to which the graduates of the top 100 out of the 4,000 or so US universities control almost every aspect of American public life (*Creation of the Future*, p. 19).

willing to borrow, in some cases, hundreds of thousands of dollars to put themselves through the private system.

Though the British lack major private universities in the American sense, and so the respective attitudes cannot be directly compared, something of the same equivocation between public and private expenditure undoubtedly exists. That distinction reflects not merely the public dislike of paying taxes (since September 11, Americans at any rate, will accept astronomical sums spent on military projects) but also a suspicion of the efficacy of public versus private expenditure that in both the US and the UK is partly justified by experience. The great private institutions are believed to demand value for money in a way that people suspect state-financed ones do not. Again, in one sense at least, that crude perception is right. No private university in the US would spend the proportion of money on unproductive monitoring of its results that the British now routinely spend. Students voluntarily complete an assessment questionnaire at the end of every course — and since they, or their parents, are paying consumers, what matters in the end is their satisfaction. In Britain or America, students are remarkably canny consumers. If you want to know what is happening within a particular course, a particular discipline, or university, student choice will tell you much more quickly than QAA inspections.

The proposals mooted at one stage by the Conservative opposition under William Hague for giving universities a substantial endowment fund rather than on-going government support was, therefore, an interesting and in many ways attractive one. It foundered for two reasons. The first is that, like many of that rather desperate party's proposals, it lacked credibility. It was never clear where the money for the enormous initial outlay required to do the job properly would come from. Secondly — and, one suspects, more seriously — it was never popular with government because it would hugely weaken central control of higher education.

Once again muddled British priorities mean that the UK falls between two stools. Many countries in the EU (from Denmark to France) support higher taxation than the UK in exchange for better-funded social and educational services. Britain tries to vie with the US for low-taxation, but gives none of the tax-breaks of the latter to support educational endowments and fees. It has rejected vouchers or greater freedom of student choice. What is at issue here, one suspects, is not educational principal, but a fear of loss of government, or more precisely, bureaucratic control.

Nevertheless, however sociologically relevant the fundamental differences between the British and American traditions in both education and health expenditure, they are brutally beside the point in terms of results. The modern research university was invented in the USA. Despite some sour-grapes condescension from the European side of the Atlantic, the very best American universities are not merely the best in the world, but the sheer vastness of their financial resources means they are steadily increasing their lead over the rest of the field.[20] Given the wealth of the US and the willingness of its citizens to invest in (private) education, it is hard to see their research lead in many of the more expensive areas of science and medicine in particular being reduced in the foreseeable future. Even in the arts and humanities the good US universities now give a quality of graduate academic training far ahead of anywhere in the British system. Nevertheless, universities are among the world's oldest continuous institutions (exceeded in age only by the Catholic Church) and their future everywhere is, we hope, much longer than what is 'foreseeable'. There is, moreover, still an immense reserve of talent at every level in British universities that could be liberated and exploited without the need for huge expenditure, but at the moment it is doubtful if the system will encourage or even allow it. In the short term Laura Spence was certainly right not to trust their quality — and that is the *real* moral of the Laura Spence saga.

What is required is a fundamental shift in British attitudes not just to education, but to social expenditure as a whole, including taxation. For those who pay sufficient taxes, university education should straightforwardly be a fully tax-deductible expense. For the rest, instead of the present (labour-inspired) tuition levels that discourage the least privileged students from applying, the charges for fee-paying students should be pitched at a level which would support at least 25% of students on scholarships. In between these extremes, a graded scale of fees should be set up not by any central authority, but by the universities themselves. Last, but not least, gifts, endowments, and legacies to universities should (as in the USA) be fully tax-deductible.

Moreover, we must recognize and *articulate* the degree to which the present system is essentially corrupt. Three very different kinds of organization have been strategically and metaphorically con-

[20] This is not to disagree with the point made earlier by Robert Grant. According to Rhodes there are 4,096 colleges and universities in the USA., but some 77% of all research expenditure, and 75% of doctorates come from the top 100 universities, Rhodes, *op. cit.*, pp. 17-19.

flated: a bureaucratic structure clothed in commercial metaphors has been imposed in the name of ethics on a previously collegiate system. In the name of better 'management' and more 'ethical' administration large sums of money are being siphoned off the educational budget at every level to support a system of testing and monitoring that in the end serves *neither* the interests of teachers *nor* of pupils. This has created a Frankenstein's Monster in the form of a new class of professional assessors, who, unlike the old inspectorate, are not there to help, but have a vested interest in maintaining their own 'management' status — in short, their own power, and who will, understandably, fight to protect their jobs with every weapon available. Similar 'management teams' are now maintained by every university simply to co-ordinate Quality Assurance and Research Assessment returns, and to give advice on improving the paperwork generated by those bodies. The muddled assumptions behind managerial ethics allow them to claim salaries to match senior management in large commercial corporations, while at the same time claiming a moral authority stemming from their role as guardians of tax-payers' money. Unlike business managers, however, they enjoy complete security of tenure, and despite a wealth of commercial metaphors there is no way of actually measuring their efficiency. Their only product is rhetoric and statistics — both, it is true, much in demand from governments, but less so from students, the real consumers.

Again North America may offer a better model. Here ranking is an important element in the competition among major universities and schools. But so far from absorbing large amounts of public money, the system is a private one, sponsored for profit either by publishers (Baron; Thomas; Gale Research; (or in Canada) Macleans) or by units within universities (Princeton; George Washington University). The obvious profitability of such exercises in the UK is shown by the way the *Times Educational Supplement,* the *Higher,* and the *Sunday Times* (all Murdoch publications) make prominent features of such league tables. Here, if anywhere, is a case for privatisation. If those major research universities in the Russell Group wish to fund such activities, that should be their choice. To force the much larger group of former polytechnics, colleges of education and further education, which at present form the rump of every league-table, and which take the vast majority of the under-funded and under-prepared mass of the expanded cohort of university entrants, to expose the paucity of their resources at their own expense is pointless. To pay for such obviously profitable productions out of public education funding is not so much an error of planning as an abuse of taxpayers' money.

Other corruptions follow from this initial misdirection of resources. These include inflated salaries for principals, vice-chancellors, and other senior administrators who have been encouraged by the prevailing jargon to see themselves not as academic leaders, or educationalists, or even civil servants, but as CEOs, chief executives of large business enterprises. Further abuses include a system of financing where second-ranking universities are encouraged to take on large numbers of students with neither the aptitude nor interest in their particular course of study, and courses of study that often serve neither the interests of the students nor (even) those of the Blunkett economy.[21]

The final corruption that must be tackled is in many ways the most interesting of the lot. It was charges of poor teaching and inadequate research that prompted the original government interference in the 1980s. Poor teachers undoubtedly existed, and many academics published little or nothing. Yet, as we have seen from the essays in this volume, as well as from anecdotal evidence elsewhere, a decade and a half of rigorous testing of children, of inspection of teaching, and assessment of research, has made the situation at least marginally worse. As Diana Mabbutt convincingly argues, much of the 'progress' boasted of by Ministers of Education rests on very soft evidence, of massaging of figures, and of restricted curricula.[22] Good teachers have left the system in droves, and gaps in school staff are made up by an increasing army of uncommitted supply teachers, tourists from Australasia[23] — and, finally, not at all.

[21]   The classic example is of course 'Media Studies' and its derivatives where students are erroneously led to believe that their degrees will lead to well-paid jobs in journalism and the media.

[22]   According to official figures, the proportion of 11-year olds reaching the expected standard in English has increased from 48 percent (1995) to 74 percent (2001). Ministers claim that this figure is a vindication of the 'literacy hour', but the first independent study of its kind indicates that the 'improvement' is probably a sham. Researchers from Durham University administered the same test of reading and vocabulary to 11-year olds in 122 primary schools for the past five years and found no improvement. Peter Tymms, head of Durham's curriculum, evaluation and management centre, concludes that 'high stakes' tests are inherently unreliable as staff are motivated to 'teach to the test'. Before the 2002 tests for 11-year olds, many primary schools did virtually no teaching for 10 weeks. Instead, day after day, pupils had to work through previous test and practice papers. This is one of the reasons why children's performance appears to dip so sharply when they are transferred to secondary schools.

[23]   This is not an insult to Australians and New Zealanders. I myself taught in the Australian system for ten years and hold dual UK/Australian citizenship.

Because the most easily measurable output of university teachers was their writings, publication was made into a measure of 'quality'. Pressure to publish on academics who may have been excellent teachers but who, justifiably, felt they had little to put into print, has resulted in a huge quantity of second-rate and unread academic publication which actually hampers the activity of the best scholars, who feel compelled to keep up with their discipline. What improvement there may have been in the quality of university faculty probably owes more to the natural retirement of the inflated cohort of staff hired too-rapidly in the 1960s than to QAA or RAE. It would probably have happened anyway. Meanwhile an increasing number of professors (two among the contributors to this book) have left the UK system for better conditions elsewhere, and those who remain are hamstrung at every turn by the demands of meaningless paperwork and a self-serving bureaucracy.

Before our universities and schools drown completely, we need to discard both the sets of heavy metaphorical clothing that have been weighing them down. We need an administrative and organizational model that is drawn *neither* covertly from the civil service *nor* rhetorically from business, but which is essentially collegial and educational. That almost certainly means a far greater degree of financial independence than of recent years. The old University Grants Committee provided much of this, but that was only with government good will. Given the temptation for government to interfere in the name of 'auditing', and the jobs that will be preserved and the empires created by doing so, it is unwise for educationalists ever to put their trust in princes or politicians again.

There is no need to think any one academic structure will serve the needs of an increasingly pluralistic society. Collegiality can allow for more pluralistic (or polyphonic) university structures. We should recognize that there can be a much wider range of possible courses and ways of structuring universities, and to allow universities to experiment with new ways of learning. The model I envisage would be more one of family resemblance than clones. Moreover, there is a wealth of such models already in existence: my own experience of Cambridge, Sussex, the Australian National, Glasgow and Duke Universities offers five very different ones. None were perfect, and the middle three have all suffered greatly from the unintended con-

---

Many of the adventurous young antipodeans who take supply-teaching jobs in British schools as a way of financing their round-the-world trips are intelligent, well-educated, and resourceful teachers. My point is that the British education system should not be relying on them to keep its head above water.

sequences described in this book, but all once possessed valuable and distinctive qualities which should not have been lost.

What is striking about the present turmoil in education is the total lack of real *new* thinking. For Woodhead, transmission of existing knowledge, culture, and values was all. The rest was 'progressive' clap-trap. The DfES, on the other hand, delivers a constant flood of so-called 'new initiatives', to the despair of headteachers struggling with lack of money to engage the staff needed to cover the day-to-day running of the school. New money is never put into the hands of the institutions to do their existing job better, however; it is always held by some central authority for schools or universities to 'bid for'. Commercial metaphors rule. The whole procedure is an example of what financial circles call 'churning': buying and selling shares with no particular rationale, but to give the amateur investor the impression of an 'active' management that is fully on top of the situation. The underlying message is, as always, clear: control is an ideology in itself.

It is a tragic symptom of the current vacuum in educational ideas that the last time radical and innovative thinking at the college or university level took place was in the 1960s, when new ideas and interdisciplinary courses were successfully pioneered by those 'New Universities' of the 1960s — Essex, Lancaster, Sussex, Sterling, and Warwick.[24] More radical still was the programme of problem-based learning initiated by McMaster University medical school, of Hamilton, Ontario, Canada, which has abandoned structured courses altogether, and simply issues students with a copy of the syllabus, the dates of the final examinations,[25] the library catalogue, and the (regular) times when members of the teaching faculty would be in their rooms for consultation. Rigorous monitoring of this revolutionary scheme over the years has revealed no statistical difference at all in (the externally monitored) exam grades between students 'trained' by this method, and those by more conventional methods. What difference there is lies the ability of the 'self-taught' students to cope with new methods and ideas, and to think origi-

[24] The creative buzz in such universities communicated itself to potential students. I recall one outstanding able student who turned down a place at Cambridge to go to Sussex simply on intellectual grounds. He was probably right to do so then; it is hard to image a first-class applicant doing so now. It is also unlikely that what he was looking for — and found — could have been measured by QAA or RAE.

[25] Not, of course, university examinations, but the nation-wide qualifying exams of the Canadian Medical Association.

nally. The point is not that *all* medical schools should be run like this, but that students and staff should have the freedom to experiment.

As Desmond Ryan has noted, the real paradox is that Blunkett's ideal of a well-trained labour force for the twenty-first century would only have been achievable by ceasing to concentrate on it as a goal, and concentrating instead on real 'education', if not in exactly Newman's sense, at least in the sense of creating a quality of mind — and allowing it to happen as part of a 'polyphonic' structure. The magic word here is a very old one: 'freedom'.

A well-trained labour force does not consist of people who have been drilled in certain ways of thinking and proceeding, but people who have been encouraged to think rigorously for themselves, to work out ideas from first principles, and to recognize when those above, or around them, are talking nonsense. As Newman first articulated, and Grant and Scruton have here argued in their own inimitable and very different ways, the only education that is in the end socially productive and useful is the education that aims to be all of these things. 'Training' is something else again. Valuable as it is, it is not education. Metaphors like 'well-trained labour force' are military images, and they tell us more about the mind-set of the people who coined it than about the products of our education system. It is in any case the wrong one for the post-industrial society of the twenty-first century. Phrases like the 'knowledge society' or 'intelligent society', clichés as they are, suggest a more realistic approach to an economy that is relying less and less on manufacturing and more and more on providing a wide range of services. Something like half the jobs now available in the UK did not exist a generation ago. There is no reason to suggest that the pace of change will slow in the next few generations.

As in any process of change, however, there is bad with the good — especially when extensive social change is combined with an active, government-led, suppression of academic freedom. Oscar Wilde commented that there were few sights less attractive than that of the British public in one of its periodic fits of morality. 'Managerial ethics' is only our latest fashion in public hypocrisy. If Roderick Floud's 2001 figures suggesting that the UK now spends at least half a billion pounds on monitoring and testing education are even remotely accurate,[26] this must make it qualify as our fastest-growing new area of employment. Maybe this is what Blunkett had in mind for his well-trained labour force.

[26] See Introduction, n. 2.

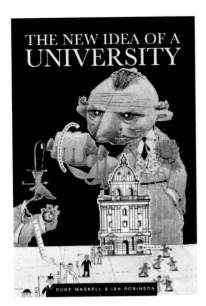

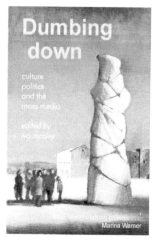

Dumbing Down: Culture, Politics and the Mass Media

Edited by Ivo Mosley

334 pp., £12.95, 0907845 657 (pbk.)

Never before in human history has so much cleverness been used to such stupid ends. The cleverness is in the creation and manipulation of markets, media and power; the stupid ends are in the destruction of community, responsibility, morality, art, religion and the natural world.

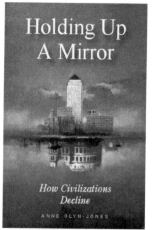

Holding Up A Mirror: How Civilizations Decline

Anne Glyn-Jones

652 pp., £14.95, 0907845 606 (pbk.)

The dynamic that promotes economic prosperity leads to the destruction of the very security and artistic achievement on which civilizations rest their claim. This book argues that the growth of prosperity is driven largely by the conviction that the material world alone constitutes true 'reality'. Yet that same dynamic undermines the authority of moral standards and leads to social disintegration.

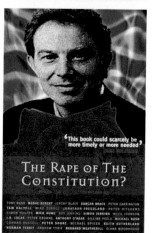

The Rape of the Constitution?

Edited by Keith Sutherland
Foreword by Michael Beloff QC

384 pp., £12.95, 0907845 703 (pbk.)

Lord Hailsham once remarked that if you removed a brick from the wall of the British Constitution, the building would collapse; yet New Labour has embarked on a reckless path of constitutional change. Has the increase in executive power turned Bagehot's 'disguised republic' into an elective dictatorship?

sample chapters/reviews/TOCs: **www.imprint-academic.com/politics**